CANADIAN LANDMARK CASES
IN FORENSIC MENTAL HEALTH

High-profile legal cases involving individuals with mental health challenges often address complex issues that confront previous decisions of the courts, influence or change existing social policies, and ultimately have a profound impact on the daily practice of mental health professionals and the lives of their patients. Providing in-depth context into milestone cases in forensic mental health, this book addresses issues such as the confidentiality of mental health records, criminal responsibility, fitness to stand trial, the right of individuals to refuse mental health treatment, and the duty of mental health practitioners to warn and protect individuals who may be at risk of harm at the hands of a patient. The authors explore the social and political context in which these cases occurred, incorporating court decisions, contemporaneous media articles, and legal reviews in the analysis.

Graham Glancy and Cheryl Regehr, who are experts in the field of forensic psychiatry, draw upon their own practice, in addition to scholarly literature, to describe the impact of the decisions rendered by the courts in the area of mental health and offer practical guidelines for professionals working at the interface of law and mental health.

GRAHAM GLANCY is an associate professor in the Department of Psychiatry and the Director of Forensic Psychiatry at the University of Toronto.

CHERYL REGEHR is a professor in the Faculty of Social Work, with cross-appointments to the Faculty of Law and the Institute of Medical Science at the University of Toronto.

Canadian Landmark Cases in Forensic Mental Health

GRAHAM GLANCY
CHERYL REGEHR

UNIVERSITY OF TORONTO PRESS
Toronto Buffalo London

© University of Toronto Press 2020
Toronto Buffalo London
utorontopress.com

ISBN 978-1-4875-0735-0 (cloth)   ISBN 978-1-4875-3608-4 (EPUB)
ISBN 978-1-4875-2504-0 (paper)   ISBN 978-1-4875-3607-7 (PDF)

Library and Archives Canada Cataloguing in Publication

Title: Canadian landmark cases in forensic mental health / Graham Glancy,
    Cheryl Regehr.
Names: Glancy, Graham, author. | Regehr, Cheryl, author.
Description: Includes bibliographical references and index.
Identifiers: Canadiana (print) 20200154192 | Canadiana (ebook)
    20200154222 | ISBN 9781487507350 (cloth) | ISBN 9781487525040
    (paper) | ISBN 9781487536084 (EPUB) | ISBN 9781487536077 (PDF)
Subjects: LCSH: Mental health laws – Canada – Cases. | LCSH: Insanity
    (Law) – Canada – Cases. | LCSH: Mentally ill – Commitment and
    detention – Canada – Cases. | LCSH: Forensic psychiatry – Canada –
    Cases. | LCSH: Psychiatrists – Legal status, laws, etc. – Canada –
    Cases. | LCGFT: Casebooks (Law)
Classification: LCC KE514.G63 2020 | LCC KF9242.G63 2020 kfmod | DDC
    346.7101 / 30874–dc23

University of Toronto Press acknowledges the financial assistance to its
publishing program of the Canada Council for the Arts and the Ontario Arts
Council, an agency of the Government of Ontario.

Canada Council   Conseil des Arts
for the Arts   du Canada

ONTARIO ARTS COUNCIL
CONSEIL DES ARTS DE L'ONTARIO
an Ontario government agency
un organisme du gouvernement de l'Ontario

Funded by the   Financé par le
Government   gouvernement
of Canada   du Canada

Canadä

Contents

Figures and Tables

Figures

Tables

Acknowledgments

We would like to thank several individuals who were instrumental in the preparation of this book: University of Toronto JD/MSW students Arielle Di Iulio and Priya Khalsa and University of Toronto law librarians Susan Barker, John Bolan, and Gian Medves, who conducted research for the book; University of Toronto alumna and graphic artist Savanna Jackson, who designed the figu es; freelance editor Marissa Heinzman; and Meg Patterson of University of Toronto Press. In addition, we would like to acknowledge the work of our friends and colleagues in criminal justice and mental health who have shaped Canadian law, policy, and practice in the area of forensic mental health over many years.

CANADIAN LANDMARK CASES
IN FORENSIC MENTAL HEALTH

1 Landmark Cases and Canadian Law

Landmark Cases

Judges arrive at legal decisions by thoroughly analysing the evidence presented to them in a court of law, reviewing relevant legislation and pertinent rulings in previous cases, and considering the degree to which these factors influence their decision latitude and possible outcomes of the current case. A landmark case – also known in Commonwealth countries as a leading case – is a judicial decision "that settles the law on some important point" (Lefroy, 1914, p. v) and has legal and historical significance. Landmark cases set new precedents, and in doing so, direct future judicial decision-making.

Landmark cases often arise out of changing societal views on particular issues. The resulting judicial decisions affect not only the interpretation of the law but also the lives of individual citizens and the society in which they live. The following are examples of Canadian landmark cases that both reflected changing societal values and resulted in changed rights and practices (Ontario Justice Education Network, 2006):

- *The right to a fair trial.* During the late 1980s and early 1990s, concerns arose within the legal community and the media regarding the rights of individuals believed to be wrongfully convicted and imprisoned for violent crimes. Criminal lawyers and activists joined forces to form the Innocence Project in the United States (Innocence Project, 2018) and the Innocence Canada Foundation (Innocence Canada, 2018), with the aim of directing resources, media attention, and political pressure toward addressing the plight of those convicted on the basis of faulty evidence. One issue of concern in Canada was the fact that the Crown prosecutor was not required to disclose to the accused and their defence counsel evidence that could jeopardize the case for conviction. In the landmark case of *R v Stinchcombe* (1991), the Supreme Court of Canada ruled that the Crown is obligated to disclose all relevant information to the accused prior to a trial. The court reasoned that failure to do so undermined the individual's right under the Canadian Charter of Rights and Freedoms (1982) to make full answer and defence to criminal charges.

- *Consent in sexual assault.* In 1992, many members of the public were horrified to see media photographs of signs saying "No Means Kick Her in the Teeth" and "No Means Harder" displayed in residence room windows at Queen's University (Johnson, 1992); these signs were posted in response to the Canadian Federation of Students' (2018) national "No Means No" campaign, which was focused on addressing issues of sexual violence on campus. Shortly thereafter, Alberta business owner Steve Ewanchuk was charged with the sexual assault of a 17-year-old job applicant. In his defence, he claimed that the young woman had given "implied consent" for sexual activity because, although she had repeatedly said no to his sexual advances, she did not leave the premises. He was acquitted by the Alberta Court of Appeal despite the fact that the "trial judge believed the complainant and accepted her testimony that she was afraid, and he acknowledged her unwillingness to engage in any sexual activity" (*R v Ewanchuk*, 1999). The Supreme Court of Canada rejected Ewanchuk's defence and ruled that implied consent does not exist as a defence for sexual assault under Canadian law (*R v Ewanchuk*, 1999).
- *Same-sex marriage.* In light of the rulings of several provincial courts that restricting marriage to a union between one man and one woman was unconstitutional, the federal government requested that the Supreme Court of Canada provide an opinion as to whether a proposed Act on same-sex marriage was consistent with the Canadian constitution. In particular, the court was asked to comment on whether the Act conflicted with the constitutional right t freedom of religion. The court found that the Act did indeed meet the equality principles under the Canadian Charter of Rights and Freedoms (Ontario Justice Education Network, 2006; *Reference re Same Sex Marriage*, 2004). As a result, in 2005, same-sex marriages were legalized in Canada with the enactment of the Civil Marriage Act.

Judicial rulings in landmark cases are based on the interpretation of legislation, for instance as to the relevance of the Canadian Charter of

Rights and Freedoms to same-sex marriage and the right to a fair trial. In judicial rulings consideration is given to the interpretation of the law by other courts and whether prior judicial decisions are correct. For instance, in the case of *R v Ewanchuk* (1999), the court made the following determination:

> The majority of the Court of Appeal also relied on inappropriate myths and stereotypes. Complainants should be able to rely on a system free from such myths and stereotypes, and on a judiciary whose impartiality is not compromised by these biased assumptions.

In this way, landmark cases set judicial standards, but also reflect and set societal standards.

Forensic Mental Health Professionals and Landmark Cases

Forensic mental health professionals (including psychiatrists, psychologists, social workers, nurses, and occupational therapists) work at the interface between law and mental health. Their work entails providing:

> expertise to judicial, administrative, and educational systems including, but not limited to, examining or treating persons in anticipation of or subsequent to legal, contractual, and administrative proceedings; offering expert opinion about psychological issues in the form of *amicus* briefs or testimony to judicial, legislative, or administrative bodies; acting in an adjudicative capacity; serving as a trial consultant or otherwise offering expertise to attorneys, the courts, or others; conducting research in connection with, or in the anticipation of, litigation; or involvement in educational activities of a forensic nature. (American Psychological Association, 2018)

Forensic mental health teams can be found in correctional centres, mental health facilities, court services, and community-based services such as the Canadian Mental Health Association, probation and parole offices, and the Office of the Children's Lawyer in Ontario. They provide assessments and treatment to both perpetrators of criminal activity and victims of crimes and accidents. Their expertise is sought by the courts and administrative tribunals, such as the Criminal Code Review Board, and by other mental health professionals on issues such as capacity and future dangerousness. Given the nature of forensic mental health practice, legislation such as Canada's Criminal Code (1985), and decisions in certain legal cases pertaining to civil and criminal law can have a profound impact on professional practice, the clients served, and the systems and organizations in which forensic professionals work. Landmark cases relevant to forensic mental health practice address:

- *Expert testimony.* The permitted nature and bounds of expert opinion provided by forensic experts and mental health practitioners.
- *Mental health defences to criminal charges.* Including issues related to insanity, criminal responsibility, whether the accused appreciated that the act was wrong, automatism, and intoxication.
- *Court processes.* Such as whether the accused has the mental capacity to participate in the court proceedings.
- *Mental health treatment.* Including the right to refuse treatment, the responsibility of a mental health practitioner to warn and protect others, and the confidentiality of mental health ecords for an individual engaged in a court process.
- *Civil litigation.* Involving assessing the level of damage experienced by individuals who were injured as a result of the negligence or wrongdoing of others.

Despite the critical influence of legislation and landmark court cases on forensic mental health practice, these laws and cases, both in the civil and criminal arenas, do not easily translate into guidelines to which a practitioner can adhere in forming a conclusion or recommendation in a specific case. For example, in the section of the Criminal Code of Canada (1985) pertaining to fitness to stand trial, one of the criteria is whether the accused person understands the nature and consequences of the proceedings. This is clearly a complicated concept. The Code does not spell out the degree of understanding an accused person must have in order to be considered fit. It does not spell out whether the accused must have the ability to articulate this understanding. Fitness to stand trial clearly cannot be determined by filling out a simple checklist or by doing a blood test. Rather, the practitioner must be aware of the legal interpretation of these terms and the reasoning behind these interpretations in order to come to a concluding recommendation. If the practitioner is cognizant of the landmark cases in this area, and the analysis and reasoning behind the legal principles leading to the landmark decision, they are better suited to understand the intricacies of the law. By studying the learned judges' analyses and complex reasoning, and the context in which the decisions were made, the practitioner can gain a better understanding of the relevant law.

Structure of the Book

This book begins with a review of the Canadian legal system, the structure of the courts, and the manner in which judicial decisions are made. Critical matters to be considered include the role of the federal and provincial legislatures in creating laws, the structure of the courts, the role of the courts in statutory interpretation, the nature of the common law tradition, and the importance of precedents or *stare decisis*. Subsequent chapters review some of the most important Canadian landmark cases in forensic mental health.

Chapter 2 considers the issue of expert testimony. It begins with the landmark case of *R v Mohan*, concerning a pediatrician who was charged with multiple counts of sexual assault. In this case, the defence sought to introduce expert testimony aimed at proving that Dr. Mohan did not fit the profile of an individual who would commit these acts. The court determined that the evidence on which the expert would base his decision was not sufficiently reliable to be of use to the trier of fact. The chapter reviews the factors that judges should consider in determining whether the testimony of an expert is admissible and whether it is relevant and necessary to the court process. In addition, when the evidence involves novel science or novel theories, the court considers whether the science or theory has been tested and peer-reviewed, and whether standards for its use have been established. Finally, the chapter reviews situations in which expert witnesses have testified on matters beyond their expertise or competence, or have expressed excessive confidence in methods or science that have not been sufficiently tested. These examples serve as cautionary tales to all working in forensic mental health.

The next few chapters discuss landmark cases related to mental health defences. In chapter 3, we begin with *R v M'Naghten*, a case that was tried in 1843 and led to the M'Naughten rules, which still stand as the basis for insanity laws in most English-speaking countries of the world. Daniel M'Naughten was found not guilty of murder on the grounds of insanity; he was thus detained at Her Majesty's Pleasure and taken to the Broadmoor Hospital, where he was treated for his mental illness until he died 20 years later. Public outcry that M'Naughten had not been held to account for his actions followed the verdict. As a result, Queen Victoria – who herself had been the intended victim of an assassination attempt three years earlier – charged the highest court in the kingdom, the House of Lords, with addressing the issue. The answers to the questions posed by the Crown have, from the time of the M'Naughten case, been interpreted as rules to guide judges and juries in cases where an accused pleads not guilty by reason of insanity. While these rules were never the substance of a particular statute, they have been subject to common law interpretation over the past 160 years and, therefore, remain the law in England today (Schneider, 2009). A version of the M'Naughton rules was included in the first Canadian Criminal Code in 1892.

For almost 100 years, the substance of insanity law remained substantially unchanged in Canada. During the 1980s, there was increasing impetus to change the insanity laws, arising from concerns in legal circles, a civil rights movement aimed at ensuring the rights of individuals suffering from mental illness, and the passage, in the 1982, of the Canadian Charter of Rights and Freedoms. *R v Swain*, discussed in chapter 4, provided the perfect illustration that Canadian laws were not consistent with contemporary understanding and treatment of mental illness, specifically that a finding of not guilty by reason of insanity resulted in mandatory detention in a mental health facility. In *R v Swain*, the Supreme Court ruled that the regime of requiring indeterminate detention, on the assumption of dangerousness, violated individual rights under the Charter. Consequently, the court struck down the existing insanity law, resulting in the need to revise the Criminal Code through the enactment of Bill C-30. Changes to the Criminal Code under Bill C-30 also clarified that accused persons seeking an insanity defence needed to prove that they were either incapable of appreciating the nature and quality of the act or omission, or that they were incapable of knowing that such act or omission was wrong.

Knowing that an act is wrong has been the subject of significant legal argument over the years. In Canada, it was generally held that *wrong* refers to legal wrongfulness, as distinct from moral wrongfulness. Chapter 5 discusses two important cases that addressed this question: *R v Chaulk* and *R v Oommen*. In the case of Robert Chaulk, the accused broke into a home and stabbed and bludgeoned the occupant to death. He presented evidence at trial that he believed, due to his delusions, that he was above the law and that therefore he had the right to kill. As a result of this, the Supreme Court defined the word "wrongfulness" as having not only a legal connotation but also a moral connotation, thereby broadening the definition of wrongfulness under the Criminal Code of Canada. This case also struck down an aspect of the insanity law, one which stated that if delusions caused the accused to believe in the existence of some phenomenon which, if it existed, would justify or excuse an act or omission, then this may lead to an acquittal on the grounds of insanity.

Soon afterwards the Supreme Court revisited the interpretation of the phrase "knowing that the act was wrong" in the 1994 case of Matthew Oommen. In this case, the accused shot and killed a female acquaintance who was sleeping at his house, believing that she was participating in a conspiracy against him. The interpretation provided by the court was based on an individual's ability to apply a rational mind to the analysis of whether an act was wrong, and has become perhaps the most commonly used basis for a defence of not criminally responsible due to mental disorder (NCR-MD). This is also helpful in guiding the assessment and subsequent defence of accused persons suffering from a mental disorder.

Cases analysed in chapter 6 address other defences related to voluntariness and intent. "Actus non facit reum nisi mens sit rea" (the act does not make a person guilty unless his mind is guilty) points to issues of intent and voluntariness. Automatism and self-induced intoxication fall into this area of consideration. In 1987, Kenneth Parks arose from his sleep on the living room couch, partially dressed, drove 23 kilometres, and attacked his in-laws, killing his mother-in-law and seriously injuring his father-in-law. The defence called evidence that Parks was sleepwalking at the time of the act and the jury acquitted him with the finding of non-insane automatism. The Supreme Court ruled that there was an onus on the *prosecution* to prove that the act was voluntary. Therefore, the accused only had to lay the proper foundation for the defence. In contrast, in the later case of *R v Stone*, the court ruled that the *accused* had to prove involuntariness in order to establish a defence of automatism.

Further cases considered the legitimacy of voluntary intoxication as a defence. In *R v Daviault*, the Supreme Court of Canada ruled that, if as a result of severe voluntary intoxication there was reasonable doubt as to whether an accused was even aware that he had committed an act, then automatism could be a defence even in general intent cases. Shortly thereafter, Parliament enacted a new section to the Criminal Code that precluded self-induced intoxication as a defence for any offence that threatens to interfere with the bodily integrity of another person. Later in *R v Bouchard-Lebrun*, a case involving a crime committed by a person while under extreme intoxication on stimulant drugs, the court ruled that self-induced states do not qualify as a disease of mind, and therefore are inadmissible as an NCR-MD defence.

In chapter 7, we turn to court processes and describe the case of *R v Taylor* (in regard to provisions for finding an accused unfit to stand trial. Dwight Taylor was a barrister and solicitor who had been found unfit to practise law by the Law Society of Upper Canada, as he suffered from a paranoid disorder resulting in mental incapacitation. Upon learning this, Mr. Taylor became enraged and stabbed a representative of the Law Society. In his criminal proceedings, Taylor was found unfit to stand trial and was subsequently found not guilty by reason of insanity (the precursor to NCR-MD). However, questions related to the suitability of the test used to determine his fitness to stand trial resulted in a retrial. The Ontario Court of Appeal ruled that the proper test for finding an accused unfit to stand trial was one the court called "a limited cognitive capacity test." According to this test, even if an accused, on the basis of firmly held delusions, is not capable of making rational decisions beneficial to himself, he may still be fit to stand trial if he understands the basic roles of the parties and procedures of the court. This test before the Ontario Court of Appeal was affirmed by the Supreme Court Canada in a subsequent case. It remains an important but controversial test for fitness

The next three chapters focus on forensic issues related to mental health treatment. Regarding the significant issue of confidentiality of psychiatric records, chapter 8 explores the cases of *R v O'Connor* and *R v Mills*. The 1995 Supreme Court of Canada decision in *O'Connor* allowed for access to treatment records of complainants (in this specific case, alleged victims of sexual violence), under certain specified conditions. In the *Mills* case, it was argued that the conditions established by *O'Connor* set the bar too low, allowing access to psychiatric and counselling records in most cases. The three competing principles, namely full answer and defence, privacy, and equality, were noted by the court not to be absolute and of equal importance. Parliament, adding emphasis to the concerns regarding the prevalence of sexual violence against women and children, set a higher threshold for access to complainants' counselling and psychiatric records by the accused. In reviewing the *Mills* case, the Supreme Court re-evaluated the issue and underlined the rights of the complainant, society's responsibility to certain groups, and the objective of promoting equality. These procedures remain in force today.

Solicitor-client privilege is the highest threshold of privilege in Canada. It has been held that if lawyers retain the services of forensic mental health professionals or other experts, this work is covered under the umbrella of solicitor-client privilege. In *Smith v Jones*, discussed in chapter 9, the Supreme Court changed the nature of confidentiality in forensic psychiatric practice, and indeed in regards to solicitor-client privilege. In the course of a forensic psychiatric assessment for defence counsel, the accused, Mr. Jones, detailed his plan to kidnap, rape, and kill prostitutes. Concerned for the safety of women in the sex trade, the psychiatrist, Dr. Smith, commenced an action entitling him to disclose the information to police. The court ruled that solicitor-client privilege is a fundamental principle, but it may be outweighed when public safety is at risk. Specificall , if there is a clear risk of serious bodily harm to an identifiable person or group, and there is an imminent danger, then the risk justifies breaching solicitor-client confidentialit .

Chapter 10 describes and analyses the issue of consent to mental health treatment by individuals in the forensic mental health system and the important case of *Starson v Swayze*. Mr. Scott Shutzman (who later changed his name to Professor Starson, despite his lack of qualiﬁ- cations) was charged numerous times with mischief, harassment, and issuing threats. During the course of psychiatric assessments, he was diagnosed as suffering from schizoaffective disorder, with symptoms that included grandiose delusions and disinhibition. He repeatedly refused medication, stating that he did not like the fact that medication would slow down his thinking. The case reviews the standard of law for provincial consent and capacity board decisions, as well as the evidence put before these boards. In the end, the Supreme Court decision defined a test for capacity that has since been cited in over 1,600 cases and tribunal decisions and has become the standard in mental health treatment in Canada.

We end with a chapter on forensic mental health practice related to civil law. It has become increasingly common for the courts to award compensation in civil cases wherein the plaintiff suffers from psychological symptoms that the court finds to be the responsibility of the tortfeasor (the individual who committed the act resulting in injury). However, it is not unusual that the plaintiff suffered from significant psychological symptoms or psychiatric illness prior to the incident that is the subject of inquiry. It is clear that the trier of fact has to decide which of these symptoms is a result of the wrongful act and which would have occurred if the act had not happened. In an important case discussed in chapter 11, *Athey v Leonati*, the Supreme Court analysed this principle. If the plaintiff suffers from symptoms due to a previous trauma or injury, prior to the current injury, from which it is likely that they would have continued to deteriorate, then this may ameliorate responsibility. In this case, it was argued that the plaintiff suffered from a pre-existing degenerative condition and may have experienced symptoms regardless of the accident. The compensation was therefore reduced, and the defendant would only pay for any additional damage. This issue became known as the "crumbling skull" rule.

Governing Legislation

In order to understand landmark cases and their relevance to practice, it is helpful to begin with an overview of the court system in Canada and of the legislative system in which the courts operate. Canada's democratic parliamentary system is derived from the British system of governance. Canada's first constitution, the British North America Act (BNA Act; also referred to as the Constitution Act of 1867), was enacted in 1867. This act was established as the supreme law of Canada and provided for the division of legislative and economic powers between the federal government and the provinces (Lefroy, 1914). The Constitution Act further set out the basic principles of democratic government and defined the three branches of government that sit under the sovereign (represented by the governor general):

1. the executive, which includes the prime minister and other ministers who answer to the legislature and are responsible for administering and enforcing laws;
2. the parliament or legislature who have the power to make, alter, and repeal laws;
3. the judiciary who interpret and apply the law (Department of Justice Canada, 2017). (See figu e 1.1)

Figure 1.1   The three branches of government in Canada

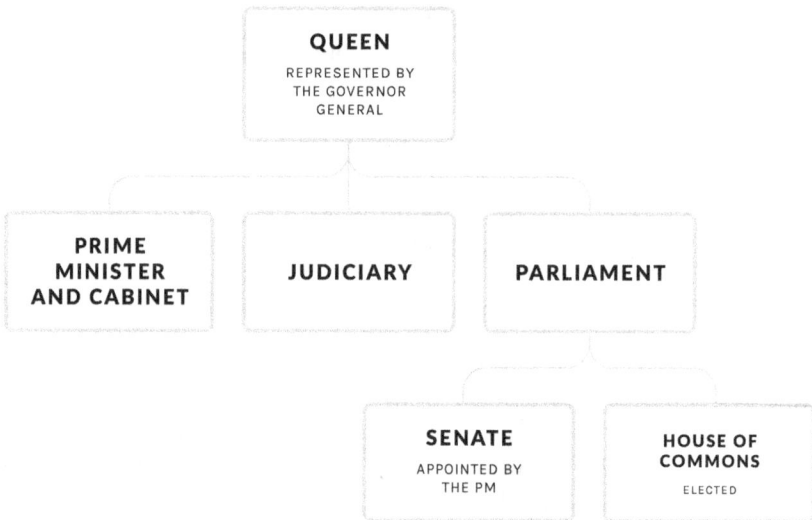

Source: Department of Justice Canada (2017)

In 1982, the Canada Act came into force, by which the British parliament agreed to surrender the power to make changes to the Canadian Constitution to the authority of the Canadian parliament. Coinciding with the Canada Act, the Constitution Act, 1982 was passed, a fundamental component of which was the Canadian Charter of Rights and Freedoms (The Charter). The Charter enshrines protection of the primary human rights of Canadians in the Constitution. Specifically, the Charter "guarantees the rights and freedoms set out in it, subject only to such reasonable limits prescribed by law as can be demonstrably justified in a free and democratic society"(s. 1). The Charter takes precedence over all federal and provincial legislation. No Canadian law or government may violate the guaranteed rights of Canadians under the Charter unless these rights threaten a free and democratic society. This requires balancing the rights of the individual against the common good. The Charter identifies the following fundamental freedoms for all Canadians:

(a) freedom of conscience and religion;
(b) freedom of thought, belief, opinion, and expression, including freedom of the press and other means of communication;
(c) freedom of peaceful assembly; and
(d) freedom of association. (Canadian Charter of Rights and Freedoms, 1982)

Rights under the Charter also include democratic rights, mobility rights, legal rights, equality rights, language rights, minority language education rights, and Aboriginal rights. A law can only violate the Charter rights of an individual if the limits placed on these rights can be shown to be reasonable, prescribed by law, and justified in a free and democratic society. However, federal and provincial governments have retained the ability to violate the Charter through a declaration under what is called the *notwithstanding clause*. This is a clause used only on rare occasions; it was invoked, for instance, by Quebec in 1988 to prohibit the use of signs in any language but French, by Saskatchewan in 1986 with respect to back-to-work legislation, and by Alberta in 2000 to define the province's marriage act as applying solely to heterosexual couples.

Types of Legislation

The Constitution provides a separation of powers between the federal parliament and provincial and territorial governments, resulting in an arrangement where Parliament can make laws (called statutes, legislation, or acts) for all of Canada on matters that the Constitution assigns, such as immigration, national defence, trade, and, for the purposes of this discussion, criminal law (Criminal Code, 1985), and youth criminal justice (Youth Criminal Justice Act, 2002). Provincial and territorial governments are empowered to enact laws on all matters of a local nature that apply only within the provincial or territorial borders, such as health and education. In turn, the provinces empower municipal governments to enact local laws or bylaws. Legislation can be understood as codified la .

There are two main categories of law in Canada: public law and private law. Public law governs the relationship between individuals and society and includes:

1. criminal law, involving the charging, trying, and sentencing of an alleged offender;
2. constitutional law, involving the relationship between federal and provincial governments and the protection of individual rights and freedoms; and
3. administrative law, involving the actions and operations of government, for instance, Criminal Code review boards. (Department of Justice Canada, 2017)

The second broad type of law is private law. Private law is used primarily to set the rules and settle disputes between citizens, that is, individuals or groups of people. This includes:

1. family law, including marriage, divorce, and custody;
2. contract law, such as employment and real estate; and
3. tort law, covering civil wrongs such as trespass and defamation.

Forensic mental health practitioners may find that individuals whom they are treating or assessing are simultaneously engaged in both criminal and civil law proceedings. For example, an individual who commits an assault may face criminal prosecution by the Crown, as well as a civil action by the injured party, one who may be seeking monetary compensation for injuries. Although criminal and civil cases may proceed simultaneously in relation to the same act, these proceedings will be entirely independent of each other (Regehr & Kanani, 2010).

Common Law

The United Kingdom, Canada, and the United States have common law legal systems under which many important laws are not created by the legislature, but rather by judges issuing decisions on a case-by-case basis and thereby creating precedents (Gennaioli & Shleifer, 2007). Prior to 1066, the dispersed nature of the English judicial system resulted in different interpretations of law by various judges and justices of the peace in various jurisdictions. Resulting decisions were thus ad hoc, that is, situation-specific without consideration for generalizable principles. It was therefore deemed necessary that judges should follow similar rules or a commonality. Over time, successive judicial interpretations of statutes – and decisions made where no statutes apply – lead to a body of judge-made decisions, known as common law. In this way, common law is uncodified; it is not based on a compilation of rules or statutes such as those that are found in legislation like the Criminal Code of Canada.

Nevertheless, case law or common law may be binding, depending on the level of court that makes the decision. Judges are asked to be consistent in their approaches across different jurisdictions by deciding whether the circumstances of a particular case are the same as previous cases that involved similar issues. If similar cases can be found, then the court must be guided by the previous decision or follow precedent. This principle is known as *stare decisis,* literally translated from the Latin as "the thing has been decided" (Winny, 2008). Case law is thus comprised of the accumulation of written decisions of judges arising from all levels of court in Canada. This promotes the principle that the law should be applied consistently throughout Canadian courts. If the circumstances in a certain case are slightly different or unique, the presiding judge may write a new decision that then becomes a new precedent. Despite this, statutes enacted by Parliament supersede any common law rule that existed beforehand.

Structure of the Courts

In order to understand the importance of landmark cases, it is critical to know how the Canadian courts are structured, beginning with a historical understanding. In 1721, seven years after Nova Scotia was ceded to the British Crown, a general court with jurisdiction over criminal and civil matters was established consisting of the governor and his council. Later, in 1749, a two-court system was established consisting of the General Court and the Inferior Court of Common Pleas, composed of five justices of the peace with jurisdiction over common law matters. Five years later, the General Court was abolished and Canada's first independent court, the Supreme Court of Nova Scotia, came into being under the Honorable Jonathan Belcher, Chief Justice of Nova Scotia.

During the mid-1800s, the Inferior Court was abolished and replaced with a county court system (Courts of Nova Scotia, 2004).

In 1760, the British captured Quebec and Montreal, giving the British control over a vast area of territory, including what we now call Ontario. Following this, the Quebec Act of 1774 established English law as the standard governing criminal matters, while allowing French law to have jurisdiction over other matters. After the end of the American Revolutionary War in 1783, population demographics changed dramatically owing to the influx of English-speaking British Loyalists who had fled the United States. These individuals, who remained British citizens, expressed resentment about the imposition of French law on their lives. This led to the Constitutional Act of 1791, which provided for two separate provinces: Upper Canada in the west and Lower Canada in the east (Ferguson, 2009).

At the turn of the century Upper Canada remained sparsely populated with few trained lawyers or judges. Most local legal issues, such as marriages, liquor licences, and taxation, were dealt with by justices of the peace, generally local gentry without formal legal training who were appointed by the governor. More serious matters were dealt with by the Court of the King's Bench in Montreal (Ferguson, 2009). Later, the Court of the King's Bench (which became the Queen's Bench in 1837) consisted of three justices sitting in the colonial capital of York (later named Toronto in 1834). The Queen's Bench exercised judgment over criminal and civil matters and heard appeals from across the province. Lay justices continued to staff the district courts, which later became county courts. This arrangement continued until as late as 1985, when the District Court of Ontario was established. In 1990, this district court was combined with a high court of justice to form the Ontario Court of Justice, now called the Ontario Superior Court of Justice (Ferguson, 2009).

On the west coast, the two founding colonies of British Columbia and Vancouver Island adopted English law in the 1800s and established a system of magistrate courts. Magistrates were individuals, often assuming the role on a part-time basis, who had little or no formal legal training. Wages for the role were either paid by the government or as a portion of fines imposed on someone found guilty. In 1947, the first educational conference of a recently formed provincial association of magistrates was held in response to federal and provincial legislation calling for increased legal training, qualifications, and continuing education for those charged with interpreting the law. The Provincial Court of British Columbia was established in 1969. It was not until 1974 that the new Provincial Court Act resulted in the retirement of the remaining lay judges (Provincial Court of British Columbia, 2014).

Provincial Courts

All provinces and territories (except Nunavut) now have three levels of courts. These are the provincial or territorial courts, the superior courts, and the appeal courts. Provincial and territorial courts deal with most criminal matters, family law matters, youth criminal justice matters, and most civil matters. On a day-to-day basis, most issues of fitness to stand trial and not criminally responsible due to mental disorder (NCR-MD), as well as the so-called therapeutic courts, such as mental health courts and drug diversion courts, are dealt with at this level.

Higher-level offences are referred to the provincial or territorial superior courts. They are divided into trial and appeals levels. Most serious civil and criminal cases appear before the trial-level courts. The appeal-level courts, sometimes referred to as divisional courts, are courts of first review and may hear appeals resulting from decisions by the trial courts (although these courts do not hear cases involving health law, which are generally heard in the provincial and territorial courts of appeal). Recently, the Ontario Court of Appeal has dealt with a large number of health law decisions as a result of the creation of an amicus program, which empowered lawyers appointed by the court to raise any issues that they believe to be relevant (Presser & Szigeti, 2017). In matters of national or significant social importance, decisions by the provincial or territorial courts of appeal are then appealed to the Supreme Court of Canada (Department of Justice Canada, 2017).

Federal Courts

In addition to the provincial territorial court systems, Parliament has established several federal courts, the most powerful being the Supreme Court of Canada (SCC). Federal courts deal with some matters over which the provincial courts do not have jurisdiction, for instance, certain drug charges. Tax courts and military courts also are under federal jurisdiction. The Federal Court of Appeal hears appeals from the Federal Court and Tax Court and conducts judicial reviews of certain federal administrative tribunals. The Canadian parliament has authority over criminal court procedures at all levels, in order to ensure fair and consistent treatment of criminal matters across the entirety of the country (see figure 1.2).

While provincial courts of appeal hear cases from the provincial courts and the district courts, the Supreme Court of Canada is the final court of appeal. The Supreme Court will agree to hear a case if it considers the matter to be of public importance or to have national significance.

Figure 1.2 The court structure in Canada

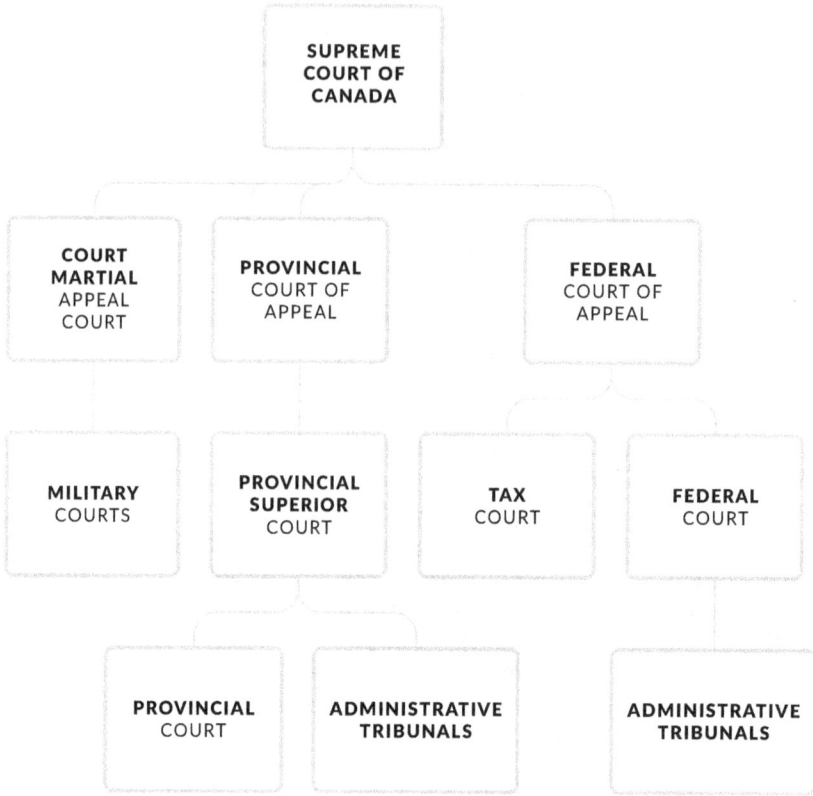

```
                    SUPREME
                    COURT OF
                    CANADA

  COURT          PROVINCIAL           FEDERAL
  MARTIAL        COURT OF             COURT OF
  APPEAL         APPEAL               APPEAL
  COURT

  MILITARY       PROVINCIAL     TAX          FEDERAL
  COURTS         SUPERIOR       COURT        COURT
                 COURT

          PROVINCIAL    ADMINISTRATIVE      ADMINISTRATIVE
          COURT         TRIBUNALS           TRIBUNALS
```

Source: Adapted from Department of Justice Canada (2017)

In addition, where a judge at the appeal level has dissented on how the law should be interpreted, there is an automatic right of appeal to the Supreme Court.

Administrative Boards and Tribunals

A significant amount of administrative law is dealt with by provincial and federal administrative tribunals. Important examples from a mental health perspective are the provincial Criminal Code review boards, which have jurisdiction over cases in which those accused are found not criminally responsible due to mental disorder (NCR-MD) or unfit to stand trial; and Consent and Capacity review boards, which deal with the issue of consent to treatment. These are technically not part of the court system and are rather "creatures of statute" (entities required by statute). Decisions from these tribunals may be reviewed in provincial courts and, in some cases, federal superior court.

Stare Decisis

As discussed above, an important concept in common law is the setting of precedents, a process that forms the basis of national, provincial, and territorial law in Canada, with the exception of Quebec, which has a civil code. Judicial precedent is embodied in the Latin phrase "stare decisis et non quieta movere," which can be translated as "to stand by decisions and not disturb settled matters" (Parkes, 2006). That is, previous legal decisions have binding authority over subsequent judicial decisions.

Stare decisis is hierarchical, implying that lower courts are bound to respect the authority and decisions of higher courts when the precedent is relevant to the case at hand, thereby limiting the discretion of any one person and ensuring consistency in courts across the country (Winny, 2008). Supreme Court of Canada decisions are binding in all courts across Canada; decisions of provincial and territorial courts of appeal are binding on all lower courts within their jurisdiction. This hierarchy is known as *vertical stare decisis*. Nevertheless, lower courts are required to follow only the *ratio decidendi* (the legal reasoning on which the case depends), not the *obiter dictum* (the judge's opinion on matters not essential to the decision). Thus, lower courts at times may refuse to follow a Supreme Court decision on the basis that the relevant part of the decision was *obiter dicta*, or a judicial aside (Parkes, 2006).

Complementary to the concept of hierarchical stare decisis is *horizontal stare decisis*. According to this concept, there should be consistency within any given court and between courts of "coordinate jurisdiction," that is, the same level of court. Before 1949, the Supreme Court of Canada held itself to the precedence of prior decisions. Similarly, the English House of Lords strictly maintained the horizontal tradition, leaving it to Parliament to correct decisions that were unjust or unworkable rather than overrule itself. However, in 1966 Lord Gardiner stated on behalf of the House:

> Their Lordships regard the use of precedent as an indispensable foundation upon which to decide what is the law and its application to individual cases. It provides at least some degree of certainty upon which individuals can rely in the conduct of their affairs, as well as a basis for the orderly development of legal rules.

Their Lordships nevertheless recognize that too rigid adherence to precedent may lead to injustice in a particular case and also unduly restrict proper development of the law. They propose therefore to modify their practice and, while treating former decisions of this House as normally binding, to depart from previous decisions when it appears right to do so. (*Practice Statement*, 1966)

In addition, there are times when precedents arising in other jurisdictions are also taken into account. While such decisions are not binding, it is generally held that decisions in certain jurisdictions have persuasive authority and may assist the court in coming to a decision (Parkes, 2006). For instance, the court of appeal in Ontario may be guided by the analysis and decision of the court of appeal in British Columbia because of parallels between circumstances of the particular cases, despite the fact that it is not binding. However, if the British Columbia case is appealed to the Supreme Court of Canada and the decision upheld, the decision does become binding. In other instances, cases from the United Kingdom (particularly if the decision is from the House of Lords or Court of Appeal), cases from other Commonwealth countries, and even cases from the United States may be considered and may have persuasive authority. For instance, the famous Tarasoff decision in the United States on the duty to warn and protect was viewed as having relevance to Canada (Glancy, Regehr, & Bryant, 1998, Chapter 9).

Despite the importance of precedence, Parkes reminds us that judges do not "slavishly adhere" to outdated principles and that rather "there remains a lively and important debate about the functions, values and limits of abiding by things decided in common law systems" (p. 135). For instance, in *R v Salituro*, the accused was charged with forging his estranged wife's name on a cheque and cashing it. Under law, she could not testify for the prosecution against her spouse. Citing a change to precedent, Chief Justice Lamer stated:

While complex changes to the law with uncertain ramifications should be left to the legislature, judges can and should make incremental changes to the common law to bring legal rules into step with a changing society when it is appropriate to do so. Since the enactment of the Canadian Charter of Rights and Freedoms, judges also have a duty to see that the common law develops in accordance with the values of the Charter. Where the principles underlying a common law rule are out of step with the Charter values, the courts should scrutinize the rule closely. If it is possible to change the rule so as to make it consistent with such values, without upsetting the proper balance between judicial and legislative action, then the rule ought to be changed. This is an appropriate case for a court to change the common law rule in order to make spouses who are irreconcilably separated competent witnesses for the prosecution. (*R v Salituro*, 1991)

Conversely, in another case involving maritime law, the Supreme Court noted that the court's power to change the common law is limited (*Bow Valley Husky (Bermuda) Ltd. v Saint John Shipbuilding Ltd.*, 1997). The court noted that lawmaking and law reform should be left to the legislature and that judges must be restrained in their lawmaking, limiting this exercise to incremental steps. Nevertheless, in chapter 4, which discusses criminal responsibility, we will see an example of the court crafting a new common law rule that overturned existing legislation.

Summarizing the challenges on this issue, Justices Steel and Freedman in *R v Neves* stated the following:

> The principle of stare decisis is a bedrock of our judicial system. There is great value in certainty in law, but there is also, of course, an expectation that the law as expounded by judges will be correct, and certainly not knowingly incorrect, which would result when a decision felt to be wrong is not overruled. The tension when these principles are in conflict can be profound. (*R v Neves*, 2005)

This type of profound conflict is exemplified in Charter challenges, as discussed below.

Statutory Interpretation and Context

> A statute is neither a literary text nor a divine revelation. Its effect therefore is neither an expression laden with innumerable overtones nor a permanent creation of infallible wisdom. It is a statement of a situation, or rather a group of possible events within a situation; as such it is essentially ambiguous. (Radin, 1930)

This statement, written in the *Harvard Law Review* in 1930, continues to have salience as the courts in Canada engage in the complex process of interpreting legislation. Legislation is usually drafted in general terms, as an attempt to deal with present and future situations, and often to mollify competing perspectives and interests. It cannot anticipate all situations to which it may apply, and, in essence, leaves this application to the courts. The process by which the courts

attempt to understand and apply legislation is called statutory interpretation (Sullivan, 2016). Three aspects of statutory interpretation
have been proposed: the literal meaning, the purpose (referred to as
the golden rule), and the consequences (referred to as the mischief
rule) (Driedger, 1974). When the literal meaning is applied, the court
believes it has little room to interpret the legislation in context. However, it is acknowledged that at times the literal interpretation will
result in an absurd outcome, and the golden rule will be applied, as
stated by Lord Wensleydale in 1857:

> In construing wills and indeed statutes, and all written instruments, the
> grammatical and ordinary sense of the words is to be adhered to, unless
> that would lead to some absurdity, or some repugnance or inconsistency
> with the rest of the instrument, in which case the grammatical and ordi-
> nary sense of the words may be modified, so as to avoid that absurdity or
> inconsistency, but not farther. (*Grey v Pearson*, 1857, p. 1234)

Finally, under the mischief rule, the court attempts to understand what
problem the statute has attempted to remedy and thus what ruling in
the current situation will affect that remedy.

In Canada, these three rules have been integrated into a single
approach: what Driedger called "the modern principle" (as cited in
Sullivan, 2016). In this approach, "the words of the Act are to be read
in their entire context and in the grammatical and ordinary sense har-
moniously with the scheme of the Act, the object of the Act, and the
intention of Parliament" (Driedger, 1974, p. 87). Critical to this is the
understanding that context is dynamic. One aspect of this is changing
technology and resulting changes in social behaviour; for instance,
how should laws governing sexual harassment be interpreted with
respect to social media? Another aspect is changing awareness, such
as changing awareness of the impact of trauma on the well-being of
individuals and groups. Yet another is changing attitudes regarding issues such as same-sex marriage. Some legal scholars suggest
that the need for statutory interpretation arises from dissatisfaction
with legislative outcomes of the political process and the view that,
at times, legislation serves the purposes of special interest groups at
the expense of broader public interests (Macey, 1986). In this respect,
interpretation of the courts takes into consideration the context and
the protection of the rights of those who are not members of the designated group or interest group.

In reading landmark cases, it is important to understand the nature
of judicial discretion. Several authors assert that years of empirical

scholarship have firmly established that the ideological views and the values of Supreme Court justices have a profound impact on their decisions (Gennaioli & Shleifer, 2007; Richards & Kritzer, 2002; Segal & Spaeth, 1996; Songer & Lindquist, 1996). As Songer and Lindquist (1996) suggest, "Justices attempt to create a policy that is as close as possible to their preferences within the constraint imposed by precedent" (p. 1050). Nevertheless, this can result in better laws that more closely reflect societal values and the day-to-day experiences of citizens. This was most saliently stated by Judge Benjamin Cardozo (1921):

> The eccentricities of judges balance one another. One judge looks at problems from the point of view of history, another from philosophy, another from that of social utility, one is a formalist, another a latitudinarian, one is timorous of change, another dissatisfied with the present; out of the attrition of diverse minds there is beaten something which has a constancy and uniformity and average greater value than its component parts. (p. 177)

Thus, in this book we describe the context in which specific cases arose, including the history of the issue, the political climate at the time the case was heard, and, where possible, the nature of past decisions made by particular judges, as knowledge of all these factors is helpful in enhancing our understanding of landmark decisions.

As we will also see throughout this book, there is often an interplay between the legislative and court processes, in which court rulings provoke legislation and legislation is interpreted by the courts. Examples include the insanity defence, fitness to stand trial, court access to records of victims of sexual violence, and consent to treatment. Each of these issues has been the source of public interest, debate, or outrage. In each case, the legislature and courts have attempted to find a balance between competing principles and demands. Another example of this is the manner in which the courts are interpreting individual rights under the Canadian Charter of Rights and Freedoms.

Charter Challenges

On 17 April 1982, a major legal event occurred that signalled Canada's final independence from the United Kingdom. Queen Elizabeth II and Prime Minister Pierre Trudeau signed the proximal of the Constitution Act, 1982. This act declared the Constitution to be the supreme law of Canada. As noted above, the Constitution contains the Canadian Charter of Rights and Freedoms (the Charter), which guarantees fundamental human rights and freedoms. Everything performed under the auspices of the Canadian government and bodies created or connected to the government, either federal or provincial, is covered by the Charter (Department of Justice, 2015). If the court decides that a law unjustifiably violates rights and freedoms guaranteed under the Charter, it may declare that particular law invalid. However, the court must perform a balancing act, considering individual interests against the interests of society. As societal values change, so do Charter rights evolve. Thus, earlier decisions may be revisited by the court. The court applies the following analysis:

1. Does the legislation infringe upon a Charter right? (The onus is on the complainant to prove that there has been an infringement of a right.)
2. If there has been an infringement, is the infringement of that right justified as a limitation in section 1 of the Charter

The Crown carries the burden of proof to prove that the limitation is justified. This is based on a two-stage test established by the Supreme Court in *R v Oakes*. In this case, David Oakes was charged with possession of narcotics for the purposes of trafficking. He made a Charter challenge, claiming that the reverse onus created by the presumption that the possession of large quantities of drugs was, by definition, for the purposes of trafficking, violated the presumption of innocence under the Charter. In ruling that the presumption of innocence lies at the very heart of criminal law and is protected expressly by the Charter, the court established that two questions be sequentially addressed. First, does the legislation have a pressing and substantial objective? The objective must be of sufficient importance to warrant overriding a constitutionally protected right or freedom. Second, are the means chosen to advance the legislation's objective reasonable and demonstrably justifiable in a free and democratic society? To answer this question, a proportionality test is applied. This test determines whether the means are rationally connected to the objective, that there must be a minimal impairment of rights, and that there must be proportionality between the infringement and the objective (*R v Oakes*, 1986).

Elements of a Landmark Case

The first page of a Supreme Court judgment begins with the reference known as the *style* or *title of the proceedings*. It then lists the *appellant*, the person on whose behalf the appeal is made. Below this is the name of the *respondent*, which in a criminal case is Her Majesty the Queen (the Crown). Included on either side may be the *interveners* (also spelled *intervenors*), who are not party to the case but are permitted to join in the proceedings without the permission of the litigants. In practice, interveners may include the attorneys general of Canada and the provinces, and groups that have an interest in the litigation, for instance, the Canadian Mental Health Association. Other information includes the date of the judgment, the date the case was heard, judges who heard the case (identified as present), lawyers for each party, a list of some of the key terms of the case, a brief summary of the facts and law in the case, and a list of cases, statutes, regulations, books, articles, and chapters that are cited or relied upon in coming to the decision.

The judgment is found under the heading of *held*, which states whether the appeal is allowed or dismissed. In simple language, if the appeal is allowed, the question that the appellant has raised, for instance, as to whether a particular law or statute is unconstitutional, has been answered in the affirmative. There are nine judges on the Supreme Court of Canada. Sometimes the decision is unanimous, and the judgment may be written by one judge representing the whole Supreme Court. In other cases, one or more judges may write a concurring decision, coming to the same conclusion, perhaps using different arguments. In a split judgment, the majority opinion holds sway and one or more of the judges may write a dissenting or minority opinion. In one of the cases that we have included (*Starson v Swayze*, Chapter 10), the decision starts with the minority opinion because the chief justice dissented. In this case, you will note that the majority opinion, written by Justice Major, does not start until paragraph 61. The case may also include *obiter dicta* (a statement made by the judge in passing and not essential to the decision); as we have noted above, this part of the decision is not binding on lower courts.

Summary of Key Concepts in Law

As we have indicated, landmark cases are studied because they have historical and legal significance in that they establish new precedents and change the manner in which an issue is dealt with by the courts. The cases selected in this book also have a significant impact on forensic mental health practice. As forensic mental health professionals, we are called to translate mental health concepts into concepts that are helpful

Table 1.1 Elements of a landmark case

Style of cause	The name of the case
Report	The case citation
Appellant	The person appealing the decision of a lower court to a higher court
Respondent	The party against whom an appeal is being brought. (In a criminal case often Her Majesty the Queen)
Present	Judges hearing the case
Interveners	Third parties who have an interest in the proceedings as the judgment may in some way affect them or others they represent
Facts	Aspects of the case taken into account by the courts
Statutory provisions	Statutes and legislation taken into account such as the Canada Evidence Act or a section of the Criminal Code of Canada
Courts below	Decisions made by courts who have made judgments prior to the appeal
Cases cited	Relevant precedents
Authors cited	Relevant literature considered
Held/holding	The decision of the court
Judgment	The opinion of the court regarding the rights and liabilities of the parties and the reasons for the decision
Dissenting opinion	A written opinion by one or more judges expressing disagreement with the majority opinion
Disposition	Final ruling on the case

in the process of coming to legal decisions. Simply reading the law does not give us clear direction for deciding concepts such as unfit to stand trial or NCR-MD. It is only by understanding the analysis and reasoning of landmark cases that we can inform ourselves sufficiently to be able to contribute meaningfully to the legal forum. In order to understand how legal decisions affect the law, it is important to understand the structure of the courts and which decisions have legal authority. Gaining familiarity with the development of common law precedents, that is, decisions made in similar cases in similar circumstances, and with the role of Parliament and legislation, are essential to our understanding of the legal process.

Table 1.2 Key concepts in law

Landmark case	Settles a point in law Often has important social or practice implications
Canadian Charter of Rights and Freedoms	Enshrines protection of the primary human rights of Canadians in the Constitution
Legislation	Laws enacted by government
Common law	A body of judge-made decisions where no statutes apply
Public law	Governs the relationship between individuals and society Includes criminal law, constitutional law, and administrative law
Private law	Also known as civil law Sets the rules and settles disputes between citizens, that is, individuals or groups of people Includes family law, contract law, and tort law
Precedent	A principle or rule established in a previous case that is binding on a court deciding a similar case
Stare decisis	Hierarchical – lower courts are bound to respect the authority and decisions of higher courts when the precedent is applicable Horizontal – there should be consistency within any given court and between courts at the same level
Statutory interpretation	The process by which the courts attempt to understand and apply legislation

2 Expert Testimony

R v Mohan

Chikmaglur Mohan, a practising pediatrician in North Bay, Ontario, was charged with sexual assault related to medical examinations performed on four female patients who were between the ages of 13 and 16. Allegations involved fondling of breasts, digital penetration without the use of gloves, and stimulation of vaginal areas while asking intrusive questions about their sexual activities. Three of the victims came forward independently and did not know the other complainants; a fourth came forward as a result of media attention to the case (*R v Mohan*, 1994).

Dr. Mohan denied the allegations against him, and, in support of his defence, his counsel indicated the intent to call a forensic psychiatrist, who would testify on characteristics of individuals that perpetrated such offences and factors that differentiated Dr. Mohan from this class of individuals. In a *voir dire*, Dr. Wood Hill testified that the perpetrator of the first three alleged offences was likely a pedophile, while the fourth was likely a sexual sadist. Further, he indicated that Dr. Mohan did not possess the characteristics of either group of offenders. The trial judge ruled that this evidence was inadmissible as it fell outside of the proper sphere of expert evidence (Glancy & Bradford, 2007). Dr. Mohan was found guilty and appealed the decision to the Ontario Court of Appeal. In 1992, the Court of Appeal ruled that the trial judge had erred in its ruling with respect to Dr. Hill's testimony. As a result, it quashed the conviction of Dr. Mohan and ordered a new trial. The Crown appealed to the Supreme Court of Canada.

Supreme Court Ruling in *R v Mohan*

The issue before the Supreme Court was whether an expert witness could be called to testify as to the fit between the character traits of the accused and the psychological profile generally believed to be associated with perpetrators of the offence (or in legal terms, putative perpetrators). Mr. Justice Sopinka, in writing for the Supreme Court, noted that the admissibility of expert evidence relies on four factors (*R v Mohan*, 1994):

1. *Relevance.* The court noted that relevant information could be excluded if the probative value is outweighed by the prejudicial effect. That is, where the evidence may distort the fact-finding p o-cess or confuse the jury.
2. *Necessity.* In order to meet the criteria of necessity, expert evidence must be outside the knowledge or experience of the judge and jury. Therefore, the trier of fact would be unable to come to a satisfactory conclusion without the assistance of the expert.
3. *Absence of any exclusionary rule.* The Canadian Charter of Rights and Freedoms (s. 24.2) specifically notes that "evidence shall be excluded if it is established that … the admission of it in the pro-ceedings would bring the administration of justice into disrepute." Examples could include misconduct by the police in the investiga-tory process (Leckie, 1997).
4. *Qualifications of the expert.* Expert evidence must be given by an individual who has acquired special knowledge in the areas in which they are testifying.

In this particular case, Mr. Justice Sopinka indicated that there was no evidence that pedophilia or psychopathy had been standard-ized to the extent that they could be matched with an individual in this specific case. Therefore, as the evidence on which the expert would base his opinion was not sufficiently reliable, the usefulness of the testimony would not outweigh the potential for misleading or diverting the jury. The appeal was thus upheld, and the evidence excluded.

Postscript on *R v Mohan*

Dr. Mohan was sentenced to nine months in jail and two years' pro-bation for his original conviction but was released from custody pending his appeal. He continued to practise as chief of pediatrics in North Bay's two hospitals and continued to see children under supervision (Gray, 1991). Subsequently, the Discipline Committee of the College of Physicians and Surgeons of Ontario concluded their proceedings and found Chikmaglur Mohan guilty of professional misconduct arising from sexual misconduct "in that he committed sexual impropriety with a patient ... [his conduct] would reasonably be regarded as disgraceful, dishonourable or unprofessional." His licence to practise was revoked (College of Physicians and Surgeons of Ontario, 1991).

Dr. Mohan was deported to India in 1996, following the Supreme Court ruling which upheld his original conviction. Nine years later, he was spotted walking along a street in North Bay by Detective Dan Webber, was arrested, and taken to Ottawa-Carleton Detention Centre by immigration officers from Canadian Border Services ("Deported Doc Faces Immigration Hearing," 2005). At a hearing the day following his arrest, he was ordered to be deported by the Immigration and Refugee Board (IRB). The Immigration and Refugee Board spokesperson, Dominique Forget, is quoted as saying that "Mr. Mohan was ordered detained because he is considered a danger to the public" ("Mohan's Deportation," 2005).

Frye v United States (and *Daubert v Merrell Dow Pharmaceuticals*)

A particular challenge in applying the criteria for allowing expert testimony arises if the opinion is based on novel or controversial theory. Retired Supreme Court justice Frank Iacobucci and barrister Graeme Hamilton, in a 2010 *Canadian Medical Association Journal* article on medical expert witnesses, provided the following examples of novel or controversial science that can be troubling for courts:

• the theory that trauma precipitates the onset of multiple sclerosis;
• the use of PET scans to diagnose mild traumatic brain injury;
• the use of mitochondrial DNA typing for forensic identification.
  (Iacobucci & Hamilton, 2010)

As demonstrated in *Smith v Jones* (1999) regarding the duty to warn and protect, discussed in chapter 9, rulings in the United States on the admissibility of expert testimony have influenced Canadian courts, in particular, concerning the manner in which the courts deal with newly emerging science. *Frye v United States* (1923) was the first American case that outlined a standard for determining whether novel subject matter could be considered expert testimony (Schwartz, 1996). During the murder trial of Mr. Frye, defence counsel offered expert witness testimony, involving the use of a systolic blood pressure deception test, that they asserted would verify the truthfulness of the defendant. The theory proffered was that truth is spontaneous and comes without conscious effort. In the case of lying, it was proposed that the effort involved would increase blood pressure, and thus lying could be detected by the test. In considering the issue, Associate Justice Van Orsdel wrote:

> Just when scientific principle or discovery crosses the line between experimental and discovery … is difficult to define. Somewhere in this twilight zone, the evidential force of the principle must be recognized … the thing from which the deduction is made must be sufficiently established to have gained general acceptance in the particular field in which it belongs. (*Frye v United States*, 1923, p. 1014)

The court concluded that the systolic blood pressure deception test had not yet gained such standing and scientific ecognition.

Frye v United States thus established the *general acceptance test*, a test that was not significantly modified until the US Supreme Court case *Daubert v Merrell Dow Pharmaceuticals* (1993), 70 years later. Jason Daubert and Eric Schuller were children born with congenital disabilities who, along with their parents, sued a pharmaceutical company asserting that the cause of the defects was the mothers' ingestion of an anti-nausea drug manufactured by the respondent. In support of their claim, they sought to introduce expert evidence by Dr. Steven Lamm, an expert on exposure to chemical substances. In considering the admissibility of scientific evidence, Justice Blackman stated

> There are important differences between the quest for truth in the courtroom and the quest for truth in the laboratory. Scientific conclusions are subject to perpetual revision. Law on the other hand must resolve disputes finally and quickly. The scientific project is advanced by broad and wide-ranging consideration of a multitude of hypotheses, for those that are incorrect will eventually be shown to be so, and that itself is an advance. Conjectures that are probably wrong are of little use, however, in the project of reaching a quick, final and binding legal judgment – often of great consequence. (*Daubert v Merrell Dow Pharmaceuticals*, 1993, p. 2798)

The US Supreme Court thus cited four additional factors for consideration when assessing whether a particular test used has a reliable foundation:

1. whether the theory or technique is testable and has been tested using valid and reliable procedures;
2. whether the theory or technique has been subject to peer review;

3. whether the error or potential rate of error has been identified and whether standards exist for controlling the technique's operation; and
4. whether this theory or technique has been generally accepted by the relevant scientific communit . (*Daubert v Merrell Dow Pharmaceuticals*, 1993)

In what has been called the *"Daubert* diaspora," this standard is now used in many jurisdictions throughout the world (Meintjes-Van Der Walt, 2011).

R v J-LJ

In 2000, the Supreme Court of Canada adopted the criteria established in the US case of *Daubert v Merrell Dow Pharmaceuticals* in *R v J-LJ*. In this case, the accused had been charged with the sexual assault of two young boys. The defence attempted to call the evidence of Quebec psychiatrist Dr. Edouard Beltrami to demonstrate that the offences would have been committed by a serious sexual deviant, and that, upon testing, it was determined that the defendant did not possess the characteristics to be so classified. Evidence on which the expert opinion was based included a psychiatric history, the MMPI-2, electromyography, and penile plethysmography (Glancy & Bradford, 2007). In writing for the court, Mr. Justice Binnie indicated that novel science should be subject to special scrutiny and included penile plethysmography in this category. He observed:

> Expert witnesses have an essential role to play in the criminal courts. However, the dramatic growth and the frequency with which they have been called upon in recent years has led to ongoing debate about suitable controls on their participation, precautions to exclude "junk science," and the need to preserve and protect the role of the trier of fact – the judge or the jury. (*R v J-LJ*, 2000, at para 25)

The judgment carefully detailed the manner in which Dr. Beltrami's evidence was consistent with the standards enunciated in *Daubert*. The court concluded that Dr. Beltrami's testimony did not meet the standard and should, therefore, be excluded. Thus, while the principles in *Daubert* were not specifically referred to the in the conclusions of the court, they were clearly relied upon, suggesting that Canadian law now recognizes the principles for the adoption of novel science (Glancy & Bradford, 2007).

White Burgess Langille Inman v Abbott and Haliburton Co

While the case of *White Burgess Langille Inman v Abbott and Haliburton Co* (referred to more generally as *White Burgess*) arises in a context far outside the bounds of forensic mental health, it nevertheless has implications for expert testimony. In this case, action was brought against the chartered accountancy firm of White Burgess Langille Inman (referred to in the judgment as "WBLI" or "the auditors") for professional negligence by a group of small businesses (referred to as "the shareholders"), led by Abbott and Haliburton Home Hardware, based on alleged irregularities discovered by a new auditing firm, Grant Thornton. White Burgess Langille Inman brought a motion seeking to have the shareholders' action dismissed. As a result, the shareholders retained a forensic accountant, Susan MacMillan, as their expert. It was alleged by WBLI that since Ms. MacMillan worked for another office of Grant Thornton, the firm that raised the original concerns, she had a financial interest in the outcome and, as a result, might tailor her evidence and not be truly impartial. In the end, the Supreme Court of Canada ruled that there were no grounds to conclude that Ms. MacMillan was biased, and that past business relations between a litigant and a proposed expert do not automatically render the expert biased (*White Burgess Langille Inman v Abbott and Haliburton Co*, 2015, at para 2).

The judgment written by Mr. Justice Cromwell identified the two-step process for determining the admissibility of expert testimony originally identified in *R v Abbey* (1982). First, the evidence must meet the threshold of admissibility using the four factors identified in *R v Mohan* (1994). At the second stage, the trial judge must determine the degree to which the expert testimony will be beneficial to the court, balanced against any potential harm to the court process. The judgment went on to discuss the duty of the expert as follows:

> Expert witnesses have a special duty to the court to provide fair, objective and non-partisan assistance. A proposed expert witness who is unable or unwilling to comply with this duty is not qualified to give expert opinion evidence and should not be permitted to do so. Less fundamental concerns about an expert's independence and impartiality should be taken into account in the broader, overall weighing of the costs and benefits of receiving the evidence. (*White Burgess Langille Inman v Abbott and Haliburton Co*, 2015)

In this respect, when looking at the relationship between an expert and a party to the case, the issue is not whether a reasonable observer would think the expert is not independent, but rather if the relationship impedes the expert's ability to be fair, objective, and non-partisan. Any witness unable to fulfil this duty should be excluded. The court concluded that the threshold requirement was whether the witness was unable or unwilling to fulfil their duty to assist the court. Generally, the fact that the expert recognizes their duty to the court is sufficient in the absence of a challenge. Any party opposing the admission of the expert must demonstrate that there is a real concern that the expert was unable or unwilling to comply with this duty. If this burden is discharged, then the burden shifts to the party calling the witness to prove, on the balance of probabilities, that the threshold requirements have been met. The court stressed that the threshold requirement was not particularly onerous and that it was likely quite rare that the expert testimony would be excluded. In the case discussed below (*R v Livingston*, 2017), the expert was a former police office , and, therefore, a higher threshold was determined to be necessary.

The main impact of *White Burgess* was that it was concluded that the lack of independence or impartiality of an expert went to the admissibility of the evidence, rather than to the weight to be given to the testimony, which had been the general rule prior to this decision. A further refinement of this occurred in *R v Tang* (2015), in which the Ontario Court of Appeal ruled that in most cases, the suggestion that the expert witness lacks independence or impartiality will go to the weight of the evidence and not its admissibility.

The ruling was subsequently used in the high-profile case of *R v Livingston*. Mr. Livingston, chief of staff to former Ontario Premier Dalton McGuinty, and Ms. Miller, the deputy chief of staff, were charged in relation to allegedly deleting emails regarding the decision of the Liberal government to cancel two gas plants, just prior to the 2011 provincial election (Jones, 2016). The case garnered considerable media attention as it called into question the credibility of the ruling government. As a result, the case was tried by Roy Richard, a Quebec-based federal prosecutor, rather than the Ministry of the Attorney General of Ontario. Clayton Ruby was retained by one of the defendants and was paid using funds the accused had raised through crowdsourcing (Jones, 2016). The defence brought a motion to exclude an expert witness called by the Crown, a former police office , on the grounds that he was not independent and impartial (*R v Livingston*, 2017).

The witness in question was a retired member of the Ontario Provincial Police Technological Crime Unit; he was referred to as Mr. Gagnon in the ruling on the admissibility of opinion evidence. Upon retirement, Mr. Gagnon began working as a systems coordinator for the Internet

Intelligence Unit before being hired for Project Hampden, the investigation that led to the charges against Mr. Livingston and Ms. Miller. In considering the evidence before him, Judge Lipson identified that the test established in *White Burgess* is now the governing test for determining the admissibility of expert testimony. Judge Lipson noted that while Mr. Gagnon's original role was as a computer forensic expert in Project Hampden, it morphed into a proactive role in the investigation, including that of giving strategic and legal advice. "Instead of maintaining his distance and independence from the day-to-day activities of Project Hampden, Mr. Gagnon did just the opposite" (*R v Livingston*, 2017, at para 51). In his decision, Judge Lipson concluded that there was a realistic concern that Mr. Gagnon was unable to provide independent, impartial, and unbiased evidence, and his opinion was excluded. It should be noted that the lack of impartiality went to admissibility rather than to the weight to be given to the evidence. This reflected the change in the gatekeeper function of the judge at the first hurdle, a development introduced in *White Burgess*.

R v Abbey and *R v Lavallee*

As a standard of practice, forensic mental health professionals interview the evaluee, collect information from collateral contacts, review medical records and other pertinent records, review literature, and possibly talk with colleagues before coming to a final opinion. This has been the subject of some scrutiny by the courts. (See, for instance, the American Academy of Psychiatry and the Law's *Practice Guideline for the Forensic Assessment*, Glancy et al., 2015.) Nevertheless, this reliance on information provided by others may conflict with what the court views as hearsay evidence. In *R v Abbey* (1982) and *R v Lavallee* (1990), the Supreme Court of Canada addressed this question.

Most pertinently, in the context of this chapter, the Supreme Court concluded that the trial judge erred in accepting hearsay evidence relayed by an expert in the course of giving an opinion as factual. Nevertheless, the court concluded that the opinion as a whole was admissible even if it was based on what was referred to as second-hand evidence. Having been admitted, it is up to the trier of fact to accept or reject this opinion they see fit. Quoting from *R v Turner* (1974), the court noted "an expert's opinion is admissible to furnish the court with scientific information which is likely to be outside the experience and knowledge of a judge and jury. If on the proven facts a judge or jury can form their own conclusions without help, then the opinion of the expert is unnecessary" (*R v Turner*, 1974, p. 83). The court noted that what is important is not the admissibility of the testimony, but the weight that it should be given. Again referring to *Turner*, the court concluded that all the facts upon which an expert bases their opinion are hearsay, except those that the expert personally observes during their examination, such as "his appearance of depression and his becoming emotional when discussing the deceased girl and his own family" (*R v Turner*, 1974, p. 82). In this case, the lord chief justice noted fairly that it is not for him to instruct psychiatrists how to prepare their reports, but he does direct lawyers who call experts as witnesses to prove the facts upon which the expert bases their opinions. The court concluded that before any weight can be given to an expert's opinion, the facts upon which the opinion is based must be found to exist.

Twenty-two-year-old Lyn Lavallee was subject to repeated violence while in a volatile relationship with Kevin Rust over the course of three to four years (*R v Lavallee*, 1990). On 30 August 1986, the couple held a boisterous party at their home. In the early hours of the morning, Ms. Lavallee and Mr. Rust argued in an upstairs bedroom. Mr. Rust was killed by gunshot from a rifle fi ed by Ms. Lavallee as he was leaving the room. Ms. Lavallee did not testify in court, but in a statement to the police, she said that during the course of the violent argument, Mr. Rust said, "either you kill me, or I'll get you" (*R v Lavallee*, 1990, at para 7). A mental health expert that was called testified that Ms. Lavallee had been terrorized to the point of feeling trapped, vulnerable, worthless, and unable to escape the relationship. In his opinion, she sincerely believed that she would be killed that night. His evidence was based on an interview with the accused, the police report, hospital reports, and an interview with Ms. Lavallee's mother. The jury acquitted Ms. Lavallee; however, the verdict was later overturned by the Manitoba Court of Appeal. The issues before the Supreme Court of Canada were whether the evidence of the psychiatrist should have been before the court and whether, if it should, the trial judge's instructions with respect to it were adequate. The appeal was allowed.

In the ruling, the court determined that expert testimony is admissible to assist the trier of fact "in drawing inferences in areas where the expert has relevant knowledge or experience beyond that of the layperson." In the case of "battered woman syndrome," there are certain areas where the court believed this to be the case (Regehr & Glancy, 1995). The court continued to state that it is not necessary for each of the specific facts underlying the expert's opinion to be proven before any weight would be given to the opinion, as long as there is some admissible evidence to establish the foundation of the expert's opinion. When the information the expert has used to form an opinion derives from one of the parties of the litigation "or from any other source that is inherently suspect, a court ought to require independent proof of that information" (*R v Lavallee*, 1990, at para 99). If this party is not called, and these facts are neither admitted nor proven, this lessens the weight of the expert opinion. The majority concluded by saying, "the judge must, of course, warn the jury that the more the expert relies on facts not proved in evidence the less weight the jury may attribute to the opinion" (*R v Lavallee*, 1990, at para 89).

Westerhof v Gee Estate

In 2010, Rule 53.03 of the Rules of Civil Procedure, RRO 1990, Reg. 194 was subject to various amendments, which included setting out the duty of an expert "engaged by or on behalf of a party" to provide opinion evidence that is "fair, neutral and nonpartisan and within the expert's area of expertise" (rule 4.1.01). It is likely that this is in response to a prevailing feeling in civil litigation that "too many experts are no more than hired guns who tailor their reports and evidence to suit the client's needs" (as cited in Osborne, 2007).

Westerhof v Gee Estate was a routine case involving the after-effects of a motor vehicle accident. In this case, a number of attending and treating physicians were called, as well as experts retained by the parties. The essence of the case was which, if any, of these provided admissible evidence. The attending or treating physicians did not sign the disclosure form required by retained experts under rule 53.03 of the Ontario Rules of Civil Procedure (2019), which sets out an agreement to abide by the duties required of experts. The trial judge thus excluded the treating doctors on the basis that they did not comply with rule 53.03; in other words, they did not sign the acknowledgment.

The Ontario Court of Appeal made the distinction between experts engaged by a party to the litigation, whom they referred to as "litigation experts," and the treating or attending physicians, whom they referred to as "participant experts." The court clarified the role of a participant expert as

[A] witness with special skill, knowledge, training, or experience who has not been engaged by or on behalf of a party to the litigation may give opinion evidence for the truth of its contents without complying with rule 53.03 where:

- the opinion to be given is based on the witness's observation of or participation in the events at issue; and

- the witness formed the opinion to be given as part of the ordinary exercise of their skill, knowledge, training and experience while observing or participating in such events. (*Westerhof v Gee Estate*, 2015, at para 60)

The court continued that if the participant expert goes further than these limits, they should comply with rule 53.03.

In another case, *Imeson v Maryvale* (2018), the Ontario Court of Appeal reviewed the analysis for admissibility of expert witnesses and created a two-stage process. The first stage is an assessment of threshold criteria: relevance, necessity, not being subject to an exclusionary rule, and being a properly qualified expert willing to provide impartial evidence. The second stage is an assessment within the *White Burgess* framework. In the *Imeson* case, the plaintiff sought damages for alleged childhood sexual abuse in Maryvale, an institution for troubled youth. The plaintiff's treating psychologist, Dr. Smith, was called to testify as a participant expert, which is very common in cases of this nature. Dr. Smith submitted reports that were prepared about a year after the conclusion of therapy and included recommendations for future treatment. It is noted that the reports went beyond the handwritten notes prepared at the time of therapy and included various comments and opinions about such things as future treatment and a theory that the plaintiff murdered an adult because of his previous sexual abuse. The court concluded that Dr. Smith's opinions went beyond what he could provide in his capacity as a participant expert, as such opinions were not based on his skills and observations made while involved in the plaintiff's treatment (Ross & Rodrigues, 2018). These cases are important in that they clarify, and, in fact, invented a name for the role of the participant expert. It also set out some boundaries for the limits of the opinion of the participant expert.

The Goudge Inquiry

The case of *R v Mohan* (1994) occurred at a time when there was considerable media interest in the issue of expert witness credibility. For instance, Texas forensic psychiatrist Dr. James Grigson was the focus of repeated media attention during the 1980s. Indeed, a 1988 *New York Times* article referred to Dr. Grigson as "Dr. Death," "Dr. Doom," and "a menace to society," as a result of his testimony in death penalty cases (Belkin, 1988). Dr. Grigson had, in fact, testified in 167 death penalty cases, most of which concluded with a death sentence. Concerns levelled against him included assertions that he could predict behaviour without interviewing or attempting to interview the defendant, that he claimed to predict dangerousness with 100 per cent accuracy, and that he frequently performed examinations without the knowledge of the defendant's lawyer. An article at the time of his death in 2004 indicated that these assertions and others led to his expulsion for unethical conduct from the American Psychiatric Association (APA) in 1995 ("Dr Grigson, Dr Death," 2004). He was described as "an outstanding communicator who really connected with the jury ... He could really talk about medical terminology and make it understandable, using emotionally recognizable phraseology. He had a great sense of humor. He just had a way" (Tolson, 2004). In 2016, issues related to Dr. Grigson continued to arise when a writ of habeas corpus was filed to stay the execution of Jeffery Lee Wood. Three years after his expulsion from the APA, Dr. Grigson had testified that Mr. Wood would most certainly commit violent crimes in the future, despite the fact he had not interviewed the defendant.

A similar concern was raised in the United Kingdom regarding the testimony of Professor Sir Roy Meadows, whose testimony resulted in six years imprisonment for Sally Clarke, accused of murdering her baby sons. It was reported in an opinion column in the *Telegraph* that during the trial, "Sir Roy announced, with all the authority of his knighthood and his professorial chair, that the odds against two natural cot deaths occurring in a single middle-class family were 73 million to one." The statistic had been arrived at by extrapolating on an article in the *Lancet* in which it was claimed that "there was a 1 in 8,543 chance of a middle-class family falling victim to cot death. Sir Roy then whipped out his pocket calculator and squared that figu e." The commentator in the *Telegraph* concluded, "there comes a point when a man, however well-meaning, must take responsibility for his conduct and beliefs, and he must be brought to account when his beliefs are shown to be stupid and false, and his conduct causes dreadful suffering to others" (Utley, 2005).

In Canada, expert testimony came under scrutiny in the case of Dr. Charles Smith, a pediatric pathologist working at Toronto's Hospital for Sick Children between 1981 and 2005. Over the course of his 24 years of practice, Dr. Smith conducted over 1,000 autopsies of children ("Dr. Charles Smith, 2009), many of which involved suspicious deaths. Over time, he became known as the leading Canadian expert on "shaken baby syndrome." "Shaken baby syndrome," a term coined by American radiologist John Caffey in 1974, had been described as the most common cause of death or serious neurological injury resulting from child abuse (Blumenthal, 2002); the condition was characterized by acute encephalopathy with subdural and retinal hemorrhages

(Harding, Risdon, & Krous, 2004). However, over the course of the 1990s, Dr. Smith was subject to increasing criticism by the judicial system regarding his methods, his competence, and, in particular, his testimony at trial (Glancy & Regehr, 2012).

In 2005, the Chief Coroner for Ontario (2005) instituted a review of 45 cases of homicide where Dr. Smith had expressed professional opinions that the death was either homicide or criminally suspicious. The review determined that Dr. Smith made questionable conclusions of foul play in 20 cases, 13 of which resulted in criminal convictions. The Coroner of Ontario's review of cases involving the testimony of Dr. Smith was described as the "last and most serious blow to public faith in pediatric forensic pathology and the central role it must play in criminal proceedings involving child deaths" (Goudge, 2008, p. 7). Six days after the report was released, the Province of Ontario established a commission chaired by Judge Stephen Goudge, charging it with two tasks: 1) to conduct a systematic review and assessment of the practice and oversight of pediatric forensic pathology in Ontario, particularly as it related to the criminal justice system; and 2) to make recommendations to restore and enhance public confidence in forensic pathology (Goudge, 2008). The review concluded that Dr. Smith actively misled his superiors, made false and misleading statements to the court, and misrepresented the nature of his expertise.

The Goudge Inquiry did not shy away from the emotive nature of this issue and the potential consequences of misleading or false expert testimony:

> In many of the 20 cases, parents or caregivers were charged with criminal offences that bear a significant social stigma. Some of those charged were convicted and incarcerated. In some cases, siblings of the deceased children were removed from the care of their parents. In [one specific case] the Court of Appeal for Ontario has determined that a miscarriage of justice occurred. (Goudge, 2008, p. 8)

The inquiry identified that the role of the forensic pathologist "is to assist the state to find out why its citizens die" (p. 8). In doing so, forensic pathologists must possess expertise in conducting specialized investigations, which, if not performed competently, undermine the service of justice. However, in addition to possessing clinical acumen, forensic experts must be trained in and develop an aptitude for the legal process. They must also be able to testify fairly and objectively in language that clearly communicates their findings and to present their written documentation in a manner that serves the justice system. The inquiry report

Table 2.1 The Goudge Inquiry: Recommendations and basic principles for practice

---

Summary of recommendations

- A one-year training program in forensic pathology
- Increased recruitment in forensic pathology, including accelerated acceptance of foreign medical graduates
- Systemic changes in oversight
- A mechanism for dealing with complaints and negative feedback
- Experts called by the Crown (prosecution) should make themselves available to meet with the defence counsel in advance of the court proceedings to discuss their opinions
- Expert witnesses should meet before trial to discuss and clarify their differences

Basic principles for forensic practice

- "Think truth" rather than "think dirty," using an objective, evidence-based approach
- Forensic pathologists must remain independent of the coroner, the police, the prosecutor, and the defence to discharge their responsibilities objectively
- Work must be reviewable and transparent
- The work product must be understandable to the criminal justice system
- Teamwork and consultation are fundamental
- Practices must be founded on a commitment to quality

Source: Adapted from Goudge (2008)

noted that "the criminal justice system values finality" (p. 11). That is, an ultimate decision must be reached regarding guilt or innocence, and culpability must be assigned. Nevertheless, paralleling the language of the judge in *Daubert*, the report acknowledges that in science, there is an evolution of findings and opinions, and this evolution requires interpretation for the purposes of the legal system. The final report of the Goudge Inquiry made a series of recommendations for systemic changes to the field of forensic pathology, outlined the basic principles for practice, and further suggested best practices for forensic experts (tables 2.1 and 2.2).

The Goudge report specifically identified several deficiencies in Dr. Smith's testimony and practice. It concluded that Dr. Smith:

- lacked any formal training in forensic pathology, was not board certified, and lacked basic knowledge about fo ensic pathology;
- was unaware of the limits of expertise and exaggerated expertise to the court;
- was disorganized, evidenced poor note-taking skills, and his work not submitted in a timely manner;
- did not account for contradictory evidence that came to attention and did not adjust opinion to account for new information;

- issued reports that did not contain the reasoning or any supporting literature that might connect the dots between findings and conclusions;
- failed to understand the expert role or the requirement to give an opinion with independence and objectivity;
- took on a role of advocate for the Crown, bolstering the prosecution case;
- was unable to separate the expert witness role from the advocacy role;
- gave evidence dogmatically, not acknowledging the existence of controversy in the field
- was willing to testify on matters outside the area of expertise, such as the profile of a perpetrator of a particular crime, even when views were unsubstantiated and not based on any objective findings

These problems were exacerbated by the fact that Dr. Smith was a very effective speaker who could be engaging and charismatic, thereby presumably increasing his impact on a jury (Goudge, 2008).

On 1 February 2011, the Discipline Committee of the College of Physicians and Surgeons of Ontario (2001) found that "in his practice of forensic pediatric pathology and his work providing expert opinion evidence in relation thereto, Dr. Charles Smith committed acts of professional misconduct, in that he failed to maintain the standard of practice of the profession in Ontario, engaged in disgraceful, dishonourable or unprofessional conduct, and is incompetent" (CPSO, 2011).

Implications for Forensic Mental Health Practice

Understanding and Explaining the Role of Expert Witnesses

Fundamental to the role of expert witnesses is understanding the duty to provide fair, objective, non-partisan assistance to the courts (*White Burgess Langille Inman v Abbott and Haliburton Co*, 2015). Gutheil and Simon (1999) acknowledge that there are inherent tensions in the relationship between forensic experts and attorneys, stemming from the essential ways in which the professions differ. The attorney is "ethically obligated to embark on zealous, vigorous, and partisan advocacy on behalf of the client," while, in contrast, the expert is obligated to strive for objectivity (p. 546). According to Gutheil and Simon, this can lead to a number of issues. An attorney may make an assumption about the nature of the opinion that the expert will eventually provide and attempt to seek agreement with this assumption before the expert has seen the primary data. Data available to the expert may be selectively withheld; time available to consider or collect data may be curtailed by impending court dates or funds available; attempts may be made to sway opinions offered through persuasion or subtle or not so subtle inducements, such as another case. Thus, the expert must not only continuously self-monitor but must be prepared to assert their specific role and obligations in the process repeatedly.

The forensic mental health professional may also feel pressure to engage in cases beyond their own level of expertise. The Goudge Inquiry, in considering the case of Dr. Smith, noted that he was a pediatric pathologist, not a forensic pathologist, and had "no forensic pathology training, and only limited exposure to criminally suspicious cases and deaths" (Goudge, 2008, p. 12). Further, it noted, "His continuing medical education, which consisted of attending conferences and reviewing the available literature, focused primarily on pediatric pathology ... He picked up his limited understanding of forensic pathology on the job" (p. 13). Thus, while the Goudge Inquiry is clear about limitations in the system and the lack of general training for forensic pathologists, it clearly held Dr. Smith accountable. This is a chilling warning for all professionals providing expert opinions for the courts. From a forensic mental health perspective, professionals are advised to ensure that they are fully familiar with the area in which they are asked to offer an opinion and to consider refusing cases that are beyond the boundaries of their expertise.

Consideration of Possible Conflicts of Interest

As noted in *White Burgess* (2015), expert witnesses have a duty to provide fair, objective, and non-partisan assistance to the courts. The American Academy of Psychiatry and the Law's *Practice Guideline for the Forensic Assessment* identifies the risk to objectivity engendered by conflicts of interest (Glancy et al., 2015), which can include legal, financial, personal, and moral or philosophical conflicts.

Legal conflicts arise when the expert has either been retained or approached by the opposing party or has prior knowledge of a case, having discussed it with others. Financial conflicts exist where the expert stands to gain by a certain verdict. This was highlighted in *White Burgess* (2015) when one of the parties challenged an expert on this basis. Of note was the decision by the court that past business relations do not necessarily constitute conflicts. This does not mean that the expert should not be paid for the work that they do. However, it should be clear that the expert is paid for the time they invest in the case, not for a certain opinion. Experts should not accept contingency fees, due to the impact on impartiality; however, lawyers, who are paid to advocate for their client, may accept such fees.

Personal conflicts may take two forms, the most obvious of which is having personal knowledge of the client, who may be a friend or colleague. The second form of personal conflict occurs when a therapist is asked to provide a forensic assessment of a patient or client that the therapist has treated. The Canadian Academy of Psychiatry and the Law (2018) has developed ethical guidelines that discourage this practice. The reason for this is that it is acknowledged that when one acts as a treating mental health professional, the primary obligation is to the patient or client. Acting as an expert in a court of law, however, requires a shift to a different ethical obligation. This is set out by Appelbaum (1997), who described the forensicist's ethical obligation to the justice system while respecting the values of truth-telling and respect for persons. In an influential paper, Strasburger, Guthiel, and Brodsky (1997) noted that a therapist who attempts to combine these roles strays into treacherous waters. One potential conflict of interest is a therapist's tendency to advocate for, or at least desire a positive outcome for, their own patient or client, be it a monetary outcome or a reprieve from incarceration in a criminal case. In addition, the dual relationship arising in this situation may compel the therapist to disclose information that was provided in therapy when the client was assured of the confidentiality of this information, thus infringing upon the therapeutic relationship. In the case of *Westerhof v Gee Estate*, the Ontario Court of Appeal made a clear distinction between litigation experts (forensic mental health professionals specifically retained for the case) and participant experts (treating or attending professionals). The Ontario Rules of Civil Procedure (2019) require that litigation experts acknowledge that they are abiding by the duties of an expert by signing a relevant form (form 53). If possible, the therapist should attempt to avoid this situation and refer the retaining third party to an impartial expert (Canadian Academy of Psychiatry and the Law, 2018).

It should be noted that a forensic mental health professional performing an evaluation for the courts is not absolved of thier duty to ensure the safety and security of the patient or of another person. For instance, if an evaluee expresses suicidal ideation, the mental health professional should take whatever steps necessary to facilitate treatment. Likewise, if an evaluee expresses the intention to cause imminent and serious bodily harm to a third person, there is a duty to warn and protect, as discussed in chapter 9.

Finally, an individual may have a conflict of interest as a result of political or ideological beliefs. While these beliefs may be noble, such as in the case of protecting vulnerable children, as noted in both the cases of Sir Roy Meadows (Utley, 2005) and Dr. Smith (Goudge, 2008), the expert must ensure that such beliefs do not colour their consideration of evidence in a particular case.

Informed Consent

Informed consent and the limits of confidentiality are addressed in several chapters of this book, including chapter 3, with respect to insanity assessments; Chapter 9, with respect to treatment of those who are victims of trauma; and in chapter 11, with respect to the assessment of damages in civil proceedings. Common features of the insanity assessment include explanations that the evaluation will be sent to the retaining party, elements of the evaluation may be disclosed in open court, the individual may refuse to answer any questions, the evaluation is not for treatment, and the evaluator may need to report information to others if there is reason to believe that others are at risk (Glancy et al., 2015). Some practitioners prefer to use a specific form so that the evaluee can read this information and sign that they have read and understood it in the presence of a witness.

Report Writing and Assessment

Court reports, though not sworn as affidavits, can be heavily relied upon by the courts and can be highly persuasive. A court report should be the end result of a well-planned, objective, and systematic search for clinical facts in order to answer a legal question. It provides a way in which professionals can structure and support their expert opinion in a manner that is understandable and accessible to the various officers of the court. It should be based on facts collected from a variety of sources including those gathered by members of a multidisciplinary team (Goudge, 2008). In keeping with the requirements articulated in *Daubert* (1993) and applied in the Canadian case of *R v J (J)* (2000), it should be augmented by tests and methods that are substantiated by the best available evidence in the field (Glancy & Saini, 2009). This evidence must be offered in an impartial manner. It is not sufficient to offer a sincere belief; what is required is logical and compelling evidence-based knowledge (Rosner, 2003).

The Goudge Inquiry report also suggests that evidence included in expert reports and testimony should be clear and accessible to

cross-examination. To this end, the report discusses the practice of taping autopsies. The use of taping in forensic mental health has been a
subject of some debate. An early report of the Task Force on Videotaping of the American Academy of Psychiatry and the Law (1999) determined that videotaping is ethical, but did not specifically endorse it as
a practice. The more recent AAPL *Guideline for the Forensic Assessment*
(Glancy et al., 2015) identifies that the usual purpose of recording is to
create a complete record that can be reviewed for report preparation,
preparation for testimony, or as evidence in the trial. It may be particularly useful when the accused is exhibiting a disturbed mental state at
the time of the interview that would likely be different by the time of
the trial.

Interestingly, the Goudge report recommends that, when there are
differences of opinion between opposing experts, they meet together to
delineate areas of agreement and disagreement. While this may seem
antithetical to the current practice of adversarial systems, such as that
found in North America, in the United Kingdom, parties must consider
with their experts whether it would be fruitful for experts to meet and
discuss the extent of the areas of agreement and any disagreement.
Legal representatives may or may not attend, but should they do so,
should not intervene in the discussion (UK Ministry of Justice, 2017).

Hearsay Evidence

Forensic mental health practitioners conducting assessments for the
courts consider a broad range of information from a variety of sources
in order to arrive at an opinion that considers various contextual and
individual factors. In court, this information is considered to be hearsay
evidence. In general, hearsay evidence is not admissible. However, in
R v Abbey (1982), the Supreme Court reflected that "Expert witnesses
may testify to their opinion on matters involving their expertise, and
may also, incidentally, base opinions on hearsay." Nevertheless, the
court continued by noting "The main concern of the hearsay rule is
the veracity of statements made. The principal justification for the
exclusion of hearsay evidence is the abhorrence of the common law
to proof which is unsworn and has not been subject to trial by fire of
cross-examination" (at para 41). Thus, while expert opinion can be
based on "second-hand evidence," such a reliance "goes to the weight"
of the evidence. This is important to the administration of justice as
juries place greater weight on hearsay evidence relied upon by experts
than other forms of hearsay (Schuller, 1995). In *R v Turner* (1974), the
court instructed lawyers who call psychiatric experts to "remember

that the facts upon which they base their opinions must be proved by admissible evidence. This elementary principle is often overlooked." This statement has critical implications for providing expert testimony in court.

It is common that an assessing forensic mental health expert will hear nothing about the case between the time that they provide a written report and when they are called to give testimony in the middle of a trial. Unless the expert specifically asks, they may not know about the evidence presented at trial. This situation can lead to an invidious position as the facts of the case may have substantially changed between the time of the original assessment and the testimony at trial. These changes could either alter the expert opinion or, at least, lessen the weight given to the opinion. Consequently, it is essential for experts to meet with the retaining lawyer immediately prior to taking the stand. During this meeting, the expert and lawyer have the opportunity to review the critical facts of the case as they have emerged during the trial. A number of pertinent questions may arise: Has the accused person testified and what was the content of this testimony? If the expert spoke to collaterals as part of the assessment, have they testified and is that testimony any different from the information that they gave the expert? Have police statements been admitted? Has other evidence been presented that might affect the expert opinion? Full awareness of the evidence can assist in providing expert testimony that is not contradicted by proven facts and, ultimately, is of the greatest use to the court.

Expert Testimony

Experts should not take an advocacy role in attempting to pursue a particular agenda regardless of the strengths of their belief in an issue (Goudge, 2008; Iacobucci & Hamilton, 2010). Where opinion evidence cannot meet the standards of scientific scrutiny, it is the contention of some authors that forensic experts have an ethical duty to refuse to testify (Levine, 1984). In the courtroom, this means conceding the limits of one's expertise and considering alternative theories and evidence (Grove & Barden, 1999). In addition, experts should inform the courts of the scientific basis of their evidence, current controversies in the field, and the level of confidence they place on this evidence (Goudge, 2008; Iacobucci & Hamilton, 2010; Levine, 1984). In this way, experts can assist the court by educating others about the difference between peer-reviewed and validated evidence and "junk science" (R v J-LJ, 2000).

Table 2.2 The Goudge Inquiry: Recommended best practices in expert testimony

---

- Practice based on the best evidence in the field and incorporate the philosophy "thinking truth"
- Language that reflects the level of confidence in the expert opinion
- Multiple sources of data
- Careful note-taking
- Multidisciplinary teamwork and an acknowledgment of the opinions of others that influence the expert testimony
- Reports containing the facts on which the opinion is based
- Reports written in plain and understandable language, not obfuscated by technical or ambiguous language
- Opinions not expressed in legal terms
- Regular training to enhance effective communication

These issues have been addressed by various forensic mental health scholars and practitioners and are attended to in the codes of ethics of professional bodies such as the Canadian Academy of Psychiatry and the Law (2018) and the American Academy of Psychiatry and the Law (AAPL, 2005). Appelbaum (1997), for instance, notes that the job of the forensic mental health professional in a forensic assessment is to advance the interests of justice. The role of the forensic professional is to step outside the usual practitioner-client relationship in order to provide expertise to the court. For instance, in the situation where a forensic mental health professional performs a risk assessment and concludes that the evaluee is dangerous, the court may increase the length of the sentence. The assessment, therefore, was not necessarily in the interests of the evaluee, but rather in the interests of justice. Nevertheless, Appelbaum (1997) cautions that the mental health professional is still bound to an ethical framework that emphasizes truth-telling and respect for persons. Adherence to the central ethical principle of striving for objectivity and honesty is also expected (Canadian Academy of Psychiatry and the Law, 2018). The notion of an additional cultural formulation, whereby the evaluee is assessed in the context of their own culture and perceptions can be considered part of the framework (Griffith, 2005; Griffith, Stankovic, & Baranoski, 2010). Other aspects of the ethical framework include compassion (Norko, 2005), robust professionalism (Candilis, 2009), and attention to the risks of therapeutic alliance (Regehr & Antle, 1997).

Training and Oversight

During the Goudge Inquiry, Dr. Smith admitted that his training had been inadequate for the tasks that he had been asked to perform and that he had not taken advantage of any continuing medical education in order to upgrade his skills and knowledge (Goudge, 2008). It is incumbent on all individual practitioners to take advantage of training opportunities and ensure that they are up-to-date on developments in the field and changes in the law pertaining to their practice. Professional licensing bodies carry a responsibility for investigating allegations of unprofessional conduct and an adherence to a reasonable standard of care to ensure public safety. If forensic professionals are not self-monitoring, others will step in to fill the void.

Summary

Expert witnesses have been relied upon by the courts since the Middle Ages. However, over the centuries, and especially in recent decades, the expansion of human knowledge has resulted in an increased reliance on expert witnesses by the courts in their search for the truth. This is because the gap between the layperson's knowledge and the specialized knowledge of experts is vast and growing in an expanding range of domains (Iacobucci & Hamilton, 2010). This increased reliance on experts has caused some consternation in the courts, and thus, in a series of successive court decisions, the courts have attempted to "scrupulously control the use of expert witnesses in legal proceedings" for a number of reasons (Iacobucci & Hamilton, 2010, p. 53). First, the courts are attempting to ensure that experts – in particular, "hired guns" who present biased evidence – do not undermine the rationality of the court process. There is a concern that a "parade of experts advancing pseudoscientific theories [will bring] the administration of justice into disrepute" (p. 54). In such cases, experts' evidence may move from assisting the trier of fact to usurping them. Next, there is a concern that fairness may be undermined in a system in which some can afford to retain certain experts, while others cannot. Finally, there is an awareness that courts are not necessarily equipped to assess the reliability and credibility of the evidence presented. These concerns have been borne out in a number of high-profile situations, and, as a result, the Goudge Inquiry and other sources provide important guidelines for forensic mental health practitioners who may serve as experts in the courts. Some professional organizations have addressed these matters by adopting a code of ethics that specifies various aspects of forensic practice, including the need for objectivity and obtaining informed consent. In addition, some organizations have instituted specialized mandatory training for forensic mental health experts. In various ways, these organizations have responded to many of the criticisms levelled against them.

Table 2.3 Key points regarding expert testimony

Frye v United States (1923)

Admissibility of expert testimony reliant on novel or emerging theories or methods	• Has gained general acceptance in the field to which it belongs

Daubert v Merrell Dow Pharmaceuticals (1993)

Admissibility of expert testimony reliant on novel or emergingtheories or methods	• Tested • Subject to peer review and publication • Known rate of error • Existence of standards • General acceptance

R v Mohan (1994)

Admissibility of expert testimony	• Relevance • Necessity • Absence of exclusionary rule • Properly qualified expert

R v J-LJ (2000)

Admissibility of expert testimony reliant on novel or emerging theories or methods	• *Daubert* criteria recognized in Canadian law

White Burgess Langille Inman v Abbott and Haliburton Co (2015)

Two-stage process	• Assess admissibility using factors identified in *R v Mohan* • Determine probative value vs prejudicial impact
Duty of experts	• Provide fair, objective, non-partisan assistance

R v Abbey (1982) *R v Lavallee* (1990)

Hearsay evidence	• Experts can rely on hearsay to form their opinion • The facts upon which the opinion is based must be found to exist

Westerhof v Gee Estate (2015)

Differentiating the role of the expert	• Participant expert – treating or attending health care professional • Litigation expert – forensic health care professional retained by a party in the proceeding

The Goudge Inquiry (2008)

Basic principles of forensic practice	• Evidence-based • Objective and independent • Reviewable and transparent • Understandable to the criminal justice system • Involves teamwork and consultation • Demonstrates commitment to quality

---

(*continued*)

Table 2.3 (*continued*)

Implications for practice

Understanding and explaining the role of expert	• Provide fair, objective, non-partisan assistance • Self-monitor • Resist attempts to sway opinion • Determine what expertise is necessary
Consider possible conflicts of interest	• Determine whether any conflicts may limit objectivity
Informed consent	• Evaluation is not for treatment • Information will be shared with retaining party • Possibility of disclosure in open court • Circumstances where mandatory reporting is required • The right to answer or decline any question
Assessment and report writing	• Objective search for clinical facts to address legal question • Augmented by evidence-based tests and methods • Ensure evidence is available for cross-examination
Hearsay evidence	• Determine which facts have been introduced and accepted by the court • Evaluate the impact of these facts on the expert opinion
Testimony	• Do not take an advocacy role • Educate the court • Concede limits of evidence and expertise
Training and oversight	• Obtain required training and credentials • Commitment to continuous augmenting and updating of knowledge

---

3 The Insanity Defence

R v Hadfield

> 15th May: As King George III entered the Royal Box at Drury Lane Theatre for a royal command performance of *She Would and She Wouldn't*, he was acclaimed by the packed house. He stood in the box, bowing to the public, when a pistol shot rang out from the very front of the pit. The bullet missed His Majesty – but only just – sending a shower of plaster around his head. There was a scuffle in the pit, and a man leapt over the orchestra rail where he was seized by some musicians and locked in the music room whilst the authorities were called. The King decided to remain in his box and ordered the performance to proceed as planned. There were loud cheers at this decision, prompted by relief that the King seemed unconcerned. It was even said that later in the performance, the King was seen to be asleep in his box during one of the quieter moments of the play. (*Over the Footlights*, 1800)

The above quote, published in a broadside in 1800, provides a first-hand account of a dramatic and perennially famous incident in which James Hadfield fired a pistol at King George III, narrowly missing his head. Newspaper accounts from the time report that once it was determined that the king was unharmed, the orchestra and audience broke into a rousing chorus of *God Save the King*.

Given that his offence involved an attempt on the life of the king, Mr. Hadfield was charged with treason (*R v Hadfield*, 1800), a crime generally committed by men of privilege. Therefore, he was afforded opportunities not commonly experienced by those accused of a crime, including time to prepare a defence, pre-emptive challenges of jurors, the ability to compel witnesses, and free access to court-appointed attorneys. Not missing the opportunity, Mr. Hadfield engaged the famed barrister Thomas Erskine to lead his defence (Moran, 1985a).

The Crown, in anticipation of an insanity defence, reminded the court that for a successful plea, the accused must "suffer from an absolute privation of reason" (Moran, 1985b, p. 499) and fail to understand the consequences of their actions. The Crown cited the precedence of Edward Arnold, accused of shooting Lord Onslow in 1723. While the court at the time accepted that Mr. Arnold was deranged, it was found that he was able to form "steady and resolute design" (Moran, 1985b, p. 500) with respect to the attack on Lord Onslow, and consequently he was found guilty. In the Arnold trial, the presiding judge, Justice Tracey, quoted the *wild beast test* first developed in the thirteenth century by Henry De Bracton, who stated that in order to be acquitted on the grounds of insanity, "a man must have no more understanding than an infant, brute, or wild beast" (Allnutt, Samuels, & O'Driscoll, 2007, p. 292). Alluring though the wild beast test may be, Schneider (2009) maintains that Judge Tracey was not arguing for this test to be rigidly applied but was merely using the vivid imagery as an example. Justice Tracey went on to rule that in order for an insanity acquittal to be made, it was necessary that the defendant "could not distinguish between good and evil, and did not know what he did, though he committed the greatest offence … for guilt arises from the mind, and the wicked will and intention of the man" (Schneider, 2009, p. 22). In the case of Mr. Hadfield, the Crown attempted to draw parallels between Hadfield and the precedent set by Arnold. In doing so, he argued that the defendant's premeditative behaviour – which included purchasing a pistol, powder, and ammunition, and concealing a weapon – was clear evidence that he had formed intent, and was thus not a madman (Simon, 1983).

Thomas Erskine then led a defence of insanity, suggesting that Mr. Hadfield's madness did not come from a "hereditary taint," but rather a blow to the head in the service of the king. At the time of the attack, the assailant Mr. Hadfield wore a military uniform that identified him as a former soldier of the Fifteenth Light Dragoons. While fighting in Flanders for the king, Mr. Hadfield received severe head injuries, resulting in facial disfiguration and a wound that reportedly exposed brain tissue. Left for dead, he was taken prisoner by the French and remained four years in a prisoner-of-war camp. Over the course of his imprisonment, Mr. Hadfield developed delusions that he was speaking directly to God, that the world would soon end, and that he, like Jesus Christ, was destined to sacrifice his life for the salvation of others. Mr. Hadfield was eventually discharged from the military on the grounds of insanity. Medical experts testified at trial that the head injuries sustained by Mr. Hadfield had caused permanent damage and that this was a likely contributor to his insanity. Friends, relatives, and fellow soldiers provided testimony to support the contention that Mr. Hadfield's mind was deranged. After merely a few minutes of deliberation, the jury returned a verdict stating, "We find the prisoner is Not Guilty; he being under the influence of insanity at the time the act was committed" (Moran, 1985b, p. 508).

The case of Hadfield was a landmark decision as it rejected two previously accepted premises: 1) that the defendant must be totally deprived of all mental faculties – Mr. Hadfield was able to function normally in many other ways and had circumscribed delusions; and 2) that insanity must be accompanied by the inability to distinguish good from evil (Simon, 1983).

Context and Legislative Implications of *R v Hadfield*

Moran (1985b) provides information about the historical context that surrounded Mr. Hadfield's case at the end of the eighteenth century. He notes that Great Britain was beset by economic and political issues, including the spread of turmoil caused by French Revolution, the emergence of gentlemen's clubs sympathetic to revolution, and political repression of religious reformists. Intermingled with reformists were millenarians who predicted an end of the world, citing contemporary examples of social decay as evidence of impending Armageddon. One such individual was Bannister Truelock, who considered himself a descendant of God. He suggested to Mr. Hadfield that Jesus Christ was coming and "we should have neither King nor soldiers." This comment was apparently interpreted by Mr. Hadfield as an instruction to kill the king. Mr. Hadfield's attempt on the life of the king was thus viewed as part of a larger threat to the monarchy and England as it was known.

Between the twelfth and sixteenth centuries, English courts were required to convict individuals with mental illness who had committed illegal acts, unless they chose to refer cases to the king, who customarily would grant a pardon to individuals with mental illness. By the late 1600s, it was well established that mental disorder and lack of criminal intent were grounds to exculpate offenders who suffered from mental health problems (Simon, 1983). As a result, individuals who were acquitted on the grounds of insanity could not be detained, unless the court believed that they might present a risk to others, in which case they could be confined under the Vagrancy Act of 1744, by order of two justices of the peace (Moran, 1985a). In essence, a successful insanity defence generally amounted to an acquittal, and most individuals were sent home.

Given general concerns about holding guilty individuals responsible for their crimes, English law required that it be demonstrated that the accused's madness was obvious and overwhelming, that the accused was totally incapable of distinguishing between good and evil, and that the accused was incapable of forming a judgment regarding the consequences of their actions. Despite this, during the latter part of the 1700s, the number of insanity acquittals began to rise, causing concern among the general public. This came to a head with the acquittal of James Hadfield for the crime of treason. Consequently, in the wake of the Hadfield finding, the House of Commons moved swiftly to pass the Act for the Safe Custody of Insane Persons Charged with Offences, also known as the Criminal Lunatics Act, of 1800. This act required the automatic and indeterminate detention of insanity acquittees until "His Majesty's pleasure be known." It also instituted a fitness to stand trial provision and limited the right to bail for mentally ill offenders (Moran, 1985a). Following his verdict, James Hadfield was duly transferred from jail to Bethlem Hospital (known colloquially as Bedlam), where he died in 1841 from tuberculosis.

The American physician Isaac Ray, in his influential book *A Treatise on the Medical Jurisprudence of Insanity* (the third edition of which was published in 1853), noted that early English common law represented two types of insanity, "*idiocy* and *lunacy*, the subjects of which were designated by the term, *non compotes mentis*" [italics in original] (Ray, 1853, p. 4). He also pointed to efforts by some jurists to classify further:

Four kinds of men who may be said to be *non compotes mentis*:

1. An idiot, who from his nativity, by a perpetual infirmity is *non compotes*;
2. He that by sickness, grief, or other accident, wholly loseth his memory and understanding;
3. A lunatic that hath sometimes his understanding, and sometime not … he is called *non compotes mentis,* so long as he has not;
4. He that by his own vicious act for a time depriveth himself of his memory and understanding, as he that is drunken. (Ray, 1853, p. 4)

Isaac Ray then proceeded to outline a scientific classification of insanity consisting of two broad categories: defective development of faculties, including idiocy and imbecility, differing from each other in terms of degree; lesion of faculties subsequent to their development, which includes mania (unnatural exaltation or depression which may affect intellect and affective powers); and dementia, which could result from consecutive mania, injuries to the brain, or senility. This book was to have a significant effect on legal thinking of the day and on the subsequent trial of Daniel M'Naughten (Diamond, 1956).

R v M'Naghten[1]

On the afternoon of Friday, 20 January 1843, Daniel M'Naughten, a Scottish wood turner who had taken rooms in London in search of work, shot Edward Drummond, secretary to Prime Minister Sir Robert Peel. At the time, Mr. Drummond was walking past the Salopian Coffee House in Charing Cross, a junction just south of Trafalgar Square, having left his brother's bank. The accused lifted a pistol that had been concealed in his pocket and fired it point blank into the victim's back, causing his waistcoat to catch fire. Mr. Drummond died of infection related to his injuries five days later.

Upon his arrest, Mr. M'Naughten is reported to have stated in reference to Mr. Drummond, "He shall not break my peace of mind any longer." At the onset of his trial, Mr. M'Naughten stated, "I am guilty of firing," but also qualified, "I was driven to desperation by persecution" (Dalby, 2006, p. 21). In his written statement, Mr. M'Naughten indicated, "The Tories in my native city have compelled me to do this. They follow me and persecute me wherever I go, and have entirely destroyed my peace of mind ... I can get no rest from them night or day ... in fact, they wish to murder me" (p. 23). Although there is much speculation, it is not clear whether or not Mr. M'Naughten mistook his victim for the prime minister.

Moran (1985a) suggests that Daniel M'Naughten had one of the best-financed defences of his time. Solicitors representing him at his arraignment succeeded in having the court return £750 that was in M'Naughten's possession at the time of his arrest. This allowed him to retain four of the ablest barristers in London for his trial, in addition to medical experts. The trial of Mr. M'Naughten was highly influence by medical testimony as to his mental condition (*R v M'Naghten*, 1843). Diamond (1956) cites defence counsel Alexander Cockburn as follows:

> I am not here to deny that the hand of the prisoner was raised against the deceased. The defence upon which I shall rely will turn, not upon the denial of the act with which the prisoner is charged, but upon the state of

---

1 Daniel M'Naughten's name is reported to have 16 spelling variants (Quen, 1968), beginning in 1843, where spellings include McNaughten, McNaughton, M'Naghten, MacNaughten (Dalby, 2006), and, more recently, McNaughtan (Moran, 1985a).

mind at the time he committed the act … I shall call before you members
of the medical profession – men of intelligence, experience, skill and un-
doubted probity – who will tell you upon their oaths that it their belief,
their deliberate opinion, their deep conviction, that this man is mad, that
he is the creature of delusion, and the victim of ungovernable impulses,
which wholly take away from the character of a reasonable and responsible being. (p. 651)

Eight medical witnesses were called by the defence. Two medical experts retained by the Crown were not called to testify, perhaps suggesting that their views did not differ from those of the defence experts. The
testimony of medical witnesses included that of two physicians, Aston
Key, of Guy's Hospital, and Forbes Winslow, author of the *Plea of Insanity in Criminal Cases*. Both attended the trial, but neither had examined
the defendant. At the end of the string of testimonies, the Lord Chief
Justice Tindal declared:

> We feel that the evidence, especially that of the last two gentlemen who
> have been examined, and who are strangers to both sides, and only
> observers of the case, to be very strong, and sufficient to induce my learned
> brothers and myself to stop the case. (Diamond, 1956, p. 654)

Lord Chief Justice Tindal charged the jury: "If on the balance of evidence in your minds, you think the prisoner capable of distinguishing
between right and wrong, then he was a responsible agent and liable to
all the penalties the law imposes. If not … then you will probably not
take upon yourselves to find the prisoner guilty. If this is your opinion, then you will acquit the prisoner" (Simon, 1983, p. 187). Daniel
M'Naughten was found not guilty on the grounds of insanity and was
moved, by order of the Secretary of State, from Newgate prison to Bethlem Hospital. Schneider (2009), after a review of the literature about
treatment at that time, concluded that M'Naughten would have been
cared for in a simple, noninvasive manner and left to recover spontaneously. Twenty years later, a new psychiatric institution for the
criminally insane was opened at Broadmoor. It is said to have had a
fine library and music in the evenings on occasion. M'Naughten was
transferred to Broadmoor and died years later of natural causes at the
age of 52 (Schneider, 2009). Of note, his defence barrister, Alexander
Cockburn, was knighted, became solicitor general the following year,
and was appointed Lord Chief Justice of the Queen's Bench in 1859
(Diamond, 1956).

Context and Legislative Implications of *R v M'Naghten*

Despite the fact that Mr. M'Naughten was detained in a mental institution, the public reacted with outrage. It was suggested that the case had been treated lightly, and M'Naughten was now whiling away his time in a retreat for idlers (Simon, 1983). Queen Victoria, who three years earlier had been the victim of an attempted assassination by Edward Oxford, was similarly outraged. Mr. Oxford was found to be insane at the time he committed the act and was acquitted of the charges (Moran, 1986). The young Queen Victoria consequently charged the law lords of the House of Lords with a review of the case and the enabling legislation.

It is also important to understand the context of the times in which the M'Naughten trial took place. Several authors refer to the fact that the trial occurred in the year that Charles Dickens's *A Christmas Carol* was published, and call the reader to visualize the images so vividly described by Dickens. London was a dirty city of over 2.25 million people, rife with social, political, and economic chaos and unrest. Class and income disparities had brought the emergence of radical movements seeking suffrage for women, reformation of child labour practices, the abolishment of workhouses, and the establishment of welfare relief (Dalby, 2006; Quen, 1968; Schneider, 2009). During the Victorian period, massive political, social, and economic upheaval led to general concern about the rule of law and the stability of the existing political order.

Given the regent's charge, the House of Lords asked 15 judges[2] to respond to the following five questions in order to determine the law of England regarding the use of insanity as a defence in a criminal trial:

1. What is the law respecting alleged crimes committed by persons afflicted with insane delusion, in espect of one or more particular subjects or persons: as, for instance, where at the time of the commission of the alleged crime, the accused knew he was acting contrary to law, but did the act complained of with a view, under the influence of insane delusion, of edressing or revenging some supposed grievance or injury, or of producing some supposed public benefit
2. What are the proper questions to be submitted to the jury, when a person alleged to be afflicted with insane delusion especting one or more particular subjects or persons, is charged with the commission of a crime (murder, for example), and insanity is set up as a defence?

---

2 Some authors contend that it was 12 judges, not 15, as reported by some sources at the time (Dalby, 2006).

3. In what terms ought the question to be left to the jury, as to the prisoner's state of mind at the time when the act was committed?
4. If a person under an insane delusion as to existing facts, commits an offence in consequence thereof, is he thereby excused?
5. Can a medical man conversant with the disease of insanity, who never saw the prisoner previously to the trial, but who was present during the whole trial and the examination of all the witnesses, be asked his opinion as to the state of the prisoner's mind at the time of the commission of the alleged crime, or his opinion whether the prisoner was conscious at the time of doing the act, that he was acting contrary to law, or whether he was labouring under any and what delusion at the time?

Lord Chief Justice Tindal replied as follows:

1. Notwithstanding the party accused did the act complained of with a view, under the influence of insane delusion, of edressing or revenging some supposed grievance or injury, or of producing some public belief, he is nevertheless punishable according to the nature of the crime committed, if he knew at the time of committing such a crime that he was acting contrary to the law.
2. Jurors ought to be told in all cases that every man is presumed sane, and to possess a sufficient deg ee of reason to be responsible for his crime, until the contrary be proven to their satisfaction; and that, to establish a defence on the ground of insanity, it must be clearly proved that, at the time of committing the act, the party accused was labouring under such a defect of reason, from disease of the mind, as not to know the nature and quality of the act he was doing, or if he did know it, that he did not know that what he was doing was wrong.
3. The mode of putting the latter part of the question to the jury on these occasions has generally been, whether the accused, at the time of doing the act knew the difference between right and wrong; which mode, though rarely, if ever, leading to any mistake with the jury, is not, as we conceive, so accurate when put generally and in the abstract … If the accused was conscious that the act was one which he ought not to do, and if that act was at the same time contrary to the law of the land, he is punishable; and the usual course therefore has been to leave the question to the jury, whether the accused had a sufficient deg ee of reason to know he was doing an act which was wrong; and the course we think is correct.
4. The answer must of course depend on the nature of the delusion: but making the assumption as we did before that he labours under such partial delusion only, and is not in other respects

Table 3.1 The M'Naughten rules

Issues related to the accused	
Presumption of sanity and burden of proof	Every person brought before the court is presumed to be sane. It is the burden of the party leading the case for insanity to prove insanity on the balance of probabilities.
Knowledge of nature and quality of act and knowing right and wrong	At the time of the commission of the act, the defendant was unable to know the nature and quality of the act he was doing, or if he did so, he did not know it was wrong.
Delusional mistake of facts	If the defendant suffered from an insane delusion at the time of the offence but was not otherwise insane, his responsibility should be judged as if the facts with which the delusion existed were real (Taylor, 1950).
Issues related to the court process	
Medical testimony	Medical witnesses who have not examined the defendant cannot testify as to his state of mind at the time of the offence; this must be left to the trier of fact. The witness can testify about matters of science if facts are not disputed.
Role of the judiciary in development of legislation	Judges cannot be asked to give opinions on bills not yet law, only existing law (Dalby, 2006).
Role of the jury	It is for the jury to decide the determination of the truth of the facts and whether the prisoner was conscious at the time of doing the act that he was acting contrary to law, or whether he was labouring under delusion at the time.

insane, we think he must be considered in the same situation as to responsibility as if the facts with respect to which the delusion exists were real.

5. We think that a medical man, under the circumstances supposed, cannot in strictness be asked his opinion in the terms stated, because each of those questions involves the determination of the truth of the facts disposed to, which it is for the jury to decide, and the questions are not mere questions on matters of science, in which case such evidence is admissible. But where the facts are admitted or not disputed, and the question becomes substantially one of science only, it may be convenient to allow the question to be put in the general form, though the same cannot be insisted on as a matter of right.

Thus, the M'Naughten rules include aspects related to the accused and the trial process, as demonstrated in table 3.1.

It should be noted that these rules were never the substance of a British statute or even the written decision of an appeal. Schneider (2009) notes that they merely represent the opinions of the law lords, and as such had no precedential value in and of themselves (although they were subsequently interpreted by the common law over the next 160 years). Schneider notes that, up to the application of the M'Naughten rules, the courts had tended toward a strict common law interpretation of insanity, that is, whether the accused person knew what he was doing was wrong. The M'Naughten rules were an attempt to codify and provide a framework so as to apply some uniformity to court decisions. Schneider (2009) is critical of the rules in that they are confusing and inconsistent. He also notes that the rules do not consider volitional or emotional factors that may bear upon the accused person's ability to know or appreciate the nature and quality of the act and know it was wrong.

M'Naughten and the International Criminal Court

Just one decade after the M'Naughten rules were established in Great Britain, they were adopted by the federal and several state courts in the United States, and remained in force there for 100 years. In 1954, the US Court of Appeals in the District of Columbia discarded the M'Naughten rules in *Durham v United States*. In this case, the defendant, Monte Durham, who was charged with breaking and entering, had a long history of mental disorder and minor crime. Justice David Bazelon determined that "an accused is not criminally responsible if his unlawful act was the *product of mental disease or mental defect* ... [and] if you did find that the accused suffered from a mental disease or defect[, he] would still be responsible for his unlawful act if there was not a causal connection between such mental abnormality and the act" (Simon, 1983, p. 190). Judge Bazelon himself is said to have become disillusioned with the broadening of the definition and the resulting power given to psychiatric experts (Miller, 2003). In 1972, the DC circuit court overruled *Durham* and adopted the Moral Penal Code test of insanity instead (Allnutt et al., 2007). This code, proposed by the American Law Institute, states:

1. A person is not responsible for criminal conduct if at the time of such conduct, as a result of mental disease or defect, he lacks the substantial capacity either to appreciate the criminality [wrongfulness] of his conduct or to conform his conduct to the requirements of law.

2. As used in this article, the terms "mental disease or defect" do not include an abnormality manifested only by repeated criminal or otherwise antisocial conduct. (Hall, 1963)

While some in the United States viewed this to be a "get out of jail free" card, particularly following the attempted murder of President Ronald Reagan by John Hinckley, others viewed it differently. Thomas Szasz (1966), for instance, in writing about the insanity verdict stated:

Excepting death, involuntary psychiatric hospitalization imposes the most severe penalty that our legal system can inflict on a human being: namely loss of liberty. The existence of psychiatric institutions that function as prisons, and of judicial sentences that are, in effect, indeterminate sentences to such prisons, is the backdrop against which all discussion of criminal responsibility must take place. (p. 271)

This is very similar to a quotation which appeared in the *Spectator* newspaper in 1843, which said, "The insane man is doomed to undergo 'the next thing to capital punishment,' said Lord Brougham on the very evening when the press was ignorantly suggesting an incentive to assassination" (Schneider, 2009, p. 257). Nevertheless, a modification of the M'Naughten rules remains the most popular test in the United States, although various changes have been made by a number of states. A full review of American applications of M'Naughten can be found in the *AAPL Practice Guideline for Forensic Psychiatric Evaluation of Defendants Raising the Insanity Defense* (Giorgi-Guarnieri et al., 2002).

The M'Naughten rules also form the foundation of the insanity defence throughout Australia and New Zealand. In these countries, all states require evidence of a mental condition causing the person to have difficulty understanding or knowing the nature and quality of their actions or that their actions were wrong, although some add the term "beyond their control." The Australian Criminal Code define mental dysfunction as a disturbance or defect of perceptual interpretation, comprehension, reasoning, learning, judgment, memory, motivation, or emotion to a substantial degree of disability (Allnutt et al., 2007).

One hundred and twenty-three states are signatories to the 1988 Rome Statute, which established the International Criminal Court (ICC) located in the Hague, effective July 2002. The statute is essentially a supranational criminal code that covers four primary crimes of an international nature: genocide, crimes against humanity, war crimes, and crimes of aggression. These crimes can be investigated by the ICC where states are unable or unwilling to do so themselves. Article 31(1)(a) of the ICC addresses the issues of insanity and states:

> A person shall not be criminally responsible if, at the time of that person's conduct:
> The person suffers from a mental disease or defect that destroys that person's capacity to appreciate the unlawfulness or nature of his or her conduct, or capacity to control his or her conduct to conform to the requirements of law.

Janssen (2004) suggests that the ICC definition creates a more rigorous test of insanity, demanding the destruction of an individual's capacity to appreciate or control, rather than the simple lack of appreciation regarding the criminal nature of the behaviour. This is understandable given the nature of crimes considered by the ICC such as genocide, for which exculpation requires extreme impairment of mental condition.

M'Naughten and the Criminal Code of Canada

It is hard to overstate the importance of the M'Naughten rules to the insanity defence in Canada. England has never, even to this day, had a unified criminal code. James Fitzjames Stephen wrote a code in 1878, which made it to a second reading in the British House of Commons but never went any further (Duhaime, 2018). A few years later, Canada's first prime minister, Sir John A. Macdonald, was a strong voice for codification, since up to that time every province had its own criminal law. Finally, in 1890, a complete criminal code was accepted for the confederation. Based on the original that had been proposed in England, it was the first such code enforced in a self-governing jurisdiction in the British Empire and thus was a major event not only in Canadian legal history but throughout the Commonwealth (Brown, 1989). Regarding the law of insanity, the Criminal Code (1892) essentially used a version of the M'Naughten rules and read as follows:

> No person shall be convicted of an offence by reason of an act done or omitted by him when labouring under natural imbecility, or disease of the mind, to such an extent as to render him incapable of appreciating the nature and quality of the act or omission, and of knowing that such act or omission was wrong.

A person labouring under specific delusions, but in other respects sane, shall not be acquitted on the ground of insanity, under the provisions hereinafter contained, unless the delusions caused him to believe in the existence of some state of things, which, if it existed, would justify or excuse his act or omission.

Every one shall be presumed to be sane at the time of doing or omitting to do any act until the contrary is proved. (pp. 37–8)

While the Criminal Code has been revised and amended several times, including a major reform in 1955, very little of the insanity provisions changed (except for a modernization of the language) until these provisions were struck down in *R v Swain* (see chapter 4). Nevertheless, the 1956 Royal Commission on the Law of Insanity as a Defence in Criminal Cases reminds us:

The rules laid down by the judges in England in answer to the questions submitted to them out of the M'Naughten case form a historical background to Canadian law, but neither the answers propounded nor the jurisprudence founded on them in England constitutes the Canadian law.

Canadian law is statutory, and as such must receive and has received interpretation and application according to the principles applicable to statute law in Canada. (McRuer, Desrochers, Kinnear, Jones, & Harris, 1956, p. 8)

Thus, the examination of subsequent cases on the law of insanity and the subsequent practice of forensic mental health is critical. It is incumbent upon practitioners to educate themselves regarding the interpretation of these rules and Canadian law – misperceptions of which are all too common. Indeed, Rogers, Turner, Helfield, and Dickens (1988) surveyed all forensic psychiatrists and psychologists practising in Canada and found the majority (88 per cent) had erroneous beliefs regarding the insanity standard.

Implications for Forensic Mental Health Practice

It has become common practice for forensic mental health professionals to be charged with the task of retrospectively assessing the mental state of persons accused by the court of a variety of crimes. Knoll and Resnick (2008) identify that the primary objectives of these evaluations are to 1) educate the court, 2) clarify psychiatric issues, 3) be honest and objective, 4) strive for accuracy, 5) offer opinions based on factual data and sound reasoning, and 6) readily acknowledge limitations. In 2006, the US Supreme Court indicated that, with respect to insanity, it views experts as providing three types of evidence:

1. Observation evidence – including a description of the defendant's speech, thought, or behaviour
2. Mental disease evidence – including whether the individual suffered from a mental disease at the time of the offence
3. Capacity evidence – whether the disease may have influenced the accused's ability to appreciate the nature and quality of his act or know it was wrong. (Knoll & Resnick, 2008)

In all, forensic mental health professionals must strive to avoid advocating for a particular psychiatric understanding of an offence in order to sway the trier of fact toward an insanity defence (Dietz, 1996). To achieve these ends, the forensic psychiatric assessment has, to a certain extent, been standardized, such as in the 2015 *AAPL Practice Guideline for the Forensic Assessment* (Glancy et al., 2015). An insanity assessment comprises all of the steps of a thorough forensic psychiatric assessment but has some specific elements as outlined in the 2002 *AAPL Practice Guidelines for Forensic Psychiatric Evaluation of Defendants Raising the Insanity Defense* (Giorgi-Guarnieri et al., 2002). General elements include a thorough psychiatric history and mental state examination. In addition, as in all forensic interviews, the assessment should begin with a consent process that clearly outlines the nature and purpose of the assessment and the limits of confidentiality (see table 3.2)

An individual seeking an insanity defence may not appear before a trier of fact for months or even years after the original crime in question, during which time the individual may have changed considerably. This situation has several implications. First, the individual should be interviewed as contemporaneously as possible to the act in question to determine and record the individual's current mental state and to assist the individual in recalling thoughts, feelings, and behaviours at the time of the offence (Knoll & Resnick, 2008). Documentation will be critical for the court process. Some in the field have argued that it is helpful to video record this interview, a practice permitted but not mandated by the AAPL *Practice Guideline*. Further, as in any forensic psychiatric assessment, all materials must be retained, as the evaluator may be asked to bring records to court or to disclose them to the parties prior to trial.

Table 3.2 Forensic assessment of insanity

Obtain referral information	• Determine if the case falls within area of expertise
Explain the limits of confidentiality	• Evaluation will be sent to retaining party • Evaluation is not for treatment • Mandatory reporting requirements • Disclosure in court • Right to decline to answer
Obtain collateral information	• Medical, psychiatric, and other records • Interviews with others • Police reports, witness statements
Conduct general assessment and history	• Personal, medical, and mental health history • Previous trauma • Substance use • Social functioning
Assess for disease of the mind	• Ability to refrain from a course of action resulting in charges • Alternative courses of action considered and rejected
Assess ability to appreciate the nature and quality of the act	• Thoughts, perceptions, and motivations leading up to, during, and following the act • Understanding of the physical nature of the act • Understanding the consequences of the act • Attempts to conceal the crime
Clarify wrongfulness	• Understanding the act was legally and morally wrong (chapter 5)
Consider malingering	• Marked discrepancies between description and objective observations • Lack of cooperation during the evaluation
Formulate opinion on insanity	• Presence or absence of psychiatric diagnosis • Ability to appreciate the nature and quality of the act • Perception of wrongfulness • Nexus between mental state and the act

Collateral information can provide invaluable data regarding prior functioning, precursors to the event, and thinking and behaviour at the time of the event and immediately thereafter. Collateral information can be obtained through witness statements and police reports, medical and psychiatric records, and interviews with the evaluee's partner or relatives. If there are discrepancies or inconsistencies, these can be investigated with the evaluee. If inconsistencies remain, the evaluator should consider the possible influence of lying, malingering, or cognitive difficulties

Disease of Mind

The first question before the court with respect to an insanity defence is whether the individual suffers from a *disease of the mind*. In Canadian law, *disease of the mind* is a legal definition, about which the judge will advise the jury. This definition was clearly articulated in *Cooper v The Queen* (1980) as follows:

> In summary, one might say that in a legal sense "disease of the mind" embraces any illness, disorder, or abnormal condition which impairs the human mind and its functioning, excluding however, self-induced states caused by alcohol or drugs as well as transitory mental states such as hysteria or a concussion. In order to support a defence of insanity the disease must, of course, be of such intensity as to render the accused incapable of appreciating the nature and quality of the violent act or of knowing that it was wrong. (at para 51)

The role of the forensic mental health assessor is to arrive at a psychiatric diagnosis according to criteria found in the most recent version of the *Diagnostic and Statistical Manual of Mental Disorders* (DSM-5), albeit one that is often retrospective given the time elapsed since the act. In addition, the evaluator should seek to determine whether the accused perceived themselves to have the ability to refrain from the specific course of action that resulted in the charges. For instance, if the individual reported hearing voices telling him that his landlady was the devil, did he consider leaving the premises and finding alternative housing? Further, what did the individual perceive would happen if he had left? In addition, the evaluator might ask whether the accused considered calling relevant authorities, and if he did, why he did not follow through upon these alternative courses of action. This line of questioning provides information on volitional control, which, although not specifically part of the M'Naughten rule, may contribute to the determination that there is presence of a mental disorder or knowledge that the act the individual committed was wrong.

Know or Appreciate the Nature and Quality of the Act

Amendments to the Criminal Code of Canada changed the word "knowing," used in M'Naughten, to the word "appreciate," which comes from the Latin word *appretiare*, to recognize the full worth of. This suggests that cognition is more than simply knowing but comprises an appraisal of the value of the act. In *Cooper v the Queen* (1980), the court noted that appreciation may involve estimation and understanding of the consequences of the act. This was reflected in the 1980 Supreme Court decision in *R v Barnier* (1980), which stated that appreciating requires more than base awareness and "is a second stage in the mental process requiring the analysis of knowledge or experience in one manner or another" (p. 1125). This has further been defined as the capacity to "foresee and measure the consequences of the act" and understand the "true significance of his conduct" (McRuer et al., 1956, pp. 11–12). However, in a later case, *Kjelsden v The Queen* (1981), the definition was confined to knowing the physical actions and the likely outcome of these actions. Therefore, an accurate record of the evaluee's account of their thinking processes at the material time is an essential part of the insanity evaluation.

The evaluator must collect information regarding the thoughts, motivations, and perceptions of the individual at the time of the offence (Giorgi-Guarnieri et al., 2002). In practice, this is often difficult to effect, given the individual's reluctance to recall and discuss a distressing experience. While questions should generally be open-ended, more directed questions will aid in determining the individual's awareness of the physical nature and consequences of the act (*Kjeldsen v The Queen*, 1981). The following are examples of such questions:

- What did you think would happen when you pushed a knife into Mr. X?
- What would happen next?
- What are the consequences of that?

One of the well-known questions that an evaluator may ask is whether the evaluee would have continued with the crime if there was a policeman at their elbow, and if not, why? (Rogers & Shuman, 2000). Although this question was originally considered in the context of irresistible impulse, which is not, in and of itself, a defence, it can open up the area of legal and moral wrongfulness. Further questioning in this area might include asking if the evaluee thought they would be arrested, charged, and prosecuted, and if they thought the police would say that they had done the right thing, such as may have been the case in *R v Oommen* (see chapter 5). This enquiry can be matched with descriptions of the evaluee's behaviour before, during, and after the act. For instance, were efforts made to avoid detection, such as wearing gloves, disposing of the evidence, attempting to evade police, or fleeing the scene? (Scott, 2018).

Malingering

Malingering is defined as "the intentional production of false or grossly exaggerated physical or psychological symptoms, motivated by external incentives," for instance, evading criminal prosecution (American Psychiatric Association, 2013). The DSM-5 suggests that, in a medicolegal context, malingering should be strongly suspected if there is a marked discrepancy between an individual's claims of stress or disability and objective findings or observations, a lack of cooperation during the diagnostic evaluation, or the presence of an antisocial personality disorder. A strong index of suspicion is therefore necessary in many insanity evaluations, which characteristically may have some or all of the preceding factors. The *AAPL Practice Guideline for the Forensic Assessment* outline useful procedures for detecting malingering (Glancy et al., 2015).

Opinion

The final opinion of the mental health professional in an insanity assessment should indicate the basis for the opinion, the presence or absence of a psychiatric diagnosis, and whether the evaluee could appreciate the nature and quality of the act or know it was wrong. Further, the expert must explain the nexus between the mental state, specific hallucinations or delusions, and knowing or appreciating the nature and quality of the act. Without this nexus, the opinion may not be helpful to the courts.

Summary

The M'Naughten rules have had a profound impact on the manner in which courts throughout the world address issues of criminal responsibility and now form the foundation for the insanity defence in most common law jurisdictions (Roach, 2009). In their original form, these rules articulated a "fairly restrictive approach to the insanity defence, one which requires mental disorder to be so extreme that it deprives the accused of the capacity to understand that nature and quality of the act or know that it was wrong" (p. viii). As we will learn in chapter 4, they remained relatively unchanged in Canada until they were repealed through legislative changes in 1992. However, the essential features of these rules still remain at the core of Canadian law.

The M'Naughten rules and the manner in which insanity and mental disorder are understood in the judicial system are foundational for

Table 3.3 History of criminal insanity

Early English law regarding insanity acquittals	• Madness must be obvious and overwhelming • Total incapability of distinguishing between good and evil • Unable to form a judgment regarding the consequences of actions • Equivalent to absolute discharge
Act for the Safe Custody of Insane Persons Charged with Offences (1800)	• Automatic and indeterminate detention of insanity acquittees until "His Majesty's Pleasure Be Known" • Fitness to stand trial provision • Limited right to bail for mentally ill offenders
R v M'Naghten (1843)	• House of Lords creates the M'Naughten rules (table 2.1)
Section 11. Criminal Code of Canada (1892)	• Incapability of appreciating the nature and quality of act or know it was wrong
R v Chaulk (1990) (chapter 5)	• Specific delusions removed • Wrong defined as legally or morally wrong
R v Swain (1991) (chapter 4)	• Struck down the insanity provision of the CCC
Bill C-30 (1991) (chapter 4)	• Replaced NGRI with NCR-MD and established procedural safeguards
Winko v Forensic Psychiatric Institute (1999) (chapter 4)	• Clarifies the definition of threat
R v Oommen (1994) (chapter 5)	• Specific delusions in the absence of insanity allowed as a possible defence – not solely the general capacity to know right from wrong
Implications for practice	
Primary objectives of insanity assessment (Knoll & Resnick, 2008)	• Educating the court • Clarifying psychiatric issues • Honesty and objectivity • Accuracy • Offering opinions based on factual data and sound reasoning • Acknowledging limitations
Aspects of forensic assessment of insanity	• Limits of confidentiality • Collateral information • General assessment and history • Make diagnosis ("disease of the mind") • Assess ability to appreciate nature and quality of the act • Assess perception of wrongfulness • Consider malingering • Formulate opinion

forensic mental health practice. Mental health professionals have a critical role in assessing and informing the court regarding the mental state of an accused and educating the court about the nature and implications of mental illness. Forensic professionals are required to conduct thorough, evidence-based assessments and communicate these assessments in an objective, fair, and impartial manner. The chapters that follow explicate various aspects of the assessment.

4 Criminal Responsibility

On 30 October 1983, in response to reports of domestic violence, Toronto police arrived at the apartment Owen Swain shared with his wife and two young children. Newspaper accounts indicate that Mr. Swain was "babbling aloud about mysterious spirits. He covered the windows with a sheet and began hitting and breaking things in the apartment with a broom" (Bindman, 1991d). He subsequently piled the broken furniture in the middle of the room and threw items out the window onto the front lawn. Next, acting in "a mad frenzy" (Makin, 1985), he awakened his 16-month-old son by "poking him with the broom," removed the child's clothing and twirled him around his head by his legs. "Swain then held his wife down and scratched an X on her chest with a meat cleaver, though the scratch was superficial and did not bleed" (Bindman, 1991d), after which, he proceeded to swing his two-month-old daughter around his head. Mr. Swain was said to be talking excessively quickly and in a ritualistic manner. Later, he explained that he believed at the time that his family was possessed by devils and the purpose of his behaviour was to exorcise them.

Owen Swain was arrested and remanded to the Toronto Jail (known locally as the Don Jail). From there, he was transferred to a maximum security hospital, the Oak Ridge unit at the Penetanguishene Mental Health Centre, pursuant to a Form 1 application under the Mental Health Act of Ontario. It is of note that this mode of transfer was somewhat of an unusual procedure in a case such as this; more commonly, an application for an assessment of fitness to stand trial would have been made under a provision of the Criminal Code (1985). While at Oak Ridge, Mr. Swain was diagnosed as suffering from a schizophreniform disorder and was treated with antipsychotic medication. Within a month, his psychiatric symptoms abated, and he was deemed well enough to be returned to jail. At his bail hearing, Mr. Swain was granted release on the condition that he see an outpatient psychiatrist regularly. Mr. Swain returned to live in the community, continued to see his psychiatrist and take prescribed medication, and remained symptom-free for 18 months. During this time, he reunited with his family (Claridge, 1986) and "was even permitted to babysit his children with the approval of the Children's Aid Society" (Craig, 1985).

On 3 May 1985, Owen Swain was tried in the District Court of Ontario. The Crown sought to adduce evidence with respect to his insanity at the time of the offence, to which Mr. Swain objected. According to newspaper reports, Mr. Swain's lawyers submitted that he did not wish to enter a plea of not guilty by reason of insanity (NGRI) as "he could be locked away for an indefinite time in a mental hospital, whereas if he was found guilty he could be placed on probation or go to jail [for a finite period of time]" (Bindman, 1991d). A *voir dire* was conducted, and the trial judge ruled that the Crown could adduce psychiatric evidence, on the basis of which Swain was found NGRI on charges of assault and aggravated assault.

Upon the finding of NGRI, and in accordance with procedures spelled out by the Criminal Code (1985, s. 542(2)), Mr. Swain was automatically ordered to be kept in strict custody "until the pleasure of the Lieutenant Governor is known." Defence counsel immediately moved to have the relevant section of the Criminal Code declared inoperative on the basis that it violated the Canadian Charter of Rights and Freedoms (1982). After considering the constitutional argument, the trial judge held that Mr. Swain's constitutional rights were not infringed. District Court Judge Hugh O'Connell indicated that "he could not accept the argument that the warrants are a form of cruel and unusual punishment, nor do they constitute arbitrary detention or unequal treatment under the law" ("Warrants Not Cruel," 1985). Justice O'Connell concluded that treatment under the warrant system is not "so excessive as to surpass the standards of decency" ("Warrants Not Cruel,"1985). Mr. Swain was thus sent to the Queen Street Mental Health Centre "until the Lieutenant Governor determines that he is ready to be released" ("Warrants Not Cruel," 1985).

Subsequently, the lieutenant governor issued a warrant to detain Mr. Swain at the Clarke Institute of Psychiatry for a psychiatric assessment; a written report was to be sent to the Lieutenant Governor's Advisory Review Board within thirty days. Defence counsel requested but was denied the opportunity to make submissions with respect to this decision. Mr. Swain was duly transported to the Clarke Institute, where he was assessed for a thirty-day period, during which a report was submitted to the review board. The subsequent hearing included evidence in chief and cross-examination of the assessing psychiatrist, as well as evidence from other psychiatrists who had been previously involved with the treatment of Mr. Swain. On the board's advice, the lieutenant governor then issued a warrant to the administrator of the facility to permit Mr. Swain to gradually re-enter into the community in a supervised manner and with close follow-up. In an unprecedented move, Mr. Swain's counsel petitioned to appear before the lieutenant governor himself in order to make submissions. The petition was duly refused.

Mr. Swain then appealed the decision of the review board to the Ontario Court of Appeal. It was noted that, in the original trial, "two psychiatrists, including the head of the forensic unit at Penetanguishene Mental Health Centre, testified that he had been successfully treated since the assault and did not need further treatment in hospital" (Claridge, 1986). In a 2–1 decision, the appeal was denied. The judgment, written by Mr. Justice Houlton, criticized the Criminal Code provisions as "unnecessarily imprecise and sketchy and too often lacking any clear expression of Parliament's purpose or intent" (Claridge, 1986) but concluded that that did not make the provisions unconstitutional. He further suggested it was not the role of the court to reform legislation. However, Mr. Justice John Brooke wrote a strong dissent, suggesting current processes were "tantamount to using the criminal process to obtain a certification which could not be obtained through the civil process because the individual's condition would not justify it" (Claridge, 1986).

Owen Swain then sought leave to appeal to the Supreme Court of Canada. The full decision of the Supreme Court will be described in greater detail below. In short, however, the court ruled that the present "law violated the constitutional rights of the mentally ill to fundamental justice and the freedom from arbitrary detention" (Bindman, 1991c). Chief Justice Lamer concluded that the law failed to distinguish between those who are still dangerous and require hospital treatment and those who can be safely released to the community. In a rare move, it gave Parliament six months to enact new legislation (*R v Swain*, 1991).

Context

As with many cases that significantly influence mental health law and criminal law in Canada, the case of *R v Swain* represents a remarkable convergence of factors that ultimately lead to its conclusion. The case came at a time when psychiatric survivor groups were speaking loudly about injustices suffered by individuals who were detained and treated in mental health facilities against their will. Books like *Upstairs in the Crazy House* (Capponi, 1992) were attracting media attention, and reporters and politicians were expressing outrage over personal stories of individual suffering.

Concomitantly, the Constitution Act, 1982 had recently come into effect, codifying the Canadian Charter of Rights and Freedoms (1982) and enshrining the protection of the fundamental human rights of Canadians in the constitution. The Charter thus took precedence over all existing federal and provincial legislation; laws could only infringe Charter rights if the limits placed on these rights could be shown to be reasonable and justified in a free and democratic society. Thus, despite adherence to the standards for involuntary commitment under provincial mental health acts, committal to psychiatric facilities could be challenged as a violation of the Charter (Savage, McKague, & Johnson, 1987). Subsequently, the court ruled that an inpatient in the Health Sciences Centre in Winnipeg had to be freed from "improper detention" (*Lussa v Health Sciences Centre*, 1983), as it violated her Charter right to "life, liberty, and the security of person" (Canadian Charter of Rights and Freedoms, 1982). Actions for malicious prosecution and false imprisonment were brought against mental health facilities. For instance, in the BC case of *Ketchum v Hislop* (1984), the plaintiff was awarded damages by the hospital owing to what were deemed to be procedural irregularities, and a determination that the statutory requirements for committal had not been met. This occurred despite the fact that the court found the patient both needed and benefite from treatment (Schneider, 1988).

Disability rights groups turned their attention to the issue of patients detained in hospitals under provincial mental health legislation. ARCH Disability Law Centre in Toronto, for instance, recited examples of such injustices to the press: a woman was held on a warrant for six months at Queen Street Mental Health Centre for refusing to pay a streetcar fare; a man was held for several months for breaking a window in an abandoned building, and another man was held for sixteen years in New Brunswick for trying to steal a woman's purse (Orwen, 1987). An article published in the *Toronto Star* stated that "the warrant system has been described as a kind of no man's land, a catch-all for use when the worlds of crime and mental illness collide." It further concluded, "A large proportion [of the 1,000 Canadians held on warrant] are murderers, rapists, and arsonists, but others are accused of minor crimes like using foul language in public" (Orwen, 1987).

"Powerhouse lawyers" supported by the Canadian Disability Rights Council (Bindman, 1991a, 1991b) became involved and harnessed the power of the press. One such lawyer, Clayton Ruby, described the law of the time as "something out of the last century" (as cited in Makin, 1990). He further suggested that most NGRI cases were minor in nature and yet all were treated like murders (as cited in McNeil, 1990). Marlys Edwardh indicated that "people who are legally insane when they committed a crime often prefer to the plead guilty rather than risk going to a mental institution indefinitely" (as cited in Makin, 1990). Criminal lawyer Frank Addario described the superior rights of those similarly accused in the United States (cited in Orwen, 1987). In addition, the conditions of the Oak Ridge, where 82 per cent of those found NGRI were sent, became part of the public discussion. Dr. Stephen Hucker, chief of the Forensic Unit at the Clarke Institute, is quoted as saying, "Penetang is an inadequate facility that compares unfavourably to those in other countries" (as cited in Makin, 1985). The Oak Ridge unit at the Penetanguishene Mental Health Centre was further described by others as a "hell hole" where "1/3 of patients sleep on concrete slabs" (Payne, 1990).

Perhaps most interesting to this discussion of context was the role of Chief Justice Antonio Lamer, author of the Supreme Court judgment. Mr. Justice Lamer had served as vice-chair of the Law Reform Commission that recommended an overhaul of the insanity law in 1976, noting at the time that someone found NGRI "is often worse off than if he had been committed" (as cited in Bindman, 1991c). However, changes recommended by the commission were not enacted. Ten years later, federal justice minister John Crosbie admitted that the insanity provisions in the Criminal Code were likely at odds with the Charter, yet revisions to the law were still not introduced in Parliament. In those intervening ten years, Mr. Justice Lamer had become chief justice of the Supreme Court of Canada, the Charter had been introduced, civil liberties of mental health patients were becoming a significant public issue, and a group of committed lawyers were consequently poised to mount a constitutional challenge against the insanity laws. As Yvonne Peters of the Canadian Disability Rights Council asserted, "We've waited long enough" (as cited in Bindman, 1991c). "After years of inaction, the Supreme Court of Canada has forced Ottawa to rewrite antiquated insanity laws ... [and do] away with 19th-century thinking" (as cited in Bindman, 1991d).

Supreme Court Decision on *R v Swain*

The case of Owen Swain was heard before the Supreme Court of Canada in February of 1990, although a decision was not rendered until May of 1992. Two relevant issues were considered by the court:

1. Whether the common law criteria allowing the Crown to raise evidence of insanity despite an accused's refusal violated the Canadian Charter of Rights and Freedoms; and
2. Whether the statutory power to detain a person found not guilty by reason of insanity violated the Charter.

Raising Evidence of Insanity

With respect to the first issue, the Supreme Court ruled that raising the insanity defence over the wishes of the accused was indeed a violation of the Canadian Charter of Rights and Freedoms. The court reasoned that the principles of fundamental justice demand respect for the autonomy and dignity of the person. It is, therefore, required that an accused person have the right to control their own defence unless the person has specifically been found unfit to stand trial (UST) and incapable of instructing their own counsel. The decision to raise an insanity defence is an integral part of the conduct of an accused's defence. The court further suggested that if the Crown were to raise evidence of insanity it would, or potentially could, interfere with 1) the accused's control over the conduct of their defence, 2) other defences being advanced by the accused, and 3) an accused's credibility before the court. The court nevertheless noted that the right to control one's own defence is not absolute. Rather, if the accused's evidence raises the issue of their mental capacity for criminal intent, then it becomes a live issue, and the Crown is entitled to tender evidence of insanity.

The court acknowledged, however, that the objective of the common law rule regarding mental health is twofold. The first objective is to avoid the unfair treatment of the accused and maintain the integrity of the criminal justice system by avoiding the conviction of an insane accused. The second objective is to protect the public from dangerous persons requiring hospitalization. The court held that while these objectives relate to pressing and substantial concerns in our society, the least intrusive common law rule that will obtain the objectives without disproportionately affecting rights must be adopted by the court.

It concluded that these two objectives could be met by replacing the existing common law rule with a rule that would allow the Crown to raise the issue of insanity only after the trier of fact had concluded that the accused was guilty of the offence and before a conviction was entered. If the accused was then found to be insane at the time of the offence, the verdict of NGRI would be presented.

This rule proposes a bifurcated trial, where it is first established on the facts that the accused actually committed the act or omission. This phase of the trial would focus on all aspects of the offence relevant to establish the limited finding of whether the accused would likely be found guilty in all other respects. Only after that finding could the Crown raise the issue of the accused's mental capacity for criminal intent and put evidence relevant to this issue to the trier of fact. The accused would continue to have the option of raising evidence of insanity at any time during the trial, including after being found guilty of the offence charged, but before a verdict of guilty was entered. If the accused raised evidence of mental impairment during the trial, the trial judge could allow the Crown to adduce evidence relevant to insanity if the Crown saw fit to do so. In this scheme, the accused's right to control their own defence is safeguarded, and the objectives of avoiding the conviction of a person who was insane at the time of an offence and of protecting the public from a person who may be presently dangerous are also achieved (Glancy & Bradford, 1999).

Automatic Detention

With respect to the second issue, the court ruled that automatic detention into "strict custody" of a person found NGRI was indeed a violation of the accused's Charter right to liberty. The mandatory nature of the procedure did not provide an opportunity for a hearing to determine current mental state, although subsequent hearings were possible. Automatic detention was, therefore, determined to be arbitrary since there was no room for judicial discretion. Further, the court concluded that automatic detention was premised on the unjustified assumption that all insanity acquittees were, by definition, dangerous.

The court did find that the objective of protecting the public and preventing crime through the detention of those insanity acquittees who are dangerous was a pressing and substantial concern. Therefore, it concluded that ordering insanity acquittees into strict custody was seen as rationally connected to these objectives. Although the detention was reviewed by the lieutenant governor on the advice of the Lieutenant Governor's Advisory Review Board, in order to fulfil the goal of protecting society from dangerous persons, the court held that whatever the length of time between the court judgment and the issue of a warrant, it still did not meet the minimal impairment component of the proportionality test. The particular case of Owen Swain made this issue clear. The trial judge did hear from two psychiatrists and one social worker as well as lay people, all of whom commented on Mr. Swain's current risk to others and the task of managing this risk; however, the trial judge was not permitted to consider this evidence.

Toward the end of his judgment, Chief Justice Lamer noted that, as a result of the manner in which the constitutional question was raised, the attorney general of Canada and the attorneys general of the provinces had not been notified of the potential change. He further contended that they might certainly have intervened if they had been aware that the constitutional validity of the whole system was being challenged. However, he concluded by saying, "I do note in passing that the lack of procedural safeguards provided for in ss 545 and 547 do, in my opinion, attract suspicion" (*R v Swain*, 1991, p. 108). Thus, the court declared the relevant section of the Criminal Code to no longer be in force. However, given the serious consequences of striking down the law, that is, compelling all persons found NGRI to be released into the community, the court allowed a six-month grace period in order for the legislation to be rewritten. For logistical reasons, the Ministry of Justice applied to the court for a further six-month extension, which was granted (Glancy & Bradford, 1999).

Legislative Changes

As noted above, the 1976 Law Reform Commission had been concerned about aspects of Canadian law regarding the issues pertinent to mentally disordered offenders, and had addressed these issues in their report. This report noted that dispositions with respect to those found NGRI were not made according to known criteria, were not of determinate length, and were not reviewable. Following this, the Department of Justice began a consultation and research process, forming the Mental Disorder Project in 1982 as part of the Criminal Law Review. A discussion paper distributed by the department on this topic described the mental disorder provisions of the Criminal Code as "fraught with ambiguities, inconsistencies, omissions, arbitrariness, and often a general lack of clarity, guidance and direction" (Pilon, 1999). Recommendations in the final report of the project submitted in 1985 were incorporated into a draft bill tabled by Minister of Justice John Crosbie in 1986. Consultations on the draft bill continued until 1988, but perhaps, in part, because *Swain* was under appeal in the Supreme Court, it did not move forward.

Table 4.1 Circumstances when a court may order a psychiatric assessment

---

A psychiatric assessment may be ordered to determine:

- if the court has reasonable grounds to believe that such evidence is necessary to determine whether the accused is unfit to stand trial;
- whether the accused was suffering from a mental disorder at the time of the commission of the alleged offence so as to be exempt from criminal responsibility;
- the appropriate disposition where the verdict of not criminally responsible on account of mental disorder or unfit to stand trial has been rendered;
- whether to revoke the finding that the accused is a high-risk accused (added in 2014, s. 672.64); and
- whether an order should be made for a stay of proceedings, where a verdict of unfit to stand trial has been rendered against the accused.

In 1991, following the Supreme Court decision, then Justice Minister Kim Campbell (who would later become Canada's first, and to date only, female prime minister) tabled Bill C-30, Proposals to Amend the Criminal Law Concerning Mental Disorder (Pilon, 1999). The goal of the new legislation was to establish a scheme that was constitutional and included principles of equality, justice, and fairness (Dupuis, 2013). The new legislation also updated language, removing archaic terms such as *natural imbecility* and *insanity*, replacing them with more modern nomenclature. The previous language had essentially remained unchanged for 100 years, despite significant changes in how mental illness has been viewed and treated. As such, the legislation substituted the term "not guilty by reason of insanity" with "not criminally responsible on account of mental disorder" (NCR-MD). It was originally proposed that the legislation include outer limits on the length of time an accused could be held under the authority of the state based on the severity of the offence. This provision was never proclaimed and appeared to disappear without much commentary or debate. Passage of this bill, established as Part XX.1 of the Criminal Code, codified a new statutory framework governing the legal management of those accused who were deemed unfit to stand trial or not criminally responsible for an act due to mental disorder.

Orders for Psychiatric Assessment

The new legislation specified that the court could order a psychiatric assessment for a variety of circumstances noted in table 4.1. In these circumstances, an assessment order may be made when the court has reasonable grounds to believe that the evidence obtained is necessary to determine any of these matters.

The Criminal Code does not specify what steps need to be taken in order to satisfy that the court has reasonable grounds to believe that such evidence is necessary.

Bill C-30 also provided criteria for determining whether an accused was unfit to stand trial, for which the Code, up to that point, gave little direction. Fitness to stand trial criteria will be discussed in greater detail in chapter 7 in the case of *R v Taylor*. In enunciating the previous insanity law, the Canadian Criminal Code had used a modified M'Naughton test (as discussed in chapter 3). Implications of this change for the psychiatric assessment will be discussed in the chapter 5 in the context of the case of *R v Oommen*.

The Role of the Review Board

The new amendments to the Criminal Code abolished the role of the provincial lieutenant governor and the Lieutenant Governor's Advisory Review Board, and established a protocol for each province or territory to appoint a Criminal Code review board responsible for dispositions concerning any accused who has been found not criminally responsible or unfit to stand trial. The new legislation made important changes to the mandate of provincial and territorial review boards, and specified membership, processes, and factors to be considered in arriving at decisions. New boards were to be chaired by a judge, or a person qualified to be a judge, and to include at least one member who was qualified to practise psychiatry. Commonly, other members include a legal representative and a layperson; quorum is three people. Decisions of the board are based on majority agreement, although in practice consensus is usually reached. When a consensus is not reached, a member may write a dissenting opinion. The attorney general may be a party or send a representative (usually an assistant Crown attorney). The participation of the attorney general varies across provinces; in Ontario, the attorney general is designated as a party as a matter of routine, while in Quebec participation of the attorney general rarely occurs.

The Code specifies that after the accused has been found NCR-MD, an initial hearing may be held if the court is satisfied that it can readily make a disposition. If the court is not satisfied, then the status quo regarding release or detention prevails until such a time as the review board makes a decision, which should be as soon as is practicable but not later than forty-five days after the verdict is rendered. Thereafter, the board must review the decision at least once a year. While the board is mandated to meet at least once a year, any party may ask for a more timely hearing. Other circumstances that arise may require that the board convene earlier.

Table 4.2 Criminal Code review boards

Bill C-30 changes to review boards

Factors Criminal Code review boards must consider in making a disposition

- The least onerous and restrictive disposition (now necessary and appropriate)
- Safety of the public (paramount)
- The mental condition of the accused
- The reintegration of the accused into society
- Other needs of the accused

Possible dispositions

- Absolute discharge: not a significant threat to the public
- Discharge with conditions: to mitigate risk to the public
- Detention into custody of a minimum, medium or maximum security hospital setting: significant threat to the public

---

The Code also sets out the factors that the review board must take into account when making a disposition. These factors include the safety of the public – which later amendments note is the paramount consideration (Bill C-14) – the mental condition of the accused, and the least onerous and least restrictive disposition (which later changed to *necessary and appropriate* with Bill C-54) in order to facilitate safe reintegration of the accused into the community. The board can make three types of dispositions depending on various factors (see table 4.2). The dispositions include 1) an absolute discharge if the board is of the opinion that the accused is not a significant threat to the safety of the public; 2) a conditional discharge if the accused has been found to be a significant threat to the safety of the public, but the board believes these threats may be mitigated through certain required conditions (although this has become the subject of subsequent multiferous litigation); 3) detention in custody in hospital with any conditions that the board deems appropriate. In practice, the board specifies whether it is necessary and appropriate for the accused to be held in conditions of maximum security, medium security, or minimum security. These conditions are not defined in the Code but are generally accepted and defined within the dialogue between the review board and the various hospitals involved. The board may also specify other conditions – including accompanied or unaccompanied passes for such purposes as attending educational programs, job training, or recreation and leisure – as may be considered appropriate in managing the risk of future harm. In practice, these concerns are subject to evidence and argument presented before the board, upon which the board provides a written decision, accompanied by reasons for the decision.

Winko v Forensic Psychiatric Institute

A further challenge to the detention of those found NCR-MD occurred with the Supreme Court of Canada case of *Winko v Forensic Psychiatric Institute*. Joseph Winko was arrested in 1983 for a knife attack against two strangers on a public street. Mr. Winko reportedly suffered from schizophrenia, resulting in multiple previous hospitalizations, and was apparently experiencing command hallucinations at the time of the attack (Balachandra, Swaminath, & Litman, 2004). Specifically, the voices said: "Why don't you go and grab a woman and do her some harm?"; "You are going to the West End to kill someone"; "You are a coward." Mr. Winko was subsequently found NGRI on charges of aggravated assault, assault with a weapon, and possession of a weapon for purposes dangerous to the public peace. He was detained in a forensic psychiatric hospital from 1984 to 1990, pursuant to a warrant from the lieutenant governor, after which he was conditionally discharged into the community. He was living in a hostel staffed by mental health workers and appeared to be doing reasonably well when he appeared before the relatively new provincial review board in 1995. He had not been aggressive since he committed his original offences in 1983. Nevertheless, the review board determined that he could present a future danger in certain circumstances and granted him a conditional discharge. Dissatisfied with the conditional discharge, Mr. Winko appealed to the BC Court of Appeal on two occasions, suggesting that denying him an absolute discharge was an infringement of his rights under the Charter, but on both occasions, his appeal was dismissed. Mr. Winko then appealed to the Supreme Court of Canada. The issues before the Supreme Court in *Winko* were as follows:

1. Does s. 672.54 of the Criminal Code infringe the rights and freedoms guaranteed by s. 15 of the Canadian Charter of Rights and Freedoms on the grounds that it discriminates against people with a mental disorder who have been found NCR-MD?
2. Does s. 672.54 of the Criminal Code infringe the rights and freedoms guaranteed by s. 7 of the Canadian Charter Rights and Freedoms on the ground that it deprives persons found NCR-MD of their right to liberty and security of the person contrary to the principal of fundamental justice?
3. If so, can these infringements be demonstrably justified in a f ee and democratic society under s. 1 of the Charter?

In dismissing the appeal, Chief Justice Lamer noted that the changes to the Criminal Code (described above) supplemented the guilt–innocence dichotomy with the NCR alternative, allowing for "individualized assessment to determine whether the person poses a continuing threat to society, coupled with an emphasis on providing opportunities to receive appropriate treatment. Throughout the process, the offender is to be treated with dignity and accorded the maximum liberty compatible with Part XX.1's goals of public protection and fairness to the NCR accused." Mr. Justice Lamer further indicated that, according to the legislation, the review board must make a disposition "that is the least onerous and least restrictive to the accused." He went on to state, "Read in this way, it becomes clear that unless it makes a positive fin -ing on the evidence that the NCR accused poses a significant threat to the safety of the public, the court or review board must order an absolute discharge." Mr. Justice Lamer noted the significant variety in cases of NCR considered by review boards with respect to the seriousness of the offence and compliance with medication and other medical directives. Nevertheless, Mr. Justice Lamer concluded that he could not accept the interpretation of the Charter proposed by the appellants and asserted that the Code as it is written does not infringe on the rights of an individual found NCR (*Winko v Forensic Psychiatric Institute*, 1999). Despite this finding, the court went on to make a number of points in its decision that have subsequently had important implications for the way the provincial and territorial review boards operate, including determining the threshold for the concept of significant threat, the present and prospective assessment of significant threat, and the characterization of the review board's function (Schneider, Glancy, Bradford, & Seibenmorgen, 2000).

The Threshold for Significant Threat

The first critical decision that a provincial and territorial review board must make is whether the accused represents a significant threat to the safety of the public. If the board determines that the accused is not a significant threat, the accused may be granted an absolute discharge, in which case, the board will no longer have jurisdiction. Prior to this, review boards had become surprisingly comfortable with the double-negative interpretation in *Orlowski v Forensic Psychiatric Institute* (1999), which stated "If the Board fails to find affirmatively that the accused is not a significant threat to the safety of the public it need not discharge the accused absolutely." This language appeared to place a reverse onus on the accused to prove that he was not a significant threat. This was interpreted by review boards to mean that if there was uncertainty as to whether the accused was not a significant threat (note the double negative again), they would not order an absolute discharge. After *Winko*, uncertainty regarding whether or not the accused presented a significant threat to others required the board to grant an absolute discharge. This was a substantial change to the way review boards considered the term *significant threat* (Schneider et al., 2000).

In *Winko v Forensic Psychiatric Institute* (1999), the court stated that the threat must be significant "both in the sense that there must be a real risk of physical or psychological harm occurring to individuals in the community and the sense that this potential harm must be serious," an important clarification of the Criminal Code. The decision also noted that the potential harm "must be serious and criminal in nature and that the minuscule risk of great harm, or a high risk of trivial harm, is not sufficient." Therefore, review boards would have to state positively that the accused is a significant threat to the safety of the public, a higher burden than the previous interpretation of the Code. It was surmised that this would lead to an increased percentage of absolute discharges, a hypothesis supported by an informal review of the figu es by the Ontario Review Board in the year following the finding (Schneider et al., 2000). This was subsequently confirmed in a research study that compared the characteristics of those individuals found NCR-MD in British Columbia, following the 1992 Criminal Code amendments, with those found NGRI prior to the revisions. Results revealed a significant increase in those entering the forensic mental health system following a finding of NCR-MD. However, individuals found NCR had shorter hospital stays and were more likely to receive absolute discharges than the earlier cohort. Of note, is that a substantially larger proportion of these individuals had been charged with relatively minor offences, suggesting that the changes may have made the NCR defence a more attractive option for defendants and their attorneys (Livingston, Wilson, Tien, & Bond, 2003).

Time Frame of Significant Threat

A second area addressed by the Court in *Winko* was the time frame of the anticipated threat. Specifically, a review board was instructed to assess the significant threat prevailing at the time of the hearing. To this point, review boards had assumed that a determination of whether an accused represented a significant threat to others took into account various circumstances. In particular, it considered the accused's future or prospective situation. Indeed, despite this statement about threat at the time of the hearing, the court does say that the board should consider the accused's compliance with treatment, living arrangements, abstinence from substances, and any other relevant circumstances. This suggests that the board is obliged to consider such factors and relapse prevention plans as relevant to the assessment of threat. Reference to future considerations may indeed reflect the court's growing awareness of the utility of violence risk assessment and prediction tools (Kamba, 2013). In practical terms, an assessment of significant threat is presented by the hospital to the review board for consideration. In the new age of structured professional judgment instruments, clinical and relapse prevention plans are a significant part of this assessment. Consequently, the assessment of significant threat continues to be a forward-looking exercise.

Role of the Review Board

The third issue that arose from the *Winko* decision was that the Supreme Court appeared to characterize a function of the review board as inquisitive. Whereas previously the board viewed itself as an adjudicative tribunal, the Supreme Court in *Winko* seems to imply that the board has a duty not only to hear the evidence and submissions but actually to gather evidence. It appears that this has been interpreted by some review boards to mean that, in practical terms, they are obliged to access and review all the relevant evidence that is available regarding any significant threat that an accused may pose. Given the relative paucity of data on outcomes for those found NCR-MD, this decision was seen as "a signal for forensic psychiatry to complete further research into treatment outcome and risk assessment in this group of patients" (Schneider et al., 2000, p. 212).

2014 Changes to the Criminal Code

Largely fuelled by media attention on tragic cases in the United States, public concern about the danger posed by those suffering from mental illnesses remained high (McGinty, Webster, & Barry, 2013; McGinty, Webster, Jarlenski, & Barry, 2014). In Canada, the public was horrified by the case of Vincent Li, who was found NCR in 2009 after decapitating a stranger on a bus. Public attitudes to those found NCR, in general, included concerns that people had been treated lightly for serious crimes (Lacroix, O'Shaughnessy, McNiel, & Binder, 2017) and that justice had not been served. In 2011, public outrage ensued when Allan Schoenborn of British Columbia was granted escorted day passes by the review board one year after being found NCR in the killing of his three children. Prime Minister Stephen Harper's government was in the process of revising several acts of Parliament through Bill C-10 (which passed in 2011). Known as the Safe Streets and Communities Act, the bill, among other things, increased minimum sentencing and limited judicial discretion on sentencing (Lacroix et al., 2017). However, political denunciation of the granting of day passes to Schoenborn, and later Li, led to calls to further modify the Code's position on the issue of presumption of least onerous and least restrictive disposition. Thus, Bill C-14 (originally introduced as Bill C-54), enacted in 2014, replaced the phrase "least onerous and least restrictive" with "necessary and appropriate." Nevertheless, even though Parliament clearly had some-thing else in mind, necessary and appropriate has been interpreted by the courts to mean the least onerous and least restrictive (*R v Ranieri*, 2015). Bill C-14 also created a new *high-risk* designation that could be imposed on someone who had committed a serious personal injury offence and was found NCR. These individuals are currently ineligible for conditional or absolute discharge and are automatically detained in a facility (Lacroix et al., 2017), thus returning to the original spirit of the Criminal Code. A recent decision by the British Columbia Supreme Court has helped interpret the meaning of the term "high-risk" in Bill C-14 (*R v Schoenborn*, 2017).

Implications for Forensic Mental Health Practice

Significant changes to the laws regarding criminal responsibility were enacted following the case of *R v Swain*. In response to the previous laws regarding not guilty by reason of insanity being struck down, new legislation was enacted in an effort to balance the goals of facili-tating humane treatment of the offender with that of the safety of the public. This legislation modernized the language of the Criminal Code of Canada, which had essentially remained unchanged for 100 years, although it did not significantly change the criteria for an accused per-son to be exempted from criminal responsibility.

A number of changes significantly altered the practice of mental health law in conjunction with the practice of forensic mental health. One of the most significant was defining the reasons and criteria that authorized the court to make orders for psychiatric assessments. These orders include assessment of fitness to stand trial, assessment of a mental disorder that indicates exemption from criminal responsibility, and recommendation of an appropriate disposition where a verdict of NCR-MD or unfit to stand trial has been rendered. Added later was a specific assessment regarding whether a finding that the accused is high-risk should be revoked. The Code specifically directed that certain statements made by the accused during these assessments may be accorded privileged status and therefore would not admissible against the accused.

The new legislation specifically codified the establishment and parameters of provincial and territorial Criminal Code review boards as independent adjudicative tribunals. These review boards replaced the role of the lieutenant governor and the Lieutenant Governor's Advisory Review Board. The Code authorizes the court to hold a disposition hearing, specifying the criteria for maintaining jurisdiction over the accused, namely, whether the accused is a threat to the safety of the public. If the court declines to make a disposition, it is specified that the review board should hold a hearing as soon as practicable, but not later than forty-five days after the verdict is rendered. Most particularly, the phrase "to be kept in strict custody" was removed. The review board can only maintain jurisdiction over the accused if the accused is found to be a significant threat to the safety of the public. If the board fails to positively conclude that the accused poses a significant threat to the safety of the public, it must grant an absolute discharge. The later case of *Winko v Forensic Psychiatric Institute* more clearly defines the nature of the significant threat. It was suggested that the emphasis of this later case on a prediction of dangerousness based on relapse prevention plans would stimulate research into this area. Current research has indeed demonstrated that the Historical Clinical Risk Management-20 (HCR-20), a structured professional judgment instrument that has moderate predictive ability, is used in most cases (Crocker, Charette, et al., 2015). This emphasis on prediction of dangerousness requires that forensic mental health professionals ensure they are knowledgeable and proficient in the use of risk assessment tools, including actuarial tools and standardized professional judgments.

The Code sets out a clear set of procedures for the operation of the provincial and territorial Criminal Code review boards. The boards are to have an adjudicative role, although the Supreme Court in *Winko* suggested they also have an inquisitorial role. Review boards must operate under the presumption of the "least onerous and least restrictive" alternative – although this was later changed to "necessary and appropriate" disposition. Nevertheless, "necessary and appropriate" has been interpreted in a subsequent case to mean least onerous and least restrictive (*R v Ranieri*, 2015).

Legislative changes in 1991 modernized the exemption from criminal responsibility and created clear procedural safeguards. These changes, coupled with the 1999 *Winko v Forensic Psychiatric Institute* decision, which directed review boards to grant an absolute discharge if a positive determination of threat could not be established, led some commentators to believe that the NCR-MD defence would be used with increased frequency, including in cases of minor crimes. One research study indeed suggested that there was an increased number of NCR defences following legislative changes, particularly for more minor crimes in British Columbia. This was accompanied by shorter hospital stays and increased rates of absolute discharge (Livingston et al., 2003). These findings were supported by an Ontario study that similarly found increased numbers of absolute discharges post-*Winko*, although the authors note that reduction in forensic beds and increased criminalization of the those with mental illnesses are possible confounds (Balachandra et al., 2004). On the other hand, a study comparing cases three years prior to *Winko* with cases three years post-*Winko* in Ontario, British Columbia, and Quebec found few significant changes post-*Winko*, with the exception that substance abuse disorders were more common in those found NCR. Rather, this study found that regional differences in index offences, mental disorder diagnoses, and prevalence of personality disorders were more significant than the effects of legislative change (Desmarais, Hucker, Brink, & De Freitas, 2008). Thus, while there may be differences in the number of absolute discharges with respect to minor crimes, it appears that, in practice, boards can make judgments that are consistent with the aim of public protection despite legislative change. This parallels research that determined that, despite legislative reform and legal decisions, involuntary admission to mental health facilities on the basis of danger to others has remained remarkably consistent (Bagby, 1987; Bagby & Thompson, 1991). This suggests that clinicians and adjudicative boards continue to consider a wide range of factors and exercise a consistent set of judgments.

These studies provide some support for the impression that the forensic mental health system has become parallel to the correctional system and the public mental health system for those with mental health problems who have contravened the law. There has been exponential growth in both inpatient and outpatients in the forensic mental health system. This had led to growth in forensic mental health teams who provide the rehabilitation leading to the recovery of these patients. A series of articles published under the auspices of the National Trajectory Project (a longitudinal study of individuals found NCR-MD in British Columbia, Ontario, and Quebec) suggests that this system works satisfactorily (Charette et al., 2015; Crocker, Charette, et al., 2015; Crocker, Nicholls, Seto, Charette, et al., 2015; Crocker, Nicholls, Seto, Côté, et al., 2015; Nicholls et al., 2015). Among a plethora of other findings, these articles demonstrated that, generally speaking, review boards were in agreement with the clinical recommendations, suggesting a common purpose and language between the clinicians and review boards. This research was able to tease out the salient characteristics that appeared to lead to absolute discharges: a lack of past defences, having a less serious index offence, and the presence of a mood disorder. In addition, those granted absolute discharges were less likely to have a diagnosis of personality disorder and evidence of substance use disorders, suggesting that these accused persons had disorders that were more amenable to treatment that lowered the risk of violence.

The National Trajectory Project also provides critical data on the three-year recidivism rate for those found NCR-MD in British Columbia (10 per cent), Ontario (9 per cent), and Quebec (22 per cent). Individuals with severe offences had significantly lower rates of recidivism (0.6 per cent), suggesting the system has appropriate safeguards to protect the public. Higher three-year recidivism rates in Quebec were associated with a greater likelihood of NCR-MD fin - ings for less serious offences, less time spent under the jurisdiction of the provincial review board, less frequent treatment of those found NCR-MD by specialist forensic services, and more frequent treatment by general psychiatric services (Charette et al., 2015). In this respect, it appears that the province of Quebec uses the NCR-MD schema as a kind of mental health diversion.

Summary

Almost exactly 100 years since the Criminal Code of Canada was written using a modified M'Naughton test, the case of *R v Swain* struck down the mental health sections of the Code. Subsequently, Bill C-30 was enacted by Parliament, providing a significant number of changes that directly affected mental health law. The new sections of the Code use language more appropriate to modern-day forensic mental health practice. These sections specified policies and procedures with the institution of provincial and territorial Criminal Code review boards replacing the role of the lieutenant governor and the Lieutenant Governor's Advisory Review Board. The Code also specified clear directions as to when the courts could order a psychiatric assessment. In a subsequent case, *Winko v Forensic Psychiatric Institute*, the court clarified the definition of significant threat and placed the onus on review boards to affirmatively find that an accused is a significant threat to the safety of the public in order to maintain its jurisdiction over the accused person. Recent studies have found that the system seems to be working satisfactorily in that hospitals and clinicians appear to share a common language and purpose with review boards. In addition, studies have found that, although differences exist in recidivism rates for relatively minor crimes, the rates of recidivism for serious crimes remain low. A summary of the key issues regarding criminal responsibility resulting from legislative changes and case law can be found in table 4.3.

Table 4.3 Key points regarding criminal responsibility

R v Swain (1991)	
Insanity defence	• Struck down the insanity provisions of the Criminal Code • Determined that raising the insanity defence over the wishes of the accused was a violation of the Charter • Found that automatic detention of those found NGRI was a violation of Charter rights
Bill C-30 (1991)	
Insanity defence	• Replaced NGRI with NCR-MD and established procedural safeguards • Stated court may order psychiatric assessment regarding fitness to stand trial or criminal responsibility
Review boards	• Abolished the the Lieutenant Governor's Advisory Board • Established provincial and territorial Criminal Code review boards • Set out structure and procedures for review boards • Stated that boards have not only an adjudicative but also an inquisitive function
Disposition	• Stated that boards must order the least onerous and least restrictive disposition, taking into account public safety • Described dispositions as including absolute discharge, conditional discharge, and custody in a minimum, medium, or maximum security hospital • Declared that dispositions must be reviewed at least once per year

(continued)

Table 4.3 (*continued*)

Winko v Forensic Psychiatric Institute (1999)

Determining threat to others	• Clarified the definition of significant threat • Stated that, unless there is a positive finding of significant threat, an absolute discharge must be ordered • Described factors in the determination of a significant threat, which include the seriousness of the offence and compliance with medication and other medical directives • Determined that the threat must focus on the risk presented at the time of the hearing, although relapse issues are considered

Bill C-14 (2014)

Disposition	• Changed "least onerous and least restrictive" to "necessary and appropriate"
Significant threat	• Codified into law the previous *Winko* description of what significant threat means (with some minor modifications)

Implications for practice

Systems issues	• The NCR-MD defence is increasingly being used for those who have committed minor crimes; concomitantly the average length of hospital stay for those found NCR has decreased, and the rate of absolute discharge has increased • The current model creates a forensic mental health system that parallels the correctional system • Forensic mental health professionals are called upon to address the risk of future violence and must be knowledgeable and skilled in the use of risk assessment tools • While three-year recidivism rates for those found NCR are 9%–22%, the recidivism rate of those with serious offences is 0.6%

---

5 Clarifying Wrongfulness

R v Chaulk

Fifteen-year-old Robert Chaulk was tried and convicted of first-degree murder in a jury trial before the Court of Queen's Bench of Manitoba for the stabbing and beating death of George Edgar Haywood, an 83-year-old resident of Winnipeg. Mr. Chaulk and his friend Francis Darren Morrissette had broken into the home of Mr. Haywood in the St. James area, a large residential community in the western section of Winnipeg, on 3 September 1985. They brutally attacked the elderly man, stabbing him 17 times, beating him, and leaving him to die (Baxter, 2017). Knives, a garden hoe, rake, bottle, and flashlight were all used in the beating. Mr. Chaulk slit Mr. Haywood's throat from behind, while Mr. Morrissette stabbed him in the stomach (Duffy, 1987). One week later the boys went to the police and confessed to the crime.

At the time of the killing, Robert Chaulk was a Grade 9 student at Sansome Junior High School; Darren Morrissette was in Grade 10 at Sturgeon Creek Regional Secondary School. According to witness Ron St. Jean, a 16-year-old friend of the two accused, Mr. Chaulk repeatedly spoke about murder prior to killing Mr. Haywood. "He [Chaulk] would say to me, 'How would it feel like to kill someone?' I knew someone would end up dying" (Murray, 1987, p. 5). Others testified that Mr. Chaulk enjoyed fantasizing about killing teachers he did not like, and that they were personally afraid of him.

Mr. Chaulk and Mr. Morrissette were said to be an inseparable pair. Mr. Chaulk, born and raised in a middle-class neighbourhood of manicured lawns and bungalows, was described as a dull loner. He found companionship in Mr. Morrissette, a gregarious youth from an abusive home who liked to be the centre of attention. According to Mr. St. Jean, Mr. Morrissette was developing a plan to use mental power to move large objects, alter the desires of others, and ultimately control the world. Mr. St. Jean admitted that he engaged with Mr. Chaulk and Mr. Morrissette in various anti-social acts such as killing neighbourhood cats: "We'd tie something to the cats and throw them in the river and watch the little bubbles come up" (Murray, 1987, p. 5). They also attempted to practise the occult, allegedly communicating with spirits by candlelight. While he was not a party to the murder of Mr. Hayward, Mr. St. Jean indicated to police that Mr. Chaulk and Mr. Morrissette recounted the murder to him in detail, laughing at their antics. Later, upon reading about the murder in the newspaper, he convinced them to go the police (Duffy, 1987).

Due to the severity of crimes the two teenagers were alleged to have committed, the legal case began with a transfer of proceedings from youth court to the Court of Queen's Bench of Manitoba. At the trial, lawyers for the accused argued that the young men both suffered from paranoid psychoses that caused them to believe that they were destined to rule the world and that they possessed superhuman powers – powers that would increase if they killed Mr. Haywood (*R v Chaulk*, 1990). As a consequence, they believed that they were not subject to laws governing other people in Canada and had the right to kill the victim (Baxter, 2017). The lawyers for the defence presented expert testimony in support of an insanity defence. One expert testified, "They fed off each other, fanning the flames of madness" (Murray, 1987, p. 5). Another: "Child psychologist Eric Ellis said the pair came to share the same twisted delusional beliefs, a rare psychiatric condition known as *folie à deux* – madness of two. If they had not met, likely neither one of them would have committed murder" (p. 5). Dr. Sheila Cantor indicated that their desire to emulate a musical hero, a teenage killer from an Iron Maiden album, may have been a catalyst. "[Heavy metal music] can have a devastating impact on the sick mind … music gets stuck in their heads and drives them nuts or pushes them to act on it" (p. 5).

The original jury rejected the insanity pleas and found the accused guilty of first-deg ee murder. Mr. Chaulk and Mr. Morrissette appealed the decision to the Manitoba Court of Appeal. Their lawyers, Heather Leonoff for Chaulk and Greg Brodsky for Morrissette, argued (among other things) that the judge had erred in his charge to the jury with respect to the influence of mental impairment on their commission of the crime. The court unanimously dismissed the appeal on 13 May 1988, determining that the judge's conduct in his charge to the jury was fair.

Lawyers John Scurfield, representing Mr. Chaulk, and Heather Leonoff, this time representing Mr. Morrissette, then appealed the decision to the Supreme Court of Canada on behalf of their clients. Legal counsel again argued that their clients should be found not criminally responsible for their acts. Mr. Scurfield was quoted as saying, "Even the prosecution psychiatrist described Chaulk as the sickest boy he had ever seen ... The delusion clearly motivated the act" (as cited in "Crown Must Prove," 1990). J.G. Dangerfield, representing the Manitoba attorney general's office, contested the suggestion that the accused were suffering from a mental disorder and countered that Chaulk "had told a youth centre employee it's easy to fake insanity. When he was packed off to hospital after the trial, he'd just drop the act, say he was sorry and be released" (as cited in "Crown Must Prove," 1990). Nevertheless, the Supreme Court upheld the appeal, and a new trial was ordered. The court also made a landmark decision in the interpretation of wrongfulness.

Following the Supreme Court ruling, Mr. Chaulk and Mr. Morrissette were again tried for murder using the revised test for understanding wrongfulness, and in 1990 they were found not guilty by reason of insanity. Mr. Chaulk was sent to a mental health centre in Manitoba for treatment and was released four months later by the Criminal Code review board.

Supreme Court Decision in *R v Chaulk*

Three major questions were before the Supreme Court with respect to the issue of insanity:

1. Whether section 16(4) of the Criminal Code, which provides that "Every one shall, until the contrary is proved, be presumed to be and to have been sane," infringes on the presumption of innocence under the Canadian Charter of Rights and Freedoms.
2. Whether the meaning of wrong in section 16(2) of the Criminal Code should be restricted to legally wrong.
3. Whether section 16(3) of the Criminal Code pertaining to specific delusions provides for an alternative defence if the conditions of section 16(2) pertaining to insanity are not met.

The Presumption of Sanity

As in the case of Owen Swain, discussed in chapter 4, the majority decision of the Supreme Court was written by Chief Justice Antonio Lamer, who had a deep and continuing interest in the rights of those suffering from mental illness in the criminal justice system. On the first issue regarding which party holds the burden of proof, Mr. Justice Lamer indicated that the intention of section 16(4) of the Criminal Code is to prevent "perfectly sane persons who have committed crimes to escape criminal liability on tenuous insanity pleas" (*R v Chaulk*, 1990).

In this respect, the court determined that criminal capacity for an adult is indeed presumed and not something that must be proven by the Crown beyond a reasonable doubt. Nevertheless, in his written ruling, Mr. Justice Lamer did differentiate between capacity in adults and children. He stated, "While the state of insanity and the state of childhood cannot be equated, the connection between these two situations for the purpose of criminal law is apparent … because of the immaturity of [the child], he or she has not yet developed the basic capacity with which justice and fairness require to be present in a person who is being measured against standards of the criminal law" (*R v Chaulk,* 1990). The court further noted that if the child was over the age of 14, their immaturity could be contested. This is of note given the age of the defendants in this case.

Returning to the question of burden of proof for insanity, the court opined that the objective of section 16(4) of the Criminal Code was to avoid placing on the Crown the impossibly onerous burden of proving sanity beyond a reasonable doubt. It stated that the burden would be impossible for three reasons: 1) the scientific knowledge regarding mental disorder remains relatively meagre, 2) the Crown is unable to force an accused person to participate in or co-operate with a psychiatric evaluation, and 3) the Crown may not know that insanity will be an issue until sometime after the event and will be unable to prove that the individual was sane in retrospect (Deutscher, 1991).

In the end, the court concluded that the law as it is written represents an appropriate balance between three interests: 1) avoiding placing an impossible burden on the Crown, 2) convicting the guilty, and 3) acquitting those who lack the mental capacity to form intent. False convictions and false acquittals may at times occur, but this was viewed as the fault of uncertain science, not legislation. Thus, Mr. Justice Lamer held that the objectives of the Criminal Code were sufficiently important to warrant limiting constitutionally protected freedoms (Deutscher, 1991).

Understanding Wrongfulness

Prior to the passage of Bill C-30 (see chapter 4), the Criminal Code of Canada section 16(2) stated:

> For the purposes of this section, a person is insane when the person is in a state of natural imbecility or has disease of the mind to an extent that renders the person incapable of appreciating the nature and quality of an act or omission or of knowing the act or omission was wrong.

In the original trial of Mr. Chaulk and Mr. Morrissette, the judge charged the jury to consider whether the accused understood that their actions were *legally wrong*.

On this issue, Mr. Justice Lamer wrote that "wrong" is intended to be broader than simply legally wrong; rather, it also encompasses morally wrong. The defence must, therefore, establish that, due to mental illness, the accused could not appreciate that their conduct does not conform to "normal and reasonable standards of society" (at para 104), and that it "breaches a standard of moral conduct" and "would be condemned" (at para 108). Thus, it is not sufficient to know the act was against formally written laws. Indeed, the person may well know that the act is against the law, but, due to their disease of mind, cannot understand that the act is contrary to societal moral standards (Schneider & Nussbaum, 2007).

In order to address fears that this would lead to an expansion of this defence beyond cases involving those who suffered from mental disorder, or "open the floodgates to amoral offenders to offenders who relieve themselves of all moral considerations" (*R v Chaulk*, 1990), Mr. Justice Lamer clarified that the presence of a mental disorder was a foundational requirement that preceded an analysis of the accused's understanding of wrongfulness. In addition, moral standards must not be judged from the perspective of the personal standards of the accused. That is, mental disorder must interfere with the accused's appreciation of *society's* standards of morality. Thus, the court was suggesting that psychopaths, who do not believe that societal standards apply to them, would not qualify for an insanity defence.

It is worthy of note that Madame Justice Beverley McLachlin wrote a compelling dissent opinion that, nevertheless, did not carry the day. She returned to the original finding of the House of Lords in *M'Naghten* and concluded, "This language [in M'Naughten] leaves no doubt that what is essential is that the accused knew that he or she is ought not to do the act in question. This condition is met if the accused knows that the act is legally wrong." She further notes that this was reaffirmed more than a century later by Lord Reading, who held that "wrong" should mean only legally wrong. In the end, she noted:

> To hold that absence of moral discernment due to mental illness should exempt a person who knows that legally he or she ought not to do a certain act is, moreover, to introduce a lack of parallelism into the criminal law; generally absence of moral appreciation is no excuse for criminal conduct ... Why should deficiency of moral appreciation due to mental illness have a different consequence that deficiency of moral appreciation due

to a morally impoverished upbringing, for example? (*R v Chaulk*, 1990, at para 258)

Madame Justice McLachlin also highlighted the difficulty in determining societal standards of morality, citing the cases of abortion and euthanasia in which wrongfulness in the view of the public may not necessarily coincide with wrongfulness according to the law.

Specific Delusions as an Alternative Defence

The final question before the court was whether section 16(3) of the Criminal Code, which pertains to specific delusions, provides an alternative defence if the defendant does not meet the criteria for insanity as defined in section 16(2). Section 16(3) states:

> A person who has specific delusions, but is in other respects sane, shall not be acquitted on the ground of insanity unless the delusions caused that person to believe in the existence of a state of things that, if it existed, would have justified or excused his act or omission.

The appellants argued that a delusion "should be interpreted in accordance with ordinary language and should mean a non-ambiguous fixed unshakable belief" and that "the words in other respects sane should be interpreted to mean that this accused does not fall within s 16(2)" of the Code (*R v Chaulk*, p. 48). They concluded that section 16(3) should be interpreted in a manner that gives the accused the right to raise this defence even if the accused was not insane as defined by section 16(2). They concluded, therefore, that the judge, as stated in the submissions of the appellants, should have instructed the jury accordingly.

The court held that section 16(3) does not constitute a separate and alternative defence. Mr. Justice Lamer, writing for the majority, explained that the application and interpretation of this particular section of the Code has always been difficult, and suggested that these problems are as result of the uncertainty of the meaning of the terms used. He concluded that it is difficult to define the nature of the specific delusions that do not render a person generally insane. The Code does not seem clear whether the phrase "in other respects sane" refers to the test set out in section 16(2) or to what Mr. Justice Lamer called "non-legal notions of sanity." He goes on to state that a number of sources, including the report of the Royal Commission on the Law of Insanity as a Defence in Criminal Cases (McRuer, Desrochers, Kinnear, Jones, & Harris, 1956), recommended that the provision be repealed on account of redundancy. As we have noted in chapter 3, this report purports that it is not possible to hold specific delusions and nonetheless be sane, suggesting that section 16(3) standing alone describes "a person who could not exist." He also quotes the Law Reform Commission of Canada (1987) report, which stated that "medical opinion rejects the idea of partial insanity and legal scholarship stresses the injustice and illogicality of applying to the mentally abnormal a rule requiring normal reactions within that abnormality ... requir[ing] him to be sane in his insanity" (*R v Chaulk*, 1990, p. 48).

Mr. Justice Lamer went on to state that it was not necessary for him to engage in the perhaps impossible task of explaining the section or of understanding the intention of Parliament in enacting the provision. He argued that a defence using this section would only be successful if the accused suffered from specific delusions that, if true, would have justified the act, even though the accused was capable of knowing that the particular act was wrong in those circumstances. In other words, if the delusions were, in fact, true, then the accused was justified in doing what he did. Justice Latimer concluded that such a case would be a logical absurdity. He gave an example that if an accused believed that the act was necessary to protect his life, in other words, it was in self-defence owing to his delusional belief, then he would not know that the act was wrong in the circumstances and would have a rational legal affirmative defence for his behaviour. He concluded that "if an accused fails to satisfy the conditions set out in s 16(2), he or she will not be able to benefit from s 16(3)" (p. 1361). A substantial minority disagreed and believed that it was preferable to leave section 16(3) open as an independent defence. Of note, the dissent included Madame Justice Beverley McLachlin, who later wrote the opinion when these issues were reopened in the case of Matthew Oommen, described below.

Postscript on *Chaulk*

In a chilling postscript to this tale, Mr. Chaulk, who remained a resident of Winnipeg, committed two further murders in 1999. By then in his late 20s, Mr. Chaulk brutally stabbed 37-year-old Mirzet Zec and 39-year-old Debra Leah Beaulieu to death. Both were neighbours in his apartment building and were unaware of his violent past (Baxter, 2017). Mr. Chaulk pleaded guilty to manslaughter and was sentenced to life in prison. Mr. Chaulk's mental illness was not an issue in the subsequent case (McIntyer, 2009).

In response to the second set of murders and the conviction for manslaughter, politicians expressed outrage at the system and vowed to strengthen the law, adding to pressure surrounding the *Swain* case and its aftermath (discussed in chapter 4). Chuck Cadman, a relatively new member of Parliament for the Reform Party and deputy co-chair of the Justice Committee at the time, is reported to have said, "We have to do something. It's far too easy to plead insanity" (Beltrame, 1999). Jay Hill, member of Parliament and the deputy justice critic for the Conservative Party, stated, "Something should be done to close the loophole. Right now, there's a law about the maximum a person can be held (in a mental health facility), but there's nothing about a minimum. If someone pleads insanity, he or she should have to be in an institution for a certain number of years" (as cited in Beltrame, 1999). The press seized on the story as evidence that the correctional mental health framework placed the public at risk. Even a decade later, the *Chaulk* case and concerns over public safety remained in the news:

> If you think people who are not criminally responsible for murder – like Vince Li – don't kill again, think again.
>
> We have an example right here in Winnipeg, where Robert Matthew Chaulk was found not criminally responsible in 1992 for the killing of an elderly St. James man, only to kill again in a 1999 double-homicide ...
>
> Had the review board kept Chaulk in custody at a mental health facility after his first murder, the second set of victims would still be alive today ...
>
> The NCR system assured the public that Chaulk was not a danger to society, just like they are assuring us now that Vince Li – who killed and beheaded Tim McLean on a Greyhound bus outside of Portage la Prairie in 2008 – is no longer a threat to society. (Brodbeck, 2013)

R v Oommen

Mathew Oommen was a 39-year-old taxi driver when he shot Gina Lynn Beaton to death in the early morning hours of 24 March 1991. Mr. Oommen was first hospitalized for what was reported to be a mental disorder in 1984 and was subsequently hospitalized again in 1988 and February 1991, shortly before the murder took place. In November 1986, Mr. Oommen was the victim of a robbery while driving his cab, during which the assailant struck him in the head. Mr. Oommen attributed this attack to an earlier event in which he had transported individuals across a picket line during the 1986 strike-lockout at the Fort McMurray Alberta plant of Suncor, a company specializing in the production of synthetic crude from the oil sands. At that time, the Alberta oil boom had gone bust, leading to a troubled economy. Employers were seeking concessions and cuts, and several industries across the province were on strike. Tempers were high, and violent eruptions between picketers and police at times occurred. Indeed, it is reported that at one point one-third of Edmonton's police force were at a plant in the city while strikers blocked gates, threw rocks and paint bombs, and smashed windows of buses entering the plant property (Museum, 2014). Accounts of the struggles were prominent in the press, particularly owing to the involvement of businessman Peter Pocklington, who also owned the Edmonton Oilers. These events became incorporated into Mr. Oommen's delusional system. He became obsessed with the idea that trade unionists wished to kill him in revenge for crossing a picket line.

Gina Beaton, age 15, was the roommate of Mr. Oommen, who was 24 years her senior. She met Mr. Oommen in December 1990 and stayed at his home, reportedly in exchange for cooking and cleaning. Apparently, Mr. Oommen had sought the advice of others about the propriety of this arrangement, wishing to ensure that others did not think it to be sexual (*R v Oommen*, 1994). Ms. Beaton then left Fort McMurray for Edmonton, returning a couple of months later to the apartment of Mr. Oommen, shortly before she was murdered in March 1991.

In the early morning hours of the night of the murder, a mischief-maker pushed the doorbells of all the apartments in the building where Mr. Oommen resided. It was later suggested that Mr. Oommen understood this to be a signal, arranged by Ms. Beaton and alleged co-conspirators, indicating the Mr. Oommen was asleep and they could enter his home to kill him ("Cabbie Cleared," 1995). Mr. Oommen fi ed up to 13 shots with a .22 calibre semi-automatic repeating rifle at Ms. Beaton as she lay sleeping on a makeshift bed in the living room of the apartment. She was struck in the chest, spine, head, and hip ("Self-defence Claimed," 1991). At around the time of the killing, Mr. Oommen repeatedly telephoned a taxi dispatcher, requesting police assistance. He then left the apartment and was seen by two neighbours, who themselves had been awakened by the doorbells. One neighbour witnessed him disposing of liquor bottles in the garbage. The other neighbour was asked by Mr. Oommen to call the police and inform them that he had just killed someone who had attacked him with a knife.

Upon their arrival, Mr. Oommen repeated to the RCMP that he had no option but to kill Ms. Beaton since she attacked him with a knife ("Self-defence Claimed," 1991). In his statement to the police, he explained that he had seen Ms. Beaton walk back and forth to the washroom, passing his bedroom door with what he believed to be a knife in her hand. He further stated that he knew that she was going to kill him, acting on the instructions of others, and that, at the time he killed her, she was merely pretending to be asleep; his options were to kill or be killed. The officer gained the impression that Mr. Oommen believed that the constable was investigating, or ought to be investigating, why the girl was trying to kill him.

Mr. Oommen was charged with second-degree murder and appeared before the court. At his trial, Dr. Louis Trichard, a staff psychiatrist at the Alberta Hospital in Edmonton, testified

> He, on that very night of the assault, was convinced that there were people outside the building that had staked out the building and were coming to attack him. He had, in fact, heard the buzzers being rung throughout the building and had incorporated this into his idea that he was being pursued ... On the night in question, he also became convinced that his assailants had incorporated the unfortunate deceased and had given her the commission that she was to kill him. So that on that night, it was him alone with her in his apartment, and it was either she was going to kill him, or he had to stop her. I believe that he was therefore acting under a delusion at the time that he committed his offence. (*R v Oommen*, 1994, at para 9)

Since the commission of the killing was uncontested, the only issue at the trial was whether the accused qualified for a defence of NCR-MD. The court noted that "psychiatrists testified that the accused possessed the general capacity to distinguish right from wrong and would know that to kill a person is wrong but that, on the night of the murder, his delusion deprived him of that capacity and led him to believe that the killing was necessary and justified under the circumstances as he perceived them" (*R v Oommen*, 1994). The trial judge then rejected the insanity defence, indicating that as the accused had the general capacity to tell right from wrong, he remained criminally responsible despite his beliefs at the time of the offence. Mr. Oommen was thus found guilty.

The case was appealed to the Alberta Court of Appeal, which ordered a new trial on the grounds that the trial judge had erred in his interpretation of the Criminal Code. The Crown then appealed the decision of the Alberta Court of Appeal to the Supreme Court of Canada. The Supreme Court dismissed the appeal. Following the Supreme Court decision, Mr. Oommen appeared before Justice E. Hutchinson of the Alberta Court of Queen's Bench charged with second-degree murder. Staff psychiatrist Louis Trichard, from the Alberta Hospital in Edmonton, again testified that Mr. Oommen suffered from a paranoid disorder

("Cabbie Cleared," 1995). Justice Hutchinson found Mr. Oommen NCR-MD.

Supreme Court Decision in *R v Oommen*

As noted above, the Crown appealed to the Supreme Court of Canada with respect to the order of the Alberta Court of Appeal to hold a new trial, posing the following legal issue:

> What is meant by the phrase "knowing that [the act] was wrong" in s 16(1)? Does it refer only to abstract knowledge that the act of killing would be viewed as wrong by society? Or does it extend to the inability to rationally apply knowledge of right and wrong and hence to conclude that the act in question is one which one ought not to do? (at para 20)

Justice McLachlin, in reviewing the evidence and delivering the decision, reached the conclusion that there was no rational motive for the killing and suggested that in order to understand it, "we must delve into the disordered workings of Mr. Oommen's mind" (*R v Oommen*, 1994, p. 509). She noted that the accused had incorporated the deceased into his delusions and had become fixated with the notion that his enemies had commissioned her to kill him. Justice McLachlin noted that Mr. Oommen had called a taxi dispatcher several times to request the police, suggesting that he had considered alternatives to murder, and they had not been helpful to him. She noted that he believed he had seen Ms. Beaton pass his bedroom door on more than one occasion that night with a knife in her hand. As a result of his delusions, he was convinced that she was going to kill him on the instructions of others, and he must, therefore, act in self-defence. Justice McLaughlin determined that the only issue at trial was whether Mr. Oommen's delusion qualified him for an NCR-MD defence. She went on to say that the evidence showed that he had the intellectual capacity to understand right from wrong, but owing to his delusional interpretation of the events, he honestly believed that killing her was justified under the circumstances. In other words, he was unable to apply his general ability to distinguish right from wrong to the actual act.

In reviewing the Alberta Court of Appeal decision, Justice McLachlin noted that presiding judge, Justice Kerans, interpreted the Supreme Court decision in Chaulk to suggest that section 16(3) of the Code on specific delusions was "superfluous." Indeed, following Chaulk, and subsequently the striking down of the law by the Supreme Court decision in *R v Swain* (1991), insanity provisions in the Code were rewritten, and the section regarding delusions had been omitted. However, Justice Kerans did not interpret this to mean that the defence stated therein was unavailable. Thus, "in his view, s 16(3) of the Code obligated the trial judge to direct his mind to the question of whether Mr. Oommen, despite no proven incapacity to understand societal views about right and wrong, lacked the capacity, because of his disease and resulting delusions, to apply that knowledge in a meaningful way at the time of the killing" (R v Oommen," 1994, p. 515).

In the mind of Justice McLachlin, the appeal focused on the meaning of the phrase "knowing that the act was wrong." On reviewing the history of the insanity provisions in detail, she concluded that the inquiry focuses on the ability to know that a particular act was wrong in the circumstances, not on the general capacity to know right from wrong. In other words, the accused must be able to apply the knowledge of right and wrong in a rational way to the alleged criminal act. She concluded that "the crux of the inquiry is whether the accused lacks the capacity to rationally decide whether the act is right or wrong and hence to make a rational choice about whether to do it or not" (R v Ooommen, p. 518). She noted that rational choice might be affected by the disordered condition of the mind, which might include delusions depriving the accused of the ability to evaluate what they are doing rationally. The crucial conclusion is contained in the following quote: "The real question is whether the accused should be exempted from criminal responsibility because of mental disorder of the time of the act deprived him of the capacity for rational perception and hence rational choice about the rightness or wrongfulness of the act" (p. 520). Justice McLachlin differentiates the situation from that where a psychopath or a person following a deviant moral code commits a crime. She notes that a psychopath is capable of knowing that his act is wrong in the eyes of society and, despite this knowledge, chooses to commit the act.

In the end, the court concluded that the evidence, in this case, supports the contention that Mr. Oommen was deprived of the capacity to know his act was wrong at the time. Given the evidence that he honestly felt that he was under imminent danger of being killed if he did not kill Ms. Beaton first, he, therefore, believed that killing her was justified. Thus, "there was evidence capable of supporting the conclusion that the accused's mental state was so disordered that he was unable to rationally consider whether his act was right or wrong in the way a normal person would" (p. 523). The appeal was, therefore, dismissed and the order directing a new trial was confirmed

It should be noted that in R v Chaulk, the court argued that section 16(3), regarding specific delusions, had no utility. Soon after this case, the court struck down section 16 in its entirety. Subsequently, Parliament passed Bill C-30, which rewrote section 16 with substantial changes, including doing away with section 16(3) altogether, since they concluded that it was redundant. However, in *R v Oommen*, the situation arose that specific delusions became the crux of the case for the defence. Subsequently, the court crafted a decision whereby specific delusions could affect the accused's capacity to assess rationally whether the act was right or wrong at the time. In this way, an accused with specific delusions, who could nevertheless appreciate the nature and quality of the act, could still successfully argue an NCR-MD defence. In our experience, this has become a common argument for the NCR-MD defence, with the tacit agreement of forensic psychiatrists and the courts.

Implications for Forensic Mental Health Practice

The Supreme Court rulings in *Chaulk* and *Oommen* have significant implications for forensic mental health practitioners with respect to two elements of the assessment of criminal responsibility: moral wrongfulness and the influence of specific delusions.

The Supreme Court of Canada ruling in Chaulk includes the interpretation of the phrase "knowing the act or omission was wrong" to include a knowledge of both legal and, for the first time, moral wrongfulness. As stated in chapter 3, Rogers, Turner, Helfield, and Dickens (1988) surveyed all forensic psychiatrists and psychologists in Canada in 1988 and found that 88 per cent had an erroneous understanding of the prevailing insanity standard. This error included a belief that moral wrongfulness was part of the Canadian insanity standard at that time, which it was not. This was demonstrated in case of the *R v Chaulk* when 10 mental health experts testified that it was their conclusion that the defendants were aware of the criminality of their actions but were nevertheless insane due to the fact that they were unaware of the wrongfulness of their actions (Rogers et al., 1988). Ironically, their collective belief was subsequently ruled into law. Since forensic psychiatry has been made a subspecialty in Canada and includes a certification examination, the standards now require forensic psychiatrists to be fully aware of the standard for a defence of NCR-MD in Canada.

Following *Chaulk* and *Oommen*, it is important to assess the evaluee's capacity to understand the moral wrongfulness of their actions at the material time or, more specificall , whether the accused lacked the capacity to decide rationally whether the act was right or wrong and subsequently make a rational choice about whether to commit the act. As part of the assessment, the forensic mental health expert must be able to elicit whether specific delusions experienced at the time of the act adversely affected the evaluee's capacity to decide rationally whether the act is right or wrong in both the legal and moral sense. Eliciting the thought processes at the material time – regarding moral wrongfulness and application of a rational choice and, therefore, the general ability to distinguish right from wrong at the time of the act – can be difficult because it involves an understanding of the moral and ethical values of the evaluee as they were able to bring them to bear in order to make a rational decision at the time of the act. The following might be directed to the evaluee:

> Please take yourself back to what you are thinking at the time of the act.

- How would God judge you?
- What would God think of your actions?
- What would your priest, rabbi, or imam think of or how would they judge your actions?
- How did you expect others in your community to judge your actions?
- Should you have done what you did?
- What were the alternatives to what you did?
- What else could you have done?
- Did you attempt to carry out any of the alternatives?
- What would have happened if you had not done what you did?

Summary

Robert Chaulk and Francis Morrissette put forward a defence of insanity in the brutal murder of an elderly man, claiming that they believed that they had the ability to rule the world and killing was the necessary means to an end. In reviewing the case, the Supreme Court considered the concept of wrongfulness and defined it as having not only a legal connotation but also a moral connotation, thereby broadening the definition of wrongfulness under the Criminal Code (*R v Chaulk*, 1990). This decision also struck down a previous clause in the Code referring to delusions in the insanity defence. The expansion of the meaning of wrongfulness is of major importance to the parties in this field, making the insanity defence more widely available than it was previously.

Subsequently, the Supreme Court ruling in the case of *Oommen* provided in-depth analysis and interpretation of the phrase "knowing that the act was wrong" (*R v Oommen*, 1994). This clear analysis and the resulting definition are now commonly used for the defence of not criminally responsible due to mental disorder (NCR-MD) in Canadian courts and have been helpful in guiding the assessment of accused persons suffering from mental disorder. This has implications for forensic mental health professionals both in terms of assessing wrongfulness and in addressing specific delusions

Table 5.1   Key points regarding wrongfulness

R v Chaulk	
Presumption of sanity	• Criminal capacity for an adult is indeed presumed and is not something that must be proven by the Crown beyond a reasonable doubt
Understanding wrongfulness	• Includes both legally wrong and morally wrong
Specific delusions	• Specific delusions cannot be used as a separate and alternative defence for individuals who do not meet the criteria of insanity
R v Oommen	
Specific delusions	• Specific delusions are a possible defence even if the individual is otherwise "sane" • Inquiry focuses on the ability to know that a particular act was wrong in the circumstances, not on the general capacity to know right from wrong • Inquiry applies a rational understanding of right and wrong with regard to the alleged offences
Implications for practice	
Wrongfulness	• Must include an assessment of both legally wrong and morally wrong
Specific delusions	• Forensic mental health professionals can assist the court by offering explanations as to the manner in which delusions can specifically influence the capacity to decide right and wrong in relation to the act in question

6 Voluntariness and Intent

R v Parks

Tired and exhausted, Ken Parks fell asleep on a Saturday night in front of the television. His life had not been going well, and he was filled with stress and anxiety about revealing to his in-laws the next day the extent of his financial and personal troubles.

He never made that confession. During the night, he drove the 23 kilometres from his house to his in-laws, stabbed his mother-in-law to death and almost killed his father [in-law].

The particular and remarkable fascination of this case is that Ken Parks did this all in his sleep. Awakening over the dead body of his mother-in-law, he drove to the police station and, with his hands severely cut and bleeding, he turned himself into the police. (Hutchinson, 1990)

In the early hours of the morning on 24 May 1987, Kenneth James Parks reported to police:

I just killed someone with my bare hands; Oh my God, I just killed some-one; I've just killed two people with my hands; My God, I've just killed two people with my hands; My God, I've just killed two people. I killed them; I just killed two people; I've just killed my mother- and father-in-law. I stabbed and beat them to death. It's all my fault. (*R v Parks*, 1990, at para 23)

Ken Parks and Karen Woods met as teenagers in Scarborough, Ontario, and soon became involved in a romance that blossomed over trips to the local shopping mall. Mr. Parks quickly became an integral part of Karen's life and family, taking her sister shopping and her brothers to hockey games. He became well known to her parents, Barbara Ann and Denis Woods, who provided him with a key to their home and regularly set a place at the dinner table to for him. Barbara Woods referred to him as the "gentle giant." At the ages of 19 and 20, respectively, Karen and Ken married. At the time of offence, three years later, they owned a townhouse in Pickering and had a five-month-old baby (Callwood, 1990).

In the summer preceding the murder, Mr. Parks, a high school dropout, bet five dollars on the horse races and won. He believed that gambling might be a way to supplement his income to obtain the luxuries in life he wished to provide for his family. But as the gambling quickly escalated, he suddenly found himself in a position of financial distress. Working as a project coordinator for an electrical contractor, he was putting in 10-hour days but remained significantly in debt. He took money from his wife's savings by forging her name on cheques and borrowed money from loan sharks, all of which he lost to gambling (Callwood, 1990). To cover his debts, Mr. Parks stole $30,000 from his employer, who, upon discovery of the theft, fi ed him and initiated court proceedings against him. The spiralling effects of his gambling caused strain in his personal relationships, but, nevertheless, his wife and parents-in-law reportedly continued to be supportive of him. The evening following the murder of his mother-in-law and beating of his father-in-law, he was scheduled to meet with them to discuss possible solutions to his situation (*R v Parks*, 1990, at para 16).

Mr. Parks was charged with first-deg ee murder in the death of Barbara Ann Woods and the attempted murder of Denis Woods. His attorney, the venerable Marlys Edwardh, brought forward a novel defence of non-insane automatism that undermined his voluntariness and ultimately his culpability. Expert testimony was provided by five physicians specializing in neurology, sleep neurology, psychiatry, and forensic psychiatry. Evidence presented from clinical interviews and sleep laboratory studies revealed that Mr. Parks had an established sleep disorder and was sleepwalking at the time of the offence. His sleep disorder included unusually deep sleep resulting in trouble awakening, grogginess for some time after wakening, nocturnal enuresis at an earlier age, and previous episodes of sleepwalking. Mr. Parks did not have a history of mental illness and reportedly demonstrated no evidence of neurological illness. He also had a strong family history of parasomnia. In the months prior to the murder and assault, it was reported that Mr. Parks was under considerable stress resulting in significant initial insomnia and nightly sleeps of only two to four hours.

The unanimous opinion of the experts was that Mr. Parks was suffering from somnambulism (sleepwalking). This evidence was not refuted by the Crown despite the fact that a sleep expert and a forensic psychiatrist consulted with the Crown throughout the trial.

In his direction to the jury, the trial judge indicated that, should the jury find that Mr. Parks was sleepwalking when he committed the offences, a finding of non-insane automatism would follow, and, therefore, Mr. Parks would be acquitted. This was indeed the finding of the jury and the outcome of the trial. The Crown appealed the acquittal to the Ontario Court of Appeal, arguing that if Mr. Parks was sleepwalking at the time of the offence, this should be considered a "disease of the mind" and he should have been found not criminally responsible due to mental disorder, which encompasses insane automatism. The Ontario Court of Appeal denied the appeal and upheld the acquittal, declaring that the judge was correct in instructing the jury that sleepwalking was not a disease of the mind. The Crown then further appealed to the Supreme Court of Canada (Glancy, Bradford, & Fedak, 2002).

Supreme Court Ruling in *R v Parks*

The Supreme Court thus considered two relevant issues. First, the nature of automatism in the form of sleepwalking, and second, which party holds the burden of proof with respect to the defence.

Disease of the Mind

The key issue for the Supreme Court was "Whether sleepwalking should be classified as non-insane automatism resulting in an acquittal or as a disease of the mind (insane automatism) giving rise to the special verdict of not guilty by reason of insanity" (R v Parks, 1992, p. 871).[3]

In this respect, the court concluded that the trial judge had correctly instructed the jury that the sleepwalking defence should be interpreted as non-insane automatism. In doing so, the judge had properly executed two tasks: 1) to consider the evidence supporting the position that the condition exists (the burden of which rests with the defence), and 2) to consider the evidence that the accused suffered from the condition at the time of the offence (the burden of which rests with the Crown to prove voluntariness). However, Mr. Justice La Forest, writing

---

3 Note that Bill C-30, which replaced not guilty by reason of insanity (NGRI) with not criminal responsible due to mental disorder (NCR-MD), was enacted in 1991, as this case proceeded through various courts.

the judgment for the court, continued to state that, in considering the distinction between automatism and insanity, the judge should also take into account policy considerations. These included whether there is a likelihood of recurrent danger – as "the purpose of the insanity defence has always been the protection of the public from recurrent danger" – whether the disorder can be easily feigned, and whether the decision would open the floodgates for using automatism as a defence (*R v Parks*, 1992).

The court noted that, in the case of Mr. Parks, medical testimony had clearly demonstrated that he was sleepwalking at the time of the incident. The testimony also was unanimous that sleepwalking was not a psychiatric illness, nor was it a neurological disorder or other illness. Rather, sleepwalking is classified as a sleep disorder – a fact not contested by Crown experts in attendance. A concern raised by Mr. Chief Justice Lamer in dissent was the risk to the public due to the possible recurrence of violence. In this respect, the majority decision written by Mr. Justice La Forest noted that the chances of recurrence were infin - tesimal, supported by the fact that the offence had occurred five years earlier and that the accused had made a considerable effort to re-establish his life. Further to this, if automatism was a disease of the mind, caused by something internal to the mind or brain of the accused, it would likely result in recurrence and thus represent a danger to the public if left untreated.

Burden of Proof

In considering the issue of burden of proof, the court ruled that because the Criminal Code relies on the assumption of sanity, it is the responsibility of the defence to prove insanity. However, the presumption of sanity does not relieve the Crown of its responsibility to prove voluntariness beyond a reasonable doubt where insanity is not at issue, such as in non-insane automatism. In short, evidence regarding whether the condition exists resides with the defence; evidence supporting that the voluntariness *was present* at the time of the offence resides with the Crown. This fundamental, historical principle was readdressed in *R v Stone*, as we will discuss below.

Postscript on *R v Parks*

In 2006, the *National Post* reported that Ken Parks, father of six children between 4 and 19 years old, was running for a seat as trustee on the Durham District School Board. The now 42-year-old auto worker reportedly stated "[The murder] has nothing to do with anything now; it was a medical issue and I'm practicing good sleep hygiene now" (Brieger, 2006). It is reported that Mr. Parks and his wife stayed together for several years after the murder but eventually separated.

Despite Mr. Parks's reported desire to move beyond the case involving the murder of his mother-in-law, the story of Ken Parks and the Supreme Court ruling continues to engender speculation, scepticism, and horror. The case was made into a 1997 movie, *The Sleepwalker Killing*, starring Hilary Swank, based on the book *The Sleepwalker*, by renowned journalist and author June Callwood (1990). It inspired a play, *Any Night*, by Stone's Throw Productions in Vancouver, which won an award for outstanding new play in 2009 (Birnie, 2009) and continues to be performed at theatre festivals across the country ("Calendar," 2016). It was the lead story in a 2010 BBC News special entitled "The Science of Defending Sleepwalkers That Kill" (Adam, 2010). The UK *Telegraph* highlighted the Parks case in a 2015 story: "Murder, Artistry and Sex: The Mysterious Horrors of Sleepwalking" (Goldhill, 2015). The case is regularly raised in talk show discussions of sleepwalking in the United States, Australia, and the United Kingdom.

R v Rabey

The distinction between insane automatism and non-insane automatism lies in the cause of the dissociative state. Grant and colleagues (1993) note that prior to *R v Parks*, Canadian law assumed that if an individual was in a dissociative state stemming from an internal factor, this would constitute a disease of the mind or insane automatism, and consequently the accused would need to put forward a mental health defence, resulting in a possible finding of not guilty by reason of insanity, or more laterally, not criminally responsible. Alternatively, if the individual suffered from a dissociative state caused by an external factor, for instance a blow to the head or involuntary intoxication from exposure to toxic fumes, a defence of non-insane automatism was possible.

The 1980 Supreme Court case of *R v Rabey* established the distinction between insane automatism and non-insane automatism. In presenting this case, it is important to note that the court ruling occurred prior to public and legislative attention to the issue of gender-based violence in Canada. For instance, Linda MacLeod's (1987) groundbreaking book *Battered But Not Beaten: Preventing Wife Battering in Canada*, which set the stage for funding of programs and shelters and legislative reform, was not published until seven years later. Similarly, the Women's Legal Education and Action Fund (LEAF), a national organization focused on advancing equality rights of women and addressing unequal treatment under the law, was not established until 1985.

Wayne Rabey, a 20-year-old University of Toronto student, became infatuated with a classmate who did not share his feelings. As he was leafing through her books one day to find an equation for an assignment they were working on together, he found a letter she had written to a friend in which she referred to Mr. Rabey as "one in a bunch of nothings." The next day, he ran into the victim and confronted her about the nature of their relationship, to which she replied that they were "just friends." Mr. Rabey subsequently grabbed the victim and struck her on the head with a rock he had taken from his geology lab, causing her to lose consciousness temporarily. Upon regaining consciousness, she discovered he had his hands around her neck and was shouting "you bitch" while choking her (*R v Rabey*, 1980, p. 518).

Mr. Rabey testified that he felt "a sort of flash," and then the next thing he remembered was that he was choking the victim. A professor who saw Mr. Rabey immediately thereafter reported that Mr. Rabey was pale, bewildered, distraught, shaky, and appeared "out of it." Similar evidence was reported by the dean and a nurse. Forensic psychiatrist Basil Orchard testified that, in his opinion, the dissociative state that occurred was comparable to that produced by a physical blow, and that it caused the physical effects observed by witnesses.

The judge allowed a defence of non-insane automatism caused by a psychological blow and Mr. Rabey was acquitted. In rejecting an appeal and upholding the acquittal, the Supreme Court stated:

> The meaning of the word "automatism," in any event so far as it is employed in the defence of non-insane automatism, is a term used to describe unconscious, involuntary behaviour, the state of a person who though capable of action is not conscious of what he is doing.
>
> ... the distinction to be drawn is between a malfunctioning of the mind arising from some cause that is primarily internal to the accused, as opposed to a malfunctioning of the mind, which is the transient effect produced by some specific external factor and which does not fall within the concept of disease of the mind. The ordinary stresses and disappointments of life which are the common lot of mankind do not constitute an external cause constituting an explanation for a malfunctioning of the mind which takes it out of the category of a "disease of the mind."

Here, it seems that the accused's infatuation with the complainant had created an abnormal condition in his mind under the influence of which he acted unnaturally and violently to an imagined slight to which a normal person would not have reacted in the same manner. (*R v Rabey*, 1980, p. 514)

Perhaps reflecting the ethos of the time, the Court took into account that "the appellant had never dated any other girl for any length of time and had only a minimal amount of sexual experience," and that he was an introvert infatuated with an attractive, outgoing young woman.

R v Stone

In March 1994, police were called to a vacant lot in Burnaby, British Columbia, where they discovered a pool of blood and a purse belonging to Donna Mae Stone, age 35. Police obtained a warrant, searched the Stones' home near Kelowna, and discovered a pickup truck, registered to Bert's Chain Link Fencing, locked in the garage of the house. The truck contained the body of Donna Stone, who had been stabbed 47 times (Middleton, 1994). A Canada-wide warrant was issued for the arrest of Bert Thomas Stone. Anyone with information was asked to contact the Kelowna RCMP ("Okanagan Man," 1994). Six weeks later Mr. Stone returned to Canada from Mexico and surrendered to the police, confessing that he had stabbed his wife of 10 months to death.

At the trial, Mr. Stone again admitted to killing his wife, but claimed to do so while in a state of automatism brought on by her verbal assaults. At trial, Ms. Stone's teenage daughter, Jessica Spiers, who lived with the couple, testified that Mr. Stone was "sneaking away to visit his children" (ages 12 and 14), who lived with their mother in Surrey, and was planning to take them to dinner since he had not seen them for several months. She added that having learned about the secret visit, Ms. Stone "freaked out" and "took off after him," having hastily borrowed a car from someone in order to do so (Hall, 1995a; Ogilvie, 1995b). As Ms. Stone had a difficult relationship with her husband's sons, she remained in the car while he spoke to them briefl , the plans for dinner abandoned. At some point during the following two hours, Mr. Stone drove to an abandoned parking lot and stabbed his wife.

At trial, Mr. Stone testified that in the midst of receiving a barrage of verbal abuse from his wife, he experienced a "whooshing" feeling wash over him from his head to his feet. His next conscience awareness was sitting and staring straight ahead with a hunting knife in his hand and his wife slumped over on the seat (*R v Stone*, 1999). Photos of the scene presented as evidence were graphic, demonstrating that Ms. Stone had grabbed the knife by the blade and had used her right arm to shield against the knife.

Upon reportedly regaining awareness, Mr. Stone moved the dead body from the truck cab into the large toolbox attached to the flatbed and drove home. There he prepared a note for his nine-year-old step-daughter reading "I'm sorry Nichole, but she wouldn't stop yelling at me" (Ogilvie, 1995b). Mr. Stone then sold his car, collected a business debt, and flew to Mexico. It was next reported that Mr. Stone awakened one morning in Mexico with the sensation that his throat was being cut. At that time, he also remembered stabbing his wife twice prior to experiencing the whooshing sensation (*R v Stone*, 1999). The court heard testimony from Jessica Spiers that her mother was "high-strung at times, took a lot of non-prescription pills and yelled on occasion" (Hall, 1995a). She described the couple's relationship as tense. Mr. Stone testified that "his wife's bizarre behaviour may have been the result of her taking pills containing codeine" (Hall, 1995b).

David Butcher, attorney for the defence, indicated that forensic psychiatrist Dr. Paul Janke had concluded that Mr. Stone was in an extreme dissociative state at the time of the killing, so he would have had no intent or awareness of committing a criminal act (Hall, 1995b). Mr. Butcher urged the jury to find Mr. Stone NCR-MD. Failing this, Mr. Butcher asserted that the jury should find Mr. Stone guilty of manslaughter "because the accused was provoked by a constant barrage of insults hurled at him by his wife during the trip to Surrey that ended in her demise" (Hall, 1995b).

The trial judge ruled that the defence had laid the evidentiary foundation for insane automatism but not non-insane automatism. The jury was thus instructed regarding the options of considering 1) insane automatism, 2) second-degree murder, based on the accused's intention, and 3) provocation for the offence. The jury found Mr. Stone guilty of manslaughter in October 1995, and he was sentenced to four years in prison. An appeal was made to the British Columbia Court of Appeal on both the conviction and the sentence, which dismissed both appeals and upheld both the conviction and the sentence in March 1997. The Crown and the defence then both appealed to the Supreme Court of Canada (*R v Stone*, 1999). While awaiting the Supreme Court hearing, Mr. Stone was released on parole to a half-way house in Prince George in July 1997, 20 months after his conviction ("Killer Gets Parole," 1997).

Context

Immediately following Bert Stone's initial conviction for manslaughter, newspapers began reporting accounts of his alleged abusive behaviour on other occasions. Elaine Smith, sister of Donna Stone, told the press, "It was an abusive relationship and the jury wasn't allowed to know that. He hit her before, but the judge ruled that evidence inadmissible" (Hall, 1995c). Brenda McFarlane, a friend of the deceased, reported that Ms. Stone had been frightened of her husband and recounted an incident in which he made a veiled threat to kill her in Ms. McFarlane's presence (Ogilvie, 1995a). Liz Barnes, the coordinator of a battered women's support group in Vancouver, expressed deep concern about the defence of provocation in this case and the effects on women in abusive relationships, suggesting that the jury in Stone's case "essentially allow[ed] him to blame her for her own murder."("Lobbyists," 1995) Others called for changes to legislation protecting women in abusive relationships ("Lobbyists," 1995).

Journalists summarized cases of those claiming dissociative states and raised concerns about credibility of the system, and the experts who testify in it. In one such article, with the headline "Loony law lets killers walk: Eager shrinks help sharp lawyers claim their clients were temporarily bonkers when they did their deadly deeds," it was pointed out that "many forensic experts and prosecutors concede that they're troubled with the growing trend to claim you killed because you were temporarily cuckoo" (Thompson, 1995).

Over 2,600 people sent letters to the attorney general of British Columbia urging an appeal of the case. In framing the Supreme Court appeal, lawyers for the attorney general stated: "The issue on appeal is of particular interest to Canadians concerned about domestic violence and to women whose sense of well-being is threatened by spousal killings and lenient sentences" (Tibbetts, 1998). The appeal pointed to a 1995 Statistics Canada report that indicated that spousal killing accounted for one of every six solved killings, that women were six times more likely to be killed by a spouse than a stranger, and that three-quarters of spousal murder victims were women. The appeal further argued that provoked killers get a double benefit in that provocation not only reduces the crime but is also considered mitigation in sentencing.

The federal, Ontario, and Alberta governments joined together in arguing for tougher sentences in cases of provoked spousal killings. Federal lawyer Graham Garton was quoted as stating: "Since society now unequivocally rejects and condemns spousal violence, it is appropriate for the courts to recognize that such conduct deserves concomitantly higher levels of retribution and denunciation" (Bindman, 1998a). Ujjal Dosanjh made legal history as the first BC attorney general to argue a Supreme Court of Canada criminal case. He urged the Supreme Court to send a very clear signal to every household in every part of the country that spousal violence will not be tolerated.

> If the court sends a message that it's all right to kill a nagging wife, and provocation will be allowed in a substantial way to mitigate the sentence, then we're sending a message to all Canadians that while we say domestic violence is unacceptable the sentences don't reflect that. (as cited in Bindman, 1998b)

In response to growing concerns, federal Minister of Justice Anne McLellan indicated that she was presently reviewing the 109-year-old provocation defence (Tibbetts, 1999). Nevertheless, following a three-year consultation, Minister McLellan reported that the majority of respondents to a 1997 consultation paper, ranging from police to women's organizations, concluded that provocation (defined as a wrongful act or insult that deprives an ordinary person of self-control) still has a place in the Canadian Criminal Code. She noted that women's groups saw the provocation defence as important to retain in cases where battered women killed their husbands (the battered woman syndrome defence) (Regehr & Glancy, 1995). As a result, changes to the Criminal Code were abandoned (Tibbetts, 2001).

Supreme Court Ruling in *R v Stone*

In the midst of these public debates and concerns, the Supreme Court, in the appeal of both the conviction and sentence of Bert Stone for killing his wife, considered the following:

1. whether the defence of non-insane automatism should also have been put before the jury;
2. whether the sentencing judge correctly considered provocation as a mitigating factor, or whether this had already been considered in reducing the charge to manslaughter;
3. whether the sentence properly reflected the gravity of the crime. (*R v Stone*, 1999)

In the end, the court dismissed both the defence's appeal of the conviction and the Crown's appeal of the sentence. It also addressed central issues regarding the defence of automatism related to burden of proof and the decision-making process.

Burden of Proof

The Supreme Court noted that the law presumes that people act in a voluntary manner. Therefore, those who assert that their actions were involuntary hold the burden of proof that this is, in fact, the case. This overturns the decision on burden of proof determined in *R v Parks*. Thus, the defence holds the burden of proving both that the condition exists and that it undermined voluntary action at the time of the offence.

A Two-Stage Process for Determining Non-insane Automatism

The court reiterated that two forms of automatism are recognized by law: 1) insane automatism in which involuntariness arises from a disease of the mind, and 2) non-insane automatism in which the involuntary action does not arise from a disease of the mind. How these two options are applied can result in very different outcomes, that is, a finding of NCR-MD or an acquittal. The Supreme Court ruled that if automatism is claimed by the accused, a two-step process must be followed.

First, the defence must provide sufficient evidence to support a claim of automatism, which involves calling supporting psychiatric evidence. In addition, the judge must consider other factors including the severity of the triggering stimulus, corroborating evidence of bystanders, a corroborating medical history of automatistic-like dissociative states, any motives that may explain the crime, and whether the alleged trigger is also the victim of the crime. In *R v Stone* (1999) the court advised that the judge must weigh all available evidence in coming to a determination. In this respect, a motiveless act lends plausibility to involuntariness, as does the fact that the trigger of the state is not the victim of the crime (Glancy et al., 2002).

In the second stage, the judge must determine whether the condition alleged is a mental disorder or a non-mental disorder related automatism. In doing so, the judge must consider the nature of the trigger and determine if a normal person would have reacted to the trigger by entering into an automatistic state. If that is not the case, the disorder is not a disease of the mind. The dissenting opinion with respect to the conviction of Mr. Parks delivered by Mr. Justice Binnie contains a level of graphic detail regarding the offence not often found in Supreme Court rulings. One excerpt reads:

> She taunted him that his former wife had been "fucking all my friends" (while the two had been married) and that "[my sons] weren't my kids at all." As the verbal abuse continued, he said, "I can see she's losing it," so

he pulled into a vacant lot and "she's still yelling at me that I'm nothing but a piece of shit." His wife then allegedly said she had told the police that he had been abusing her and that they were about to arrest him, and threatened to get a court order to force him out of their home leaving her in the house, collecting alimony and child support. He said she told him she felt sick every time he touched her, that he was a "lousy fuck" with a small penis and she would never have sex with her again. (*R v Stone*, 1999, p. 303)

This evidence may have swayed some into believing that Mr. Stone was indeed suffering from automatism in the manner that any normal person would to such a trigger. It may have swayed others to believe that this constituted motive, undermining a claim of automatism.

R v Daviault

On the request of his wife, Henri Daviault went to visit a partially paralysed and wheelchair-bound 65-year-old female friend. Mr. Daviault arrived carrying a 40-ounce bottle of brandy, of which the complainant consumed a small glass before falling asleep in her wheelchair. Part way through the night, she awoke to the go to bathroom. Mr. Daviault suddenly appeared, wheeled her into the bedroom and threw her on the bed where he sexually assaulted her. Established facts at trial included that the accused had consumed the rest of the bottle of brandy between his arrival at 6 p.m. and the following morning at 3 a.m. when the assault occurred, and that he drank seven or eight bottles of beer at a bar earlier in the day. Mr. Daviault testified that he had a glass of brandy upon his arrival at the apartment but had no recollection of what occurred between that time and when he awoke naked in the complainant's bed. A pharmacologist testified that an individual who had consumed such an amount of brandy might suffer a blackout and lose contact with reality, wherein the brain is temporarily dissociated from normal functioning, likely resulting in an individual being unaware of his actions and unable to recall them the next day. The trial judge acquitted Mr. Daviault, stating that he had a reasonable doubt about whether he, by virtue of his extreme intoxication, possessed the minimal intent necessary to commit the offence of sexual assault (*R v Daviault*, 1994). The Crown appealed, and the Quebec Court of Appeal ordered a guilty verdict, reasoning that the defence of self-induced intoxication resulting in a state equivalent to automatism is not available as a defence to a general intent offence. The defence subsequently appealed to the Supreme Court of Canada.

The court ordered a new trial on the basis that it was unconstitutional for Mr. Daviault to be denied the defence of being sufficiently intoxicated to the point that he could not form the minimal intent necessary to commit sexual assault (Baker & Knopff, 2014).

In the court's reasoning in *R v Daviault*, the majority decision referred to *Leary v The Queen*. In this case, British Columbia resident Allan Leary appealed a conviction for rape to the Supreme Court of Canada on the grounds that the judge had erred in directing the jury that drunkenness was not a defence for a charge of rape (*Leary v The Queen*, 1978). The trial judge followed a previous common law rule that indicated that while intoxication could be a defence for criminal offences involving "specific intent," it could not be used for "general intent" defences (Baker & Knopff, 2014). Baker and Knopff (2014) differentiate between the two types of intent: in specific intent someone must intend something beyond the immediate act, for instance intending to strike someone with the aim of killing them; whereas general intent is limited to the particular act, such as striking someone. Relying on a recent case in the House of Lords (*D.P.P. v Majewski*, 1976), which concluded that acceptance generally of intoxication would undermine criminal law (Gold, 1978), the Supreme Court of Canada in *Leary* ruled that as rape was a crime of general intent, intoxication was not an excuse. It stated that the recklessness shown by an accused in becoming voluntarily intoxicated is sufficien to constitute the fault element needed to find that the general intent offence had been committed. This became known as the "Leary rule" and its purpose was to ensure that a person accused of dangerous acts committed while impaired could be successfully prosecuted (Lawrence, 2017). In effect, under the Leary rule, the accused's intention to drink is substituted for the intention to commit a dangerous act.

In *Daviault*, the majority judgment written by Justice Cory ruled that the strict application of the Leary rule, which states that the *mens rea* of a general intent offence cannot be negated by self-induced intoxication, offends the presumption of innocence specified in section 11(d) of the Canadian Charter of Rights and Freedoms. The court reasoned that the mental aspect of an offence has long been recognized as an integral part of a crime and to ignore it deprives an accused of fundamental justice. "To deny that even a very minimal mental element is required for sexual assault offends the Charter in a manner that is so drastic and so contrary to the principles of fundamental justice that it cannot be justified under s. 1 of the Charter" (*R v Daviault*, 1994). The court emphasized that the wrongful intention to become dangerously drunk cannot substitute for the intention or *mens rea* to commit a crime of sexual assault (Baker & Knopff, 2014). The court did not accept the argument that this would open the floodgates to this defence, since the jury would not acquit unless there was clear evidence that the drunkenness was of such a severity that there was reasonable doubt as to whether the accused was even aware that he had committed the prohibited act.

The court in *Daviault* noted that a crime must consist of two elements. The first is a physical element of committing a prohibited act. The second is that the conduct in question must be willed; this is usually referred to as voluntariness. The decision in *R v Parks* noted that, in principle, absence of volition is always a defence to a crime. Absence of volition, or involuntariness, instigates a complete and unqualified acquittal. The fact that the defence of automatism, therefore, "exists as a middle ground between criminal responsibility and legal insanity is beyond question" (*R v Rabey*, 1980). While noting that automatism would apply only in rare cases of extreme intoxication, the *Daviault* decision concludes: "finall , then there must be a contemporaneous mental element comprising an intention to carry out the prohibited physical act or omission to act; that is to say a particular state of mind such as the intent to cause, or some foresight of, the results of the act or the state of affairs" (*R v Daviault*, 1994, p. 11).

Context and Legislative Response to *R v Daviault*

The public and media response to the *R v Daviault* decision was swift and predictable. One newspaper reported that "judges across Canada admit to being under fire because of the perception that the Supreme Court of Canada has given drunken men an excuse to rape women" (Vienneau, 1994, p. A4). Scott Newark, a former Crown prosecutor and spokesperson for the Canadian Police Association noted: "There is an academic and unrealistic view of the law … This court does not seem to appreciate the consequences of its actions – more people will now try to use drunkenness as an excuse" (as cited in Chisholm, 1994, p. 100). Lee Lakeman, a representative of the Canadian Association of Sexual Assault Centres and an employee at the Vancouver Rape Relief and Women's Shelter, noted, "Whether or not this is good law, it's lousy politics … How many excuses for male violence can there be?" (as cited in Chisholm, 1994, p. 102). Federal Minister of Justice Allan Rock agreed and issued a statement: "The question of where to draw the line with extreme drunkenness and insanity is now too uncertain to leave it the way it is" (as cited in Chisholm, 1994, p. 100). Nine months later, the Chrétien government introduced Bill C-72 and enacted section 33.1 of the Criminal Code of Canada (1985), re-enacting an element of the Leary rule regarding self-intoxication. Under the changes, self-intoxication is excluded as a defence for general intent offences related to bodily integrity, such as assault, but not for other types of criminal behaviour.

Section 33.1 states that

1. It is not a defence to an offence referred to in subsection (3) that the accused, by reason of his self-induced intoxication, lacks the general intent or the voluntariness required to commit the offence, where the accused departed markedly from the standard of care as described in subsection (2).
2. For the purposes of this section, a person that departs markedly from the standard of reasonable care generally recognized in Canadian Society and is thereby criminally at fault where a person, while in a state of self-induced intoxication that renders the person unaware of, or incapable of consciously controlling, their behaviour, voluntarily or involuntarily interferes or threatens to interfere with the bodily integrity of another person.
3. This section applies in respect of an offence and that this act or any other act of Parliament that includes an element of an assault or any other interference or threat of interference by a person with the bodily integrity of another person.

This section of the Code does not apply in cases where the Crown failed to prove that the intoxication was self-induced, for instance, in situations where the accused ingested prescribed medication without knowing that it might be dangerous.

It is noteworthy that the amendments to the Code were accompanied by a lengthy preamble. In it, the Parliament of Canada identified grave concern with the incidence of violence in Canadian society, the impact of violence on women and children, the close association between violence and intoxication, and the shared moral view that those who violate the physical integrity of others while in a state of self-induced psychosis should be held accountable. Nevertheless, this situation remains far from settled. In the summer of 2018, newspapers reported the ruling of Superior Court Justice Nancy Spies that federal law preventing excessive intoxication as a defence against sexual assault charges was unconstitutional (McQuigge, 2018; *R v McCaw*, 2018). Nevertheless, in a ruling delivered in December 2018, Cameron McCaw of Toronto was found guilty of sexual assault despite his claims that he was so intoxicated that he was unaware of his actions. The judge indicated that there was no evidence that

McCaw was in a state of automatism and did not know what he was doing (Shum, 2018).

R v Bouchard-Lebrun

At five o'clock on the morning of 25 October 2005, Tommy Bouchard-Lebrun and a long-time acquaintance illegally entered the home of another acquaintance for the purposes of beating him for the "real or imagined reason that he wore an upside-down cross around his neck." A neighbour, hearing the commotion, attempted to intervene but was thrown down the stairs and had his head violently stomped on by Mr. Bouchard-Lebrun, leaving him severely and permanently disabled. Evidence at trial showed that Mr. Bouchard-Lebrun had smoked marijuana and ingested amphetamines the day before and subsequently purchased and ingested ecstasy pills prior to the offence (*R v Bouchard-Lebrun*, 2011).

At trial, Mr. Bouchard-Lebrun admitted that he had committed the acts but claimed that at the time he had been suffering from a psychotic condition. This included an obsession with God, the Devil, and the upside-down cross, which he associated with the Apocalypse. Two psychiatrists agreed that he suffered from "a severe psychosis that made him incapable of distinguishing right from wrong" (*R v Bouchard-Lebrun*, 2011, p. 583). The Crown's expert, whose evidence was accepted, concluded that, at the material time, the appellant had been suffering from a toxic psychosis, in other words, a psychosis caused by the consumption of toxic substances. The psychotic condition, which diminished gradually over the next four days, was unprecedented. It was noted that Mr. Bouchard-Lebrun had no underlying mental disorder and was not addicted to any particular substance. The trial judge accepted this evidence and convicted Mr. Bouchard-Lebrun on the counts of aggravated assault. He was found not guilty on the counts of breaking and entering because of extreme intoxication. The judge noted that section 33.1 of the Criminal Code provides that self-induced intoxication cannot be a defence to an offence against the bodily integrity of another person. He sentenced Mr. Bouchard-Lebrun to five years for the offence of aggravated assault and three months concurrent for that of common assault.

Mr. Bouchard-Lebrun appealed both the verdict and the sentence to the Quebec Court of Appeal. He argued that he had acted under the influence of a toxic psychosis and that the defence of not criminally responsible due to a mental disorder was applicable since both psychiatrists at trial agreed that he had been incapable of distinguishing right from wrong at the material time. The court rejected his arguments, pointing out that section 33.1 had limited the defence of self-induced intoxication to non-violent general intent offences. Mr. Bouchard-Lebrun then appealed to the Supreme Court of Canada.

The Supreme Court rejected the appeal in a unanimous decision (*R v Bouchard-Lebrun*, 2011). In reaching this conclusion, the court considered the rules for intoxication set out by the British House of Lords in 1920 (*D.P.P. v Beard*, 1920) as follows. First, that intoxication could be a ground for an insanity defence if it produced the disease of mind. Second, that evidence of drunkenness could be considered as a factor rendering the accused incapable of forming the specific intent and should be taken into consideration with the facts proved in order to decide whether the accused had formed the specific intent. Third, that evidence of intoxication falling short of a proven incapacity to form the necessary intent and that "merely establishing that his mind was affected by drink so that he more readily gave way to some violent passion, does not rebut the presumption that a man intends the natural consequences of his acts" (Lord Birkenhead, as cited in *R v Bouchard-Lebrun*, 2011, p. 589).

Referring to section 33.1 of the Criminal Code, the court noted that if the accused was intoxicated *and* in a psychotic state at the material time, the problem faced was "to identify a specific source for his or her mental condition, namely self-induced intoxication or a disease of mind" (*R v Bouchard-Lebrun*, 2011). In *Bouchard-Lebrun*, the appellant submitted that the exclusion of "self-induced states" applies only to the normal effects of intoxication. His counsel went on to argue that if a toxic psychosis resulting from intoxication is an abnormal effect, then it would not be excluded as a defence under the Code. The court noted that the definition of mental disorder in *Cooper v The Queen* (1983) recommended a contextual approach that was intended to strike a fair balance between the need to protect the public from an accused's mental state that is inherently dangerous and the desire to impose criminal liability solely on persons who are responsible for the state that they were in at the time of the offence. Therefore, the concept that toxic psychosis is always a disease of mind was not acceptable to the court. The court emphasized that the question of whether a psychiatric diagnosis is a mental disorder is a question of law to be decided by the trial judge. The role of the psychiatrist is to describe the accused's mental condition and how it is considered from the medical point of view (Watts, 2013).

The court adopted what it referred to as a holistic approach, derived from *R v Stone*, in which two analytic tools were suggested: 1) determining whether the causal factors for the offence are internal (clarifying the degree to which the individual differs from a normal person without a disease of the mind) or external (external factors do not fall under section 16 of the Code), and 2) determining whether the condition presents a recurring danger (*R v Stone*, 1999). In the case of *Bouchard-Lebrun*, it was determined that the cause was external, since a normal person could develop a toxic psychosis as a result of consuming ecstasy and the symptoms of psychosis coincided with the duration of intoxication. Further, the court concluded that the mental condition of the accused was not inherently dangerous, providing that he abstained from such drugs in the future, "which he is capable of doing voluntarily." Therefore, his mental condition poses no threat to the public safety.

Watts (2013) concludes that this case is important for a number of reasons. First, it reminds forensic practitioners that the judge remains the gatekeeper in deciding what is a disease of mind or mental disorder. Psychiatric evidence may be helpful regarding the nature of the mental illness. Second, the decision lays out an analytic approach for the judiciary to apply in cases of states where self-induced intoxication produces psychiatric symptoms.

Implications for Forensic Mental Health Practice

The forensic assessment with regard to the defence of automatism is particularly difficult given the fact that automatism is a legal term, and that the diagnostic criteria and exclusionary criteria found in the DSM-5 and other familiar psychiatric sources do not offer guidance. It is, therefore, necessary to turn to legal texts for an interpretation of the term. Lord Denning in *Bratty v Attorney General for Northern Ireland*, defines automatism as follows:

> ... An act which is done by the muscles without any control by the mind, such as spasm, a reflex action, or a convulsion; or an accident by a person who is not conscious of what he is doing such as an act done while suffering from concussion or while sleep walking. (*Bratty v Attorney-General for Northern Ireland*, 1963, p. 409)

Lord Denning's definition focuses on involuntary muscle movements. In considering this, Arboleda-Flórez (2002) surmises that in a case where a motorcyclist is driving erratically while being stung by a swarm of bees, or where a person while sneezing flails their arms and hits a candle thereby starting a fi e, the individual would likely be found not guilty. However, cases referred for forensic assessment are rarely so simple and instead involve complex actions that may be considered involuntary and unconscious. This is reflected in the definition of automatism in Canadian law, that is, "the state of a person who though capable of action, is not conscious of what he is doing" (*R v Rabey*, 1980, p. 514). Unconscious, in this context, is generally taken to mean that the person is not fully aware of what is happening and is not reacting to outside stimuli, either because of a medical condition causing a disturbance in the brain – which can be triggered by internal factors, such as hypoglycemia, or external ones, such as a blow on the head – or a serious psychological blow that causes an analogous condition. In other words, the person is acting in an involuntary manner and in legal terms does not possess *mens rea* or the intention or knowledge of wrongdoing.

Arboleda-Flórez (2002) distinguishes between automatism in medicine, a set of behaviours that are outside the conscious control of the patient and that connote something medically serious has taken place, and automatism in law, which is tied to a defence against a criminal charge and has deep social and political implications. In neurology, examples of conditions that can result in automatism include epilepsy and traumatic brain injury (Arboleda-Flórez, 2002). In psychiatry, schizophrenia is commonly associated with automatistic states; other disorders associated with automatism include dissociative reactions associated with personality disturbances and emotional shock or acute stress reactions (Arboleda-Flórez, 2002). Further forms of automatism may potentially arise from sleepwalking, which has more recently been established as a sleep disorder, not a psychiatric or neurological disorder (*R v Parks*, 1992) and severe intoxication (*R v Bouchard-Lebrun*, 2011; *R v Daviault*, 1994).

A critical issue in law is the differentiation between insane automatism and non-insane automatism. This was addressed in the English case of *R v Quick* (1973) in which a nurse was charged with assaulting a paraplegic patient, causing a fractured nose, black eyes, and other bruising. The accused, who suffered from insulin-dependent diabetes mellitus, argued that he was in a state of hypoglycemia at the time of the act, caused by excessive insulin administration. The judge ruled that the condition of the accused constituted insanity, a decision that was overruled on appeal. The Court of Appeal reasoned that the mental state was caused by an external factor, and, therefore, a finding of non-insane automatism applied. The court did add, however, that if the hypoglycemia had been self-induced or foreseeable then this defence could not have been used. In Canada, defining cases have been *R v Stone*, in which Bert Stone claimed to kill his wife in a state of automatism, and *R v Parks*, in which Ken Parks was acquitted of killing his mother-in-law on the basis on non-insane automatism while sleepwalking.

Sleepwalking

Somnambulism as a form of automatism has long been a source of intrigue. Umanath, Sarezky, & Finger (2011) chronicle the history of reports of sleepwalking beginning with Hippocrates and Aristotle. During the medieval period, Western culture tied it to religious veneration and the consequences of either divine appointment (God) or diabolical agency (Satan). In the early fourteenth century, instances of murder committed by individuals who were sleepwalking were reported by courts in southern France and Italy (Ekirch & Shneerson, 2011). Sleepwalking was a cause for speculation in Shakespeare's time, displayed in the descriptions of Lady Macbeth. Some physicians at that time attributed sleepwalking to "severe disturbances of the spirit, sinning, and the devil, while others pointed to melancholic and diseased minds and/or agitation of the brain" (Umanath et al., 2011, p. 264). Almost 200 years later, in 1796, Erasmus Darwin asserted that "somnambulism was not madness because the train of ideas is kept constant by the power of volition" (as cited in Umanath et al., 2011, p. 256).

In reviewing the scientific evidence on sleepwalking (or confusional arousal) and violence, Pressman, Mahowald, Schenck, and Bornemann (2007) suggest that such episodes do not occur spontaneously. Rather they arise from a complex set of factors, including those that are predisposing (genetic and familial), priming (sleep deprivation, medication, fever, alcohol, or situational stress), and precipitating proximal triggers (sleep disordered breathing, noise, or touch), which produce arousals but do not fully wake the individual. As higher cognitive functions are absent or impaired, primitive behaviours can thus appear unexpectedly. Among 64 individuals referred to a sleep clinic for sleep terrors or sleepwalking, 59 per cent were reported to have harmful behaviours and 41 per cent were classified as seriously violent. The majority of those who were violent to others were males who reported high levels of stress, excessive caffeine use, and drug abuse, and who showed less stage 4 sleep (Moldofsky, Gilbert, Lue, & MacLean, 1995). Overall among individuals with sleep disorders, males comprise approximately 97 per cent of those who inflict injuries and 80 per cent of those who exhibit potentially lethal behaviour (Siclari et al., 2010).

While violence occurring in the nocturnal period may be the result of a number of disorders such as dementia or dissociative disorders,

Table 6.1   Sleep disorders with the potential for violence

Disorder	State	Features	Occurrence of violence
Confusional arousal	Dissociation Wake/non-REM	Incomplete awakening, mental confusion, reduced vigilance, impaired cognition, amnesia	When being forced awake from sleep
Sleepwalking	Dissociation Wake/non-REM	Like confusional arousal but with ambulation	On an encounter with another person
Sleep terror	Dissociation Wake/non-REM	Incomplete awakening, abrupt fear, often with alarming vocalizations, autonomic arousal (mydriasis, tachycardia, tachypnea, diasphoresis)	Linked to a frightening image in a dream
Rapid eye movement sleep behaviour disorder	Dissociation Wake/REM sleep	Acting out dreams	Linked to acting out a dream
Epileptic nocturnal paroxysmal dystonia	Possible in all sleep stages	Twisting, limbs moving	Accidental in relation to seizures
Epileptic nocturnal wandering	Possible in all sleep stages	Like sleep walking, more violence possible	Accidental when approached by another person

Source: Adapted from Siclari et al. (2010)

it occurs in a state of wakefulness and, unlike the violence that occurs with violent parasomnias and nocturnal seizures, is not true sleep-related violence (Siclari et al., 2010). The International Classification of Sleep Disorders Classification Manual has more than 60 types that are largely classified into insomnias (inability to sleep), hypersomnias (inability to stay awake), sleep-related breathing disorders, and parasomnias (unwanted or abnormal behaviours during sleep) (Idzikowski, 2014). Parasomnias include disorders of arousal (confusional arousal, sleepwalking, and sleep terror), rapid eye movement sleep behaviour disorder, nocturnal paroxysmal dystonia, and epileptic nocturnal wandering (Siclari et al., 2010) (see table 6.1). Disorders of arousal usually occur during partial arousal from slow-wave sleep; the individual is usually completely amnesic regarding behaviours that occur in them (Umanath et al., 2011). Awakening from these states is difficult: behaviour can be complex, accompanied by talking or shouting, and eyes are often described as glassy. Sleepwalking, a specific parasomnia, is frequently found in other members of the individual's family and is long-standing; 89 per cent of male sleepwalkers and 84.5 per cent of female sleepwalkers have positive histories of sleepwalking as children (Idzikowski, 2014).

Voluntary Intoxication

A further form of automatism is that caused by excessive intoxication, which in and of itself is difficult to assess, and is made more complex when the intoxication is self-induced. The psychiatric community does not provide clarity about the relationship between certain substances and psychotic disorders. The DSM-5 defines substance-induced psychotic disorder as a disorder with delusions and hallucinations that developed during or soon after substance intoxication or withdrawal and that the involves substances capable of producing the symptoms (American Psychiatric Association, 2013). It also requires that the disturbance is not better explained by an independent psychotic disorder, the evidence for which could include the following: the symptoms preceded the onset of the substance use, the symptoms persisted for a substantial period of time (somewhat arbitrarily defined as "about one month" after the cessation of acute withdrawal or severe intoxication), or there is other evidence of an independent psychotic disorder. The criteria also include the fact that the disturbance does not occur exclusively during the course of a delirium.

Fiorentini and colleagues (2011) review the literature on this complicated issue. They point out that substance-induced psychosis is commonly observed in clinical practice; however, they note that the literature has yet to clarify the differentiation between primary and substance-induced psychoses as well as best practices in terms of treatments and outcomes. A recent paper published in the *American Journal of Psychiatry* noted that 32 per cent of patients with substance-induced psychosis converted to either bipolar or schizophrenia spectrum disorders between three and four and a half years after the initial onset (Starzer, Nordentoft, & Hjorthøj, 2017). This reflects the confusion regarding the state of knowledge in this area within the psychiatric community. The court decision in *Bouchard-Lebrun* reflects the as yet incomplete ability of the mental health community to understand and explain substance-induced psychosis. The decision also emphasizes the gatekeeper function of the court in defining mental disorder and the role of the court in exempting accused persons with mental disorder from criminal liability, while simultaneously protecting the public from dangerous persons (Watts, 2013).

Forensic Assessment

From a psycho-legal perspective, a primary role of the expert in cases of automatism is to assist the court with the two-stage process. First, was the accused suffering from automatism at the time of the offence? Second, if the automatism did occur, what was the cause of the automatism – specifically, was it caused by a disease of the mind? In addition, the expert must consider the issue of recurring danger, assessed in mental health, not legal, terms. In providing assessments in this complex area of practice, expert witnesses are advised to ensure that their opinions are well supported by evidence and to heed the words of Lord President Cooper, which define the role of the expert as follows:

> [Expert witnesses'] duty is to furnish the judge or jury with the necessary scientific criteria for testing the accuracy of their conclusions, so as to enable the judge or jury to form their own independent judgement by the application of these criteria to the facts in evidence … [it is] the decision of the judicial tribunal and not an oracular pronouncement by an expert. (*Davie v Magistrates of Edinburgh*, 1953, at p. 40)

The forensic mental health assessment of a case of possible automatism involves all the facets of a full forensic assessment, a subject discussed in chapter 3. In addition, however, it also requires the consideration of factors identified by the Supreme Court in *R v Stone* (see table 6.3) and other factors identified in table 6.2. Fenwick (1990) distinguished a number of characteristics of automatism that are of practical value to the forensic mental health assessment: 1) the person experiences involuntariness and lack of control; 2) the act is inappropriate for the circumstances and shows a lack of judgment; 3) the act can, however, be complex, coordinated, purposeful, and goal-directed; and 4) there is usually amnesia or confused recollection in recounting the events. As in any assessment, it is necessary to elicit a thorough subjective account of the circumstances leading to the offence, at the time of the offence, and following the offence. This assessment includes an account, at each of these junctures, of the evaluee's thoughts, feelings, and perceived actions, and of any motives for the crime, such as jealousy, revenge, or money. Although there may be some complicated psychodynamic

Table 6.2 Forensic assessment of automatism

Presence of automatistic state	• Corroborating witnesses • Corroborating history of dissociative states • Consideration of possible malingering
Nature of the automatistic state (disease of the mind?)	• Presence of psychiatric illness • Presence of medical illness • Presence of sleep disorder • Effects of alcohol • Medical and psychiatric history • Family history • Laboratory results
Precipitant or trigger	• Severity of the triggering event • Source (did the eventual victim trigger the event?) • Context (accused's interpretation of the trigger)
Priming or vulnerability factors	• Substance use • Life stressors • Sleep deprivation
Amnesia	• Presence and duration • Cause: organic, functional condition; alcohol blackout, conscious attempt to distort • Incomprehension and possible horror on return to awareness
Motive	• Possible gains • Link between the victim and the trigger
Specific issues in sleep-related violence	• History of sleepwalking or other parasomnias • Evidence the individual was asleep prior to the offence • Duration of sleep • Concurrent factors (fatigue, drugs, alcohol) • Source of arousal (touch, noise) • Proximity of offence to arousal
Specific issues in severe intoxication and substance-induced psychosis	• No independent psychotic disorder • Symptoms did not precede substance use • Symptoms do not persist after the cessation of acute withdrawal or severe intoxication • Disturbance does not occur exclusively during the course of a delirium
Risk of recurrence	• Unique nature of the trigger • Treatment for disorder leading to automatism

Source: Adapted from Arboleda-Flórez (2002), Idzikowski (2014), Idzikowski & Rumbold (2015), Pressman et al. (2007), *R v Stone* (1999).

factors at play, generally speaking, if there appears to be an explanatory motive, this might mitigate against automatism.

The personal and medical history of the evaluee should include a careful account of previous states that are similar to the state in question, and personality and functioning between any episodes. Special emphasis should be placed on collateral information, particularly where there is amnesia and the individual is unable to provide a description of the putative state. Collateral information might include a history from the family, close friends, or partners, police observations, and statements from witnesses who observed the state of the evaluee before, during, or after the event.

If the incident is postulated to be sleep-related, then a history of sleep-related events since childhood is important. Sleep studies performed by a specialist may demonstrate characteristic patterns of sleep in the individual that predispose them to risk. In addition, consultations with a neurologist, neuropsychiatrist, or endocrinologist, and adjunctive investigations, including tests for diabetes, electroencephalograms, or brain imaging, may be useful. In the case of suspected substance-induced psychosis, efforts should be made to obtain information about the nature and amount of suspected intoxicant. This may assist the mental health expert to attempt a best estimate of the effect that a similar type and dose of intoxicant may have on a normal person, and compare this estimate to the effect on the evaluee in the present case.

The courts are generally sceptical about automatism as a defence, as evidenced in one case where the judge noted: "Automatism (is) a defence which in a true and proper case may be the only one open to an honest man, but it may just as readily be the last refuge of a scoundrel" (R v Szymuziak," 1972, p. 608). Thus, the forensic mental health professional should be alert to the possibility of malingering and consider referral to a forensic psychologist with special expertise in assessing for malingering.

Summary

Actus non facit reum nisi mens sit rea (the act does not make a person guilty unless the mind is guilty) serves as the fundamental basis for British law and the law of jurisdictions based on British law. This principle assumes that an act must be voluntary for the *actus reus*, or guilty act, to have occurred. Nowhere is this concept tested to a greater degree than when violent behaviour, and in particular murder, is claimed to have occurred in a state of automatism.

In the 1980 Supreme Court case of *R v Rabey*, involving a 20-year-old university student who attacked a woman with whom he was

Table 6.3 Key points regarding voluntariness and intent

R v Rabey (1980)

Definition of automatism	• Unconscious, involuntary behaviour • The state of a person who is not conscious of what he is doing
Insane automatism	• Malfunctioning of the mind arising from a cause internal to the accused, e.g., psychological makeup, emotional makeup, organic pathology
Non-insane automatism	• Transient effect caused by an external factor, e.g., a blow to the head, exposure to toxic fumes

R v Parks (1992)

Insane automatism	• Disease of the mind • Positive finding results in an NCR-MD
Non-insane automatism	• Not a disease of the mind • Positive finding results in acquittal
Burden of proof	• Evidence supporting that the condition exists resides with the defence • Evidence supporting that the condition was present at the time of the offence (voluntariness) resides with the Crown

R v Stone (1999)

Two-step process for determination	• First step is to determine existence of automatism (that the accused acted in an involuntary manner) • Second step is to determine whether the involuntariness is due to a mental disorder or non–mental disorder automatism
Factors for consideration	• Involuntariness • Presence of psychiatric illness • Severity of triggering stimulus • Corroborating evidence of bystanders • Corroborating medical history of automatistic-like dissociative states • Evidence of motive for the crime • Whether the alleged trigger of violence is also the victim
Burden of proof	• The law presumes that people act voluntarily • The burden of proof regarding voluntariness resides with the defence

R v Daviault (1994)

Self-induced intoxication	• The Leary rule, which states that the mens rea of a general intent offence cannot be negated by self-induced intoxication, offends the presumption of innocence under the Charter • Wrongful intention to become dangerously drunk cannot substitute for the intention to commit a crime of sexual assault • Automatism may apply in rare cases of extreme intoxication

---

(continued)

Table 6.3 (*continued*)

Bill C-72 (1995)	
Voluntary intoxication	• Self-intoxication is excluded as a defence for general intent in offences related to bodily integrity
R v Bouchard-Lebrun (2011)	
Role of the forensic mental health professional	• The question of whether a psychiatric diagnosis is a mental disorder under the law is decided by the judge • The role of the mental health professional is to describe the nature of the mental illness
Toxic psychosis	• Is the psychosis caused by internal or external factors? • Would a person without a disease of the mind experience the same effects? • Does the condition present a recurring danger?
Implications for practice	
Assisting the court with the two-stage process	• Was the accused suffering from automatism at the time of the offence? • Was the automatism caused by a disease of the mind?
Aspects of a forensic assessment	• Presence of automatism • Nature of automatism • Precipitant or trigger • Priming factors • Presence of amnesia • Motive • Specific sleep-related issues if applicable • Risk of recurrence

infatuated following a rejection, the court distinguished between two types of automatism: insane automatism caused by internal factors, such as psychological makeup or organic pathology, and non-insane automatism, caused by some external factor such as a blow to the head or exposure to toxic fumes. These definitions were further refined in the 1987 case of *R v Parks*. In this case, Kenneth Parks arose from his sleep, drove 23 kilometres, killed his mother-in-law, and seriously injured his father-in-law. Lawyers for the accused called evidence that Mr. Parks was sleepwalking at the time of the act and put forward a defence of non-insane automatism, arguing that a positive finding should result in acquittal. The court then determined that insane automatism fit the legal definition of a disease of the mind and thus the correct ruling would be not criminal responsible due to mental disorder. On the other hand, non-insane automatism was determined not to be a disease of the mind, resulting in acquittal. It was determined that Mr. Parks's sleepwalking was non-insane automatism and he was duly acquitted (*R v Parks*, 1992).

The issue of non-insane automatism was further tested in the case of *R v Stone*, in which the defendant killed his wife in what was claimed to be a state of automatism. The court identified the social risks of using the defence of automatism too broadly, particularly in the case of interpersonal violence. It clearly identified a process for determining the existence and cause of automatism, outlining factors for consideration, and, contrary to earlier findings, lay the burden of proof on the defence for determining that automatism existed and that it undermined voluntariness.

Forensic mental health professionals have been key contributors to the deliberations of the court regarding whether automatism existed at the time the offence in question occurred and whether the automatism was caused by a disease of the mind. Factors to be considered in the assessment have been defined by the courts and by scientific inquiries (see table 6.2).

7 Fitness to Stand Trial

R v Taylor

The afternoon of 6 January 1987 was like any other Tuesday afternoon on the forensic psychiatry unit at the Clarke Institute of Psychiatry. As people went about their business, seeing patients and writing reports, a well-dressed man sat in the small lobby that served as a waiting room and entrance to the elevators. He appeared to be a lawyer, visiting the unit either to speak to his client, who was presently a forensic inpatient, or to confer with one of the forensic psychiatrists. The visitor identified himself as Dwight Taylor and asked the receptionist if he could see the chief of forensic psychiatry, Dr. Steve Hucker. The receptionist noted that Mr. Taylor did not have an appointment, but nevertheless contacted Dr. Hucker. Dr. Hucker requested that the gentleman be informed that he could not be seen that afternoon. Upon hearing the news, Mr. Taylor did not leave but rather became increasingly demanding and agitated. Eventually the receptionist notified security, who then escorted the visitor from the building.

Approximately half an hour later, Mr. Taylor arrived at the offices of the Law Society of Upper Canada, located one kilometre away in Osgoode Hall. Law Society discipline counsel Robert Conway was on the second floor of the building when, according to Staff Sargeant Ian Russell of Toronto Police Services, Mr. Taylor "appeared unannounced, confronted him and an altercation took place" ("Lawyer Charged," 1987). Mr. Conway was approached by Mr. Taylor in the hallway, where Mr. Conway was stabbed twice in the chest and once in the finger with a kitchen knife. Mr. Taylor was then overpowered by other lawyers and was subsequently charged with aggravated assault and possessing a weapon dangerous to the public peace ("Lawyer Stabbed," 1987). Mr. Taylor appeared briefly in court the following day and was remanded into custody for a psychiatric assessment ("Stabbing Suspect," 1987).

Mr. Taylor had been suspended from practising law by the Law Society of Upper Canada in June 1983 "by reason of illness." He was to remain under suspension "until such time as the Society is satisfied that Mr. Taylor is recovered and able to practice" ("In Brief," 1983). Mr. Taylor sought reinstatement and met on several occasions with Law Society counsel Mr. Conway, who advised him that he required a psychiatric evaluation for consideration at the hearing. An evaluation was conducted and the report had been provided to Mr. Taylor. "In an extensive and detailed report, the psychiatrist advised the Law Society that, in his opinion, the appellant suffered from a paranoid disorder and was incapable of practising law" (*R v Taylor*, 1992). Newspaper reports attributed the stabbing to a dispute between Mr. Conway and Mr. Taylor over the reinstatement hearing ("Stabbing Suspect," 1987). The Crown's theory was that Mr. Taylor was angered by the content of the report, which he believed to be false, and stabbed Mr. Conway, whom he believed to be responsible (*R v Taylor*, 1992).

Three weeks after the stabbing incident, on 30 January 1987, the Law Society commenced proceedings to disbar Mr. Taylor. In response to a request to defer the proceedings until after the criminal trial was concluded, Stephen Sherriff, the Society's senior discipline counsel, indicated that this would only occur if Mr. Taylor was found fit to stand trial by the court. Prophetically he is quoted as saying, "The Society can't wait while an over-crowded criminal court system grinds away for two, three, four years." ("Law Society," 1987). On 6 March 1987, Mr. Taylor was found unfit to stand trial, as he was unable to instruct counsel or conduct his own defence, and was remanded to the Oak Ridge Division of the Penetanguishene Mental Health Centre until such time as he became fit ("Lawyer Is Declared Unfit," 1987). According to his lawyer, Eric Lewis, Mr. Taylor verbally "attacked me, the psychiatrists and everybody" in court when the case was called (as cited in "Lawyer Is Declared Unfit," 1987). Psychiatrists who examined Mr. Taylor reported that he suffered from paranoid schizophrenia and from delusions of persecution.

Following the court finding of unfit to stand trial, Mr. Taylor filed a complaint with the Ontario Human Rights Commission, "alleging that his right to equal treatment with respect to his membership in the law society had been infringed because of the 'perception' that he had a mental handicap" (Haliechuk, 1988). While the Human Rights Commission acknowledged a ten-year history of psychiatric problems and paranoia, the chief commissioner nevertheless indicated that "normal proceedures of investigation and conciliation" would continue as "there was no evidence that Mr. Taylor's complaint was trivial, frivolous, vexatious, or made in bad faith" (Haliechuk, 1988). Mr. Sherriff of the Law Society responded with outrage at the thought of conciliation. "Bob and I are afraid for our safety and well-being. The whole point is that every time we confront [Mr. Taylor], it gets worse and worse, the delusions get deeper and deeper ... We'd like to publicly expose the irresponsible position of the commission" (Haliechuk, 1988).

In October 1988, after having been found fit to stand trial by the Lieutenant Governor's Advisory Review Board, Mr. Taylor returned to court and was found not guilty by reason of insanity. Justice Borins indicated that he was convinced that the assault had been committed owing to Mr. Taylor's inability to distinguish delusions from reality and a belief that he was acting in self-defence ("For the Record," 1988). Mr. Taylor was ordered to be detained at the pleasure of the lieutenant governor.

Court of Appeal in *R v Taylor*

In 1991, the Supreme Court decision in *R v Swain* struck down the insanity provisions of the Criminal Code of Canada, Bill C-30 was proclaimed, and Dwight Taylor again returned to court. At this time, the not guilty by reason of insanity verdict was set aside by the Ontario Court of Appeal as evidence supporting the finding had been introduced by the Crown, not the defence as now required under the law (see chapter 3).

Mr. Taylor began the March 1992 trial by refusing to cooperate with counsel, asserting that his court appointed legal counsel was an incompetent fraud. Two psychiatrists then testified: Dr. Glen Cameron, clinical director at Oak Ridge, and Dr. Angus McDonald, staff psychiatrist at the Metropolitan Toronto Forensic Services at the Clarke Institute of Psychiatry. Quoting from an opinion letter by Dr. Jones, director of the Social Management Unit at Oak Ridge, Dr. Cameron concluded that Mr. Taylor suffered from paranoid schizophrenia and was delusional, paranoid, easily agitated, threatening, and represented a danger to others. Dr. Jones' letter further stated, "His delusional system is focussed on the judicial system and the participants in it. As such, in my view he would be unable to participate meaningfully in the proceedings as his delusional system would preclude accurate perception of events occurring before him" (*R v Taylor*, 1992). Dr. McDonald similarly testified that that he did not believe Mr. Taylor was fit to stand trial. "It would be hardly surprising if he is uncooperative with the lawyer assigned to represent him and I do not believe by any stretch of the imagination he could effectively represent himself." (*R v Taylor*, 1992). In the end, Mr. Justice Wren found that Mr. Taylor continued to be unfit to stand trial, five years after the initial offence, and ordered that he be dealt with by the newly formed Ontario Criminal Code Review Board. The board similarly found him unfit to stand trial and he was returned to Oak Ridge.

However, the Ontario Court of Appeal, in a judgment written by Mr. Justice Maurice Lacourcière, found that Mr. Justice Wren erred in finding the accused unfit to stand trial. It was determined that Mr. Taylor failed to meet the first two criteria regarding a finding of being unfit as enunciated in in section 2 of the Criminal Code (1985). That is, he fully understood the nature and object of the proceeding and the consequences that may follow. Indeed Dr. Cameron had conceded under cross-examination that Mr. Taylor was "technically fit in the sense that he is cognizantly aware of the charges against him, the officers of the court, the pleas available to him, all the technicalities of the court" (*R v Taylor*, 1992, at para 8).

However, the Court of Appeal opined that the critical question was whether Mr. Taylor met the third criteria regarding his ability to instruct counsel. Both psychiatrists testified that Mr. Taylor would be unable to trust his counsel, was likely to misconstrue evidence provided by witnesses, and was unable to distinguish reality from fantasy. While these views were not disputed, the court determined that the trial judge, in finding Mr. Taylor unfit, had adopted an *analytic capacity* test for the third criteria regarding the ability to instruct counsel, specificall , requiring the accused to be able to act in his own best interest in order to meet the criteria. Rather, the Court of Appeal stated that analytic capacity "imposes too high a threshold," and instead asserted that the required test was *limited cognitive capacity*, "under which the presence of delusions does not vitiate the accused's fitness to stand trial, unless the delusion distorts the accused's rudimentary understanding of the judicial process. The Ontario Criminal Code Review Board (OCCRB) also erred in adopting a test that required the appellant to be capable of making rational decisions beneficial to him in his relationship with counsel" (*R v Taylor*, 1992, at para 44). The court thus reasoned that the limited cognitive capacity test was in keeping with the accused's rights under the Charter to 1) have a speedy resolution to their legal matters, and 2) choose their own defence even if it does not appear to be in their best interests (as previously determined in *R v Swain*).

Two further twists on fitness to stand trial occurred in *R v Whittle*, which considered fitness to testify, and *R v Morrissey*, which considered traumatic amnesia as a qualifier for fitnes

R v Whittle

Douglas Whittle was panhandling on the street in Oshawa, Ontario, when Constable Trim, a police officer who happened to be driving by, noted his strange behaviour and the concern he was eliciting from pedestrians. Constable Trim stopped to question Mr. Whittle, and during a routine computer check, noted three outstanding committal warrants against him issued by Toronto Police Services. Mr. Whittle was cautioned, arrested, and transported to 42 Division in Toronto. While in custody, Mr. Whittle confirmed officers' suspicions that he suffered from schizophrenia and further indicated to police that he "had been involved in some heavy matters about which he wished to clear the slate" (*R v Whittle*, 1994, p. 920). Initially, Mr. Whittle disclosed that he had been involved in a series of robberies in Windsor, Ontario. However, a few hours later he indicated that he had killed his roommate, Frank Dawson, six weeks earlier by hitting him on the back of the head with an axe. Police officers in Toronto were familiar with Mr. Whittle, having removed him from doughnut shops and abandoned cars in the past, and were sceptical of the confessions. Nevertheless, they confirmed that a suspicious death had occurred in Oshawa. Mr. Whittle continued to speak incessantly about the murder, describing actions he had taken to hide the murder weapon, dispose of his clothing, and remove his finger prints. He then stated that he bought drugs with money stolen from the wallet of the deceased. Police later located the murder weapon at the location provided by Mr. Whittle.

While Mr. Whittle repeatedly refused to speak to an attorney, the police nevertheless contacted one on his behalf: Robert Nuttall. Mr. Nuttall later testified that Mr. Whittle told him "he had voices in his head, that he had to talk, that he had a pain in his head, and that he could see dead babies in the cement ... he needed to talk to police in order to stop the voices" (*R v Whittle*, 1994, p. 922). Against his lawyer's advice, Mr. Whittle participated in a video statement in which he reiterated his confession.

At Mr. Whittle's trial for murder, both Dr. Andrew Malcolm, who testified for the defence, and Dr. Angus McDonald, who testified for the Crown, opined that the accused suffered from schizophrenia and experienced auditory hallucinations. Dr. Malcolm contended that although the accused may have been rationally aware of the consequences of his confession, he was driven by command hallucinations. The judge concluded that the video confessions were inadmissible and instructed the jury to acquit Mr. Whittle. The Crown appealed the acquittal to the Ontario Court of Appeal, who set aside the verdict on the grounds that the statements were admissible and ordered a new trial. This decision was further appealed to the Supreme Court of Canada.

The Supreme Court held that the appeal should be dismissed. In writing for the court, Mr. Justice Sopinka determined that the statements of Mr. Whittle were voluntary and were not obtained in a manner that breached his rights under the Charter. He stated, "In exercising the right to counsel or waiving that right, the acused must possess the limited cognitive capacity that is required in fitness to stand trial. The accused must be capable of communicating with counsel to instruct counsel, and understand the function of counsel and that he can dispense with counsel even if it is not in the accused's best interest. It is not necessary to possess analytical ability" (*R v Whittle*, 1994, p. 917). Such a capacity to confess is described by the legal term "operating mind." Mr. Justice Sopinka further stated that "inner compulsion, due to conscience or otherwise, cannot displace the finding of operating mind," and, therefore, the fact that he could not resist the compulsion of voices could not be a basis for exclusion p. 917).

R v Morrissey

Distraught over the break-up with his girlfriend, Melissa Pajkowski, three weeks earlier, Peter Morrissey broke into his father's gun cabinet and took a .22 calibre pistol. He then picked up Ms. Pajkowski from her home and began speeding up Bathurst Street in Newmarket, just north of Toronto. He raced through a radar trap, causing a police officer to initiate a squad car pursuit, with lights flashing and the siren wailing. During the chase, Mr. Morrissey fatally shot Ms. Pajkowski and shot himself in the head, causing severe brain trauma, as testified by Dr. John Salmon at the trial.

At the time of the murder, Mr. Morrissey was living at home with his parents, Drs. John and Claire Morrissey. During his adolescence, he had been treated for depression and drug use. He struggled with learning disabilities and at times contemplated suicide. More recently, he had dropped out of George Brown College and was not working. His relationship with Ms. Pajkowski was described as turbulent. After the break-up, he made threats toward her when he learned she was dating other men, and a few days before the homicide, attempted suicide on the front lawn of the home she shared with her parents.

At his trial for first-deg ee murder, Mr. Morrissey's counsel requested a hearing on fitness to stand trial. Dr. Salmon testified that

Mr. Morrissey had retrograde amnesia and, as a result, might confabulate testimony. Forensic psychiatrist Dr. Hy Bloom testified that while Mr. Morrissey did suffer from organic amnestic disorder and frontal lobe syndrome and may confabulate, he was fit to stand trial in that he could communicate with counsel. Forensic psychologist Dr. Nathan Pollock also testified on the issue of fitness. Dr. Pollock opined that despite his many limitations, particularly with respect to written language, Mr. Morrissey "would be quite capable of participating in his defence." It was argued that since he had no memory of the event, he could not testify. The judge, Mme. Justice Fuerst, did not accept the defence's contention that testimonial competence was required for a finding of fitness to stand trial and Mr. Morrissey was found fit. This finding was appealed to the Ontario Court of Appeal as the accused contended that his memory loss from brain damage fatally impaired his right to make full answer and defence, because he was incompetent to testify (*R v Morrissey*, 2007).

On behalf of the Court of Appeal, Mr. Justice Blair dismissed the appeal, noting that testimonial competence is not a component of the definition of unfit to stand trial. In citing both *R v Taylor* and *R v Whittle*, Mr. Justice Blair noted that the limited cognitive capacity test had been accepted by courts across the country, including by the Supreme Court of Canada. He further noted that the test requires a relatively rudimentary understanding of the judicial process, sufficient to conduct a defence and instruct counsel. Thus, the finding of *R v Taylor* was seemingly upheld.

An interesting approach to amnesia is found in an earlier case from the US District of Columbia Court of Appeals in which the appellant, Robert Wilson, was charged and convicted of five counts of assault with a pistol and robbery (*Wilson v United States of America*, 1968). Having stolen the car of one of his victims, Mr. Wilson was spotted by police. The ensuing chase ended with Mr. Wilson crashing the car, which killed his accomplice and left him with retrograde amnesia following a three-week period of unconsciousness. In the original trial, the judge determined that although Mr. Wilson could not recall the events of the offence, he suffered no mental disorder and had a rational understanding of the charges against him. He was, therefore, competent to stand trial. The Court of Appeal, in considering Mr. Wilson's conviction and competence, suggested that the vital point was whether the amnesia prevented him from providing crucial details to his counsel for the purposes of constructing and presenting the defence. In this case, it was determined that sufficient information was available from other sources for this purpose. In considering the issue, the court listed six factors that should be considered when determining the effect of amnesia on the fairness of a trial:

1. the amnesia's effect on the defendant's ability to consult and counsel
2. the amnesia's effect on the defendant's ability to testify
3. whether the evidence could be constructed from other sources
4. whether the government assisted the defendant and counsel in reconstructing evidence
5. the strength of the prosecution's case
6. any other factual circumstances. (*Wilson v United States of America*, 1968)

Critiques

Forensic practitioners and scholars have expressed concern that court decisions regarding fitness to stand trial have oversimplified complex mental health issues. Competence to stand trial depends on a variety of circumstances, which include the complexity of the case (Buchanan, 2006). In other words, complicated cases require more mental capacity and, therefore, should require a more demanding threshold for competency; currently there is no process for the measurement of this threshold available under the law. Schneider and Bloom (1995) suggest that difficulties in the relationship between psychiatry and the law occur when the law "in the course of preserving an interest it holds sacred, tries to reconfigure psychiatric wisdom and expertise to fit its perceived needs. Doing so is akin to forcing the wicked stepsisters' feet into the glass slipper destined for Cinderella" (p. 183). These authors make the point that mental illness affects not only cognitive processes, but also the "afflicted individual's judgment, motivation, insight, emotional status and capacity for willful behavior (i.e. volition)" (p. 199). They go on to suggest that these complex phenomena affect one's self-evaluative and self-preservation functions and one's very capacity for successful survival. They point out that a certain type of accused person, such as a one suffering from severe depression, may feel profoundly guilty and actively seek punishment. Similarly, a paranoid accused, as in the case of *Taylor*, may believe that legal proceedings against them are a perversion of justice and are merely part of a process to harass or harm them in some way. On the basis of this, Schneider and Bloom argue that the limited cognitive capacity test may not provide adequate protection for a significant percentage of accused individuals with mental disorders. Rather, a fully functioning accused makes decisions based on considered tactics in concert with their counsel, not as a result of the irrational or deluded thinking of mental illness. Schneider and Bloom argue that the court in *R v Taylor* had gone to great lengths to balance the objectives of the Criminal Code with the constitutional right of the accused to choose their own defence, as noted in *R v Swain* (1991). However, they say that this right to choose is only meaningful if this choice is rational and not based on mental illness. In other words, in a case where a person has a serious mental illness, it would seem to be worth delaying making a choice about the nature of the defence undertaken on their behalf, until they are well enough to make a rational choice.

In a complicated case in the Ontario Court Supreme Court, this issue was central to the proceedings (*R v Adam*, 2013). Roble Adam was charged with the first-deg ee murder of the office manager of a Toronto residence for persons with mental health issues. His fitness to stand trial was repeatedly in question over the three years between his alleged offence and his ultimate trial. While he was found unfit at his first fitness hearing, he was subsequently found fit at a second hearing, and his trial commenced. During a *voir dire* related to the admissibility of evidence, a further fitness assessment and a subsequent fitness hearing were ordered. Mr. Adam was diagnosed with undifferentiated schizophrenia and harboured suspicions about his lawyers. Consequently, the judge appointed an amicus curiae. Mr. Adam repeatedly asked for the amicus to be removed because he believed that the lawyer was colluding with others to work against him. During the *voir dire*, he complained that he had received "bad medication" as a result of interference by the "Canadian Intelligence Agency," and professed his belief that the judge was involved in the conspiracy. He claimed that videotaped police evidence was fabricated, and the person appearing in the video was not him, but rather an impostor. Acting as his own lawyer, he spent considerable time cross-examining an expert witness, focusing on themes of sorcery and magic.

In his analysis, Judge Trotter noted that the fitness inquiry demands an assurance that the accused person is able to receive a fair trial, which, by necessity, includes the ability to defend oneself. Quoting the decision in *R v Morrissey*, he contended that fitness requires that the trial meets "minimum standards of fairness in accordance with the principles of fundamental justice ... and the right to make full answer and defence. Meaningful presence and meaningful participation at the trial, therefore, are the touchstones of the inquiry into fitness" (*R v Morrissey*, 2007, p. 17). Judge Trotter cites Schneider and Bloom (1995) in stating that the issue is not whether a person makes the right choice, but whether they have the capacity, unimpaired by mental disorder, to make that choice. He stated, "It cannot seriously be contended that rationality has no role to play in this determination. Moreover, the three arms of the fitness test are not free-standing fitness criteria to [be] mechanically applied; instead, they are tools to assist in determining whether a mentally ill accused person is able to defend him or herself" (*R v Adam*, 2013, p. 9). Judge Trotter concludes that the question becomes whether, because of mental disorder, the accused is able to meaningfully participate in his trial by defending himself. He concluded that Mr. Adams was unable to do so owing to his mental illness.

Similarly, Felthous (2011) notes that the US Supreme Court land-mark case of *Dusky v United States* (1960) has been interpreted in such a manner to suggest that competence to stand trial requires rational understanding. The author argues that in *Dusky*, it is noted that the standard includes whether the defendant "has sufficient present ability to consult with his attorney with a reasonable degree of rational under-standing and whether he has a rational as well as factual understand-ing of the proceedings against him" (p. 403). Felthous makes the case that factual information is not meaningful if it is understood and acted on in a delusional or psychotic manner, a concept which he believes is implicit in the *Dusky* standard. He goes on to note that several state legislatures adopted the *Dusky* standard verbatim, but that recent deci-sions by the US Supreme Court have eroded the rationality standard and therefore the standard is diminishing. He notes "[Dusky's] signiÃ-cance is fading" (p. 21) and "its important requirement for rationality is slipping into oblivion with nary a word" (p. 21).

Implications for Forensic Mental Health Practice

The concept of fitness to stand trial is foundational to fairness in the judicial system. The American Academy of Psychiatry and Law's (2018) *Ethical Guidelines for the Practice of Forensic Psychiatry* traces it back to eighteenth-century England, during which the Blackstone (1825) *Commentaries on the Laws of England* were written:

> Thus, common-law held that a defendant who was "mad" should "not be arraigned ... because he is not able to plead to [the charge]" nor should he undergo trial "for how can he make his defence?" In a late 18th century case in England, the trial was postponed until the defen-dant "by collecting together his intellects, and having them entire, shall be able to model his defense and to ward off punishment of the law." (Mossman et al., 2007, p. S4)

While the concept has been enshrined in common law for centuries, in Canada the rules for determining fitness to stand trial were clarified by Bill C-30 in the 1991 amendments to section 2 of the Criminal Code as follows:

> Unfit to stand trial ... means unable on account of mental disorder to conduct a defence at any stage of the proceedings before a verdict is rendered or to instruct counsel to do so, and, in particular, unable on account of mental disorder to
> (a) understand the nature or object of the proceedings
> (b) understand the possible consequences of the proceedings, or
> (c) communicate with counsel

Shortly thereafter, these rules were interpreted in the Ontario Court of Appeal case of *R v Taylor* (1992). This case considered a previous ruling that suggested that the accused should have the analytic capacity to determine what is in their best interest and act accordingly in order to be fit to stand trial. The Court of Appeal rejected this interpretation, indicating that it set too high a threshold. Rather, the Court of Appeal determined that the individual must possess only limited cognitive capacity in order to be found fit to stand trial. Although the court does not actually define the limited cognitive capacity test, it suggests that the inquiry is limited to whether the accused can instruct counsel and relate the necessary facts to counsel in order to present a defence. Specificall , the court has stated it is not necessary that the accused person is acting in their own best interests, even if the motivation is driven by delusions.

Under section 672.11 of the Criminal Code, a judge is entitled to order an assessment of the mental condition of an accused if there are reasonable grounds to believe that such evidence is necessary to determine whether the accused is unfit to stand trial. The Code limits the prosecutor's application for an assessment to the situation where the accused has raised the issue of fitness, or if the prosecutor is able to satisfy the court that there are reasonable grounds to doubt that the accused is fit. However, there is little information regarding the nature or level of evidence to be adduced in support of an assessment order and to meet the standard of "reasonable grounds." Two cases, *R v John Doe* (2011) and *R v Muschke* (1997), suggest that at least *some* evidence is required, such as oral evidence from a probation office , historical medical records, or a letter from a doctor. The Ontario case of *John Doe* also suggests that where the assessment order is contested, the evidentiary burden is greater and expert opinion evidence may be required.

While concerns about the accused's fitness to stand trial are usually identified early on in the proceedings (Davis, 1994), the Criminal Code allows for concerns to be raised at any stage of the proceedings before verdict is rendered. It is interesting to note that the Criminal Code does not address the situation where an accused becomes unfit at the sentencing stage. Schneider (1998), in addressing this issue, identifies that "older common-law and related case-law suggests that it is nevertheless a proper (indeed, imperative) concern of the courts. The law reviewed suggests the ability to choose must be present from the moment of arraignment through to the conclusion of the sentencing process" (p. 272). He further argues that the accused should always have the necessary mental ability, especially when their freedom could be affected. Indeed, in a subsequent case, *R v B (D)* (2003), the accused became unfit following a verdict of guilt during the sentencing stage. The trial judge reasoned that it was unjustifiable that the accused could not be found unfit at this stage of proceedings and therefore read section 2 to include fitness to be sentenced

Assessment

Assessment of fitness to stand trial represents the most common reason for legal referrals to forensic mental health professionals (Mossman et al., 2007; Nussbaum, Hancock, Turner, Arrowood, & Melodick, 2008; Rogers, Grandjean, Tillbrook, Vitacco, & Sewell, 2001). It has been estimated that in the United States there are 60,000 competency evaluations requested each year (Scott, 2018); 20 years ago, it was estimated that there were 6,000 in Canada (Schneider & Bloom, 1995).

It is not often that a decision in the Court of Appeal makes the day-to-day work of the forensic mental health professionals simpler. However, in practice, *R v Taylor* narrowed down the evaluation of fitness to stand trial to whether the accused is able to understand the nature, object, and possible consequences of the proceedings (what is referred to in *Taylor* as "technical fitness"). This suggests that simple questions – such as whether the accused understands the nature of the charges against him and the roles of the judge, Crown attorney, and defence counsel – would suffice with respect to the nature of the proceedings. In addition, questions that determine an understanding that the accused may plead guilty or not guilty would satisfy whether they understood the possible consequences of the proceedings. The Criminal Code definition clearly states that the issue is whether mental disorder has affected the capacity for the requisite task.

Table 7.1   Assessment of fitness to stand trial

Presence of mental disorder	• Generally thought to be a serious mental disorder
Ability to instruct counsel to conduct a defence	• Not necessary to comprehend or act in own best interests • Not necessary to recount an accurate version of the facts
Understanding nature or object of the proceedings	• Understand the trial process • Understand the roles of the parties, etc.
Understand the possible consequences of the proceedings	• Understand the pleas available
Communicate with counsel	• Give and receive legal advice

As previously discussed in chapters 1 and 5, "disease of the mind" is a legal term, one which would be defined by the trial judge if there were any dispute and is quite broadly defined in theory. In practice, it likely corresponds with what forensic mental health professionals would understand to be serious mental disorder.

The next arm of the test, "communicate with counsel," has also been interpreted to have been narrowly defined in *R v Taylor*. What is required is that the accused "can recount to his/her counsel the necessary facts relating to the offence in such a way that counsel can then properly present a defence" (*R v Taylor*, 1992). In the case of *R v Morrissey* (2007), the court differentiated testimonial competence from fitness to stand trial. In adopting a lower standard for testimonial competence, the court concluded that the ability to communicate with counsel requires only the ability to seek and receive legal advice. Therefore, being unable to recount the facts immediately connected with the event giving rise to the charges does not render a person unfit to stand trial

Various instruments with acceptable psychometric properties are available to aid the forensic mental health professional when assessing fitness or competency to stand trial (Nussbaum et al., 2008; Rogers & Johansson-Love, 2009). These instruments may be used as screening tests, *aides-memoire*, or adjuncts to clinical examinations, and, as some argue, may promote homogeneity in understanding and communicating the issues. Generally, tests are specific to various jurisdictions; those that have been developed for Canadian use include the FIT-R (Roesch, Zapf, & Eves, 2006)) and the METFORS fitness test (Nussbaum et al., 2008).

Disposition

Once an accused has been found unfit to stand trial, they become subject to a disposition under the territorial or provincial review board. The relevant review board then makes a disposition based on the same factors that would be considered if the accused had been found NCR-MD. The accused is entitled to a hearing at least once per year; however, in practice, the hospital would likely inform the review board if and when the accused person becomes fit to stand trial, and a new hearing would be held. If the review board agrees that the accused is fit to stand trial, the court is notified and the prosecution continues in the normal manner.

The only place in the Criminal Code that a court can actually order medical psychiatric treatment is contained in section 672.58. This section allows the court to direct treatment of an accused found not fit to stand trial for a period not exceeding 60 days. The Code identifies certain conditions associated with court-ordered treatment. One condition is that the accused is "not detained in custody," meaning that they are not in a jail or correctional centre. A related provision sets out the conditions of treatment. The Code specifies that any treatment undertaken be likely to address aspects of the accused's disorder within the 60-day period, and that the treatment undertaken is intended to treat the mental disorder that prevents the accused from being fit to stand trial. It appears that this particular standard is reasonable and workable in practice. Chaimowitz, Furimsky, Singh, and Kolawole (2018), in reviewing charts of 199 defendants assessed for fitness to stand trial, found that 92 per cent of those issued a treatment order recovered within the specified 60-day period. In addition, the benefits of the treatment must outweigh the harm. It is specified that the treatment must be the least restrictive and least intrusive treatment option, which is strange leakage of legal language to a medical treatment. Finally, the facility to which the individual is being sent must agree to provide treatment and admit the accused to that facility.

In 2004, the Supreme Court ruled on a case of an accused who was unlikely to regain fitness to stand trial (*R v Demers*, 2004). In this case, the accused was moderately intellectually disabled. He was charged with sexual assault and was subsequently declared unfit to stand trial. He remained in hospital until he was discharged three months later. The Code, as it stood at the time, dictated that he remain under the jurisdiction of the provincial review board until either he became fit to stand trial or the Crown failed to establish a prima facie case against him. In other words, an absolute discharge was not available to an accused who is likely permanently unfit. Mr. Demers appealed to the Supreme Court of Canada. The court concluded that this legislation breaches the liberty interest and infringes upon the rights and freedoms guaranteed by section 7 of the Canadian Charter of Rights and Freedoms. Therefore, the appeal was allowed.

Bill C-10, which was enacted in 2006 and became section 672.851, addressed this issue. It allowed the review board to make a recommendation to the court to hold an inquiry to determine whether a stay of proceedings should be ordered if the review board is of the opinion that the accused is permanently unfit and does not pose a significant threat to the safety of the public. If the court holds this inquiry, it is directed to order an assessment of the accused. On the basis of the information before the court, it may order a stay of the proceedings if a stay is in the interests of the proper administration of justice and the accused is permanently unfit. Although it is not directly addressed, it appears that the standards that apply to review boards and courts regarding accused who are NCR apply to this section. In other words, the principles as determined in *Winko v Forensic Psychiatric Institute*, described in chapter 4, regarding whether the accused represents a significant threat, are likely applicable.

Summary

The concept of fitness to stand trial is a central tenet of our legal system and "developed from necessity that a person should not only be physically present for the trial but should be mentally present as well" (Bloom, 2006, p. 211). From a forensic mental health perspective, this is also the most common form of assessment.

In 1992, Bill C-30 introduced changes to the Criminal Code of Canada that specified the criteria for a finding of unfit to stand trial. The landmark case *R v Taylor* (1992), which followed that same year, established the threshold for fitness as a limited cognitive capacity to understand the nature, object, and consequences of the proceedings and to communicate with counsel. It does not include whether an accused has the analytic ability to act in their own best interest. The finding in *Taylor* was reaffirmed in *R v Whittle* (1994), with respect to capacity to testify and the admissibility of a confession, and in *R v Morrissey* (2007). In practice, this means that assessments of fitness to stand trial are relatively straightforward and can be addressed by a few simple questions. This has raised several critiques with respect to the impact on those with severe mental disorders, especially those suffering from delusional thinking (Schneider & Bloom, 1995). Nevertheless, forensic

Table 7.2   Key points regarding fitness to stand trial

Criminal Code of Canada	
Definition of unfit to stand trial Bill C-30	Unfit to stand trial means unable on account of mental disorder to conduct a defence at any stage of the proceedings before a verdict is rendered or to instruct counsel to do so, and, in particular, unable on account of mental disorder to (a) understand the nature or object of the proceedings (b) understand the possible consequences of the proceedings, or (c) communicate with counsel
R v Taylor	
Analytic capacity	• Determined to be too high a threshold for fitness to stand trial • Requires the accused to act in their own best interest in order to meet the criteria
Limited cognitive capacity	• Threshold required for fitness to stand trial • Does not require the accused to act in their own best interest • "Strikes an effective balance between the objectives of the fitness rules and the constitutional rights of the accused to choose his own defence and to have a trial within a reasonable period of time" • Presence of delusions does not vitiate the accused's fitness to stand trial unless they distort the accused's rudimentary understanding of the judicial process
R v Whittle	
Capacity to testify Admissibility of confession	• Same criteria as fitness to stand trial, that is, limited cognitive capacity • Must be capable of communicating with counsel, and understand that they can dispense with counsel, even if not in their own best interest
The operating mind	• An aspect of the confession rule • Requires the accused to have sufficient mental capacity to understand what they are saying and what is being said • Includes the ability to understand a caution that evidence can be used against the accused • Not necessary to possess analytic capacity
R v Morrissey	
Testimonial competence	• Not a component of fitness to stand trial

(*continued*)

Table 7.2 (*continued*)

Implications for practice	
Assessment	• Limited to a few simple questions on the capacity to understand the court processes and implications and ability to instruct counsel
Disposition	• 60-day orders can be issued to treat an accused in order to render them fit to stand trial • Those permanently unfit can have a stay of proceedings if it is determined by the relevant review board that they no longer pose a threat to society

mental health professionals must restrict their judgment to fit within the confines of the law. The Criminal Code also specifies methods to handle those found unfit, including treatment orders, and disposition options for those who remain permanently unfit

8 Access to Treatment Records

R v O'Connor

> Bishop Hubert Patrick O'Connor has denounced as "a vicious attack" published reports that he was investigated by police for alleged child molestation several decades ago.
>
> In a letter to the B.C. Catholic, a church newspaper, the bishop for Prince George denied ever sexually abusing children.
>
> "It is very important for me to tell you that, before the Great Judge who will judge all of us, I did not then or ever in my life sexually abuse any child, be it male or female," the bishop writes in the latest issue of the church newspaper. His signed comments appeared under the headline *Bishop O'Connor to His People*. ("B.C. Bishop Disputes," 1991)

In December 1990, a month before the church publication was issued, unnamed sources had indicated that a bishop, later identified to be Bishop O'Connor, was under investigation for sexual abuse allegations relating to a former residential school for Indigenous children run by the Oblate order, located 550 kilometres north of Vancouver, near Williams Lake ("Bishop Denies Vicious Report," 1991). Bishop O'Connor countered that another priest had been convicted and sentenced in 1988 for repeatedly molesting 17 young boys who were attending St. Joseph's, the school in question. He indicated that others seemed to be inferring that because he was principal of the school for a period of two years, he was complicit in the abuse, either directly or by not acting on knowledge of the abuse ("Bishop Denounces Vicious Allegation," 1991).

Herbert Patrick O'Connor was born in Huntington, Quebec, and became an ordained priest in the Missionary Oblates of Mary

Immaculate (OMI) order of the Roman Catholic Church in 1955. Six years later, he was sent to British Columbia, where he served as the principal of the St. Joseph's mission school (also known as Cariboo Indian Residential School) for the next two decades. The school was in operation for over 90 years, between 1890 and 1981. Upon its closure in 1981, O'Connor was appointed the bishop of White-horse and subsequently of Prince George in 1986 ("Bishop Faces," 1991). On 4 February 1991, Bishop O'Connor was charged with two counts of sexual intercourse without consent, three counts of inde-cent assault, and one count of gross indecency for assault, allegedly occurring against adult women between 1964 and 1967. He was the third person charged with offences related to the St. Joseph's school ("Bishop Faces," 1991). The four complainants were former stu-dents that were employed by the school at the time of the assaults, and, therefore, under the direct supervision of Bishop O'Connor (*R v O'Connor*, 1995).

One month later in Saskatoon, at a national meeting on Indian residential schools, the Catholic bishops offered the following statement:

> For two days we listened, discussed, struggled and prayed about our relationship with the aboriginal peoples in the context of Indian Residen-tial Schools.
>
> We identified and acknowledged the positive and negative aspects of the schools, began an analysis of the current situation and explored possibilities for a new relationship with the aboriginal peoples.
>
> We are sorry and deeply regret the pain, suffering and alienation that so many experienced. We hear their cries of distress, feel their anguish and want to be part of the healing process.
>
> We recognize that the negative experiences in the Residential Schools cannot be considered in isolation from the root causes of the indignities and injustices suffered by aboriginal peoples in our country. (Canadian Council of Catholic Bishops, 1991)

In July 1991, a preliminary inquiry was held with respect to the charges against Bishop O'Connor; the tiny courtroom was filled over capacity with observers, primarily members of the four Indigenous communities from which many children were taken to be enrolled in the school (Kenna, 1991). That same week, it was announced that Pope John Paul II had accepted Bishop O'Connor's resigna-tion, a move welcomed by Indigenous leaders, many of whom had called for his removal some months earlier. That same month, the Oblate Conference of Canada president, Reverend Doug Crosby, apologized for the Oblates' role in the residential school system, calling the abuses "inexcusable, intolerable, and a betrayal of trust in one of its more serious forms" (as cited in Mate, 1991). The OMI ran approximately half of the residential schools in Canada. The following May, seven women filed a civil suit with the BC Supreme Court, alleging that they were assaulted by Bishop O'Connor and claiming damages.

Access to Records

From a legal perspective, the focus of the criminal case then moved to evidentiary issues, specifically access to records that related to the alleged victims. The defence counsel for Bishop O'Connor applied for and obtained a judicial order requiring disclosure of the complainants' entire medical, counselling, and school records. Defence counsel justified this request on the need to test the complainants' credibility, as well as to determine issues such as complainant corroboration. Judge Campbell made an order to produce these records. One month later, on 10 July 1992, the Crown applied to the BC Supreme Court for direction regarding the disclosure order. The Crown argued that the therapists' notes should not be disclosed on public policy grounds and informed the court that the complainants were not prepared to comply with the order for disclosure. The court expressed surprise that the earlier disclosure order had not yet been followed (*R v O'Connor*, 1992).

On 16 October 1992, Bishop O'Connor applied for a judicial stay of proceedings. By this time the Crown did have possession of the records, and the trial judge requested that the therapy records be provided to the court. At a further hearing on 19 November, the Crown opposed the disclosure of the records on the grounds that they were not relevant, but this argument was rejected by the trial judge. The trial was due to start in ten days. After seven days, Bishop O'Connor made another application for a judicial stay of proceedings based on the nondisclosure of several items, items which included not only the medical records but also the transcripts of interviews between Crown counsel and the complainants. It had apparently come to the attention of the defence that one of these interviews contained contradictory statements that had been made by one of the witnesses, which corroborated the evidence of Bishop O'Connor.

In the course of submissions, one of the Crown counsels noted that since there were two Crown counsels from different cities, there were difficulties concerning communication and organization. She stated that this was the reason the transcripts of the interviews had not been disclosed, reporting that she had "dreamed" that the transcripts had already been disclosed. However, she also submitted that the uninhibited disclosure of medical and counselling records would re-victimize the victims and that the request of defence counsel for disclosure exhibited gender bias.

The trial judge dismissed the application for a judicial stay, noting that the failure to disclose the records had been an oversight. He also found that the failure to disclose the transcripts of the interview did not prejudice the accused since this evidence had been known to the defence for some time. He concluded that the conduct of the Crown was "disturbing" (*R v O'Connor*, 1992, at para 37) but stated that he did not believe that there was a "grand design" (at para 36) to conceal evidence nor a "deliberate plan to subvert justice" (at para 37). He was, nevertheless, quite critical of the Crown's behaviour. On the weekend before the trial, Crown counsel agreed to waive any privilege with respect to the contents of the Crown's file and to prepare a binder in relation to each of the complainants containing all the information in the Crown's possession. However, when the court resumed, the Crown acknowledged that the binders they had undertaken to provide to the defence counsel were not complete.

Approximately one week later, the judge handed down a judicial stay of proceedings on all four counts. He noted that, by now, the trial was now under way, and witnesses had already been called by the Crown and cross-examined by the defence. In particular, he emphasized a significant dispute between the Crown and the defence regarding diagrams provided by one complainant that the Crown had not disclosed to defence counsel. The judge, therefore, concluded that the accused had suffered prejudice as a result of this nondisclosure. He noted that the repeated nondisclosure by the Crown had created "an aura" that had pervaded and ultimately destroyed the case. He concluded that to allow the case to proceed would taint the integrity of the court and, therefore, ordered a stay of proceedings. One newspaper reported, "A Roman Catholic bishop walked out of court a free man yesterday after a judge ruled that prosecutors had botched the criminal sex charges against him … B.C. Supreme Court Justice Allan Thackray ruled that the prosecutors had refused an order to disclose parts of their case to the defence" (Edge, 1991). Another reported, "This could have been avoided by reasonable efforts by the Crown counsel" ("Judge Quashes," 1992).

Court of Appeal and Supreme Court of Canada Decisions in *R v O'Connor*

The attorney general of British Columbia was taken to task for "undermining the already tenuous confidence that the native community [had] in the justice system" (Hunter, 1992) and responded by appointing a special prosecutor who appealed the ruling to the BC Court of Appeal. The Court of Appeal allowed the Crown's appeal, concluding that in order to establish an abusive process, an accused must demonstrate conduct on the part of the Crown that is so oppressive, vexatious, or unfair as to contravene the fundamental notions of justice and undermine the integrity of the judicial process.

In discussing the Crown's obligation to disclose information, the court considered *R v Stinchcombe* (1991), in which Mr. Justice Sopinka stated, "it is made clear that counsel for the Crown is under a general duty to disclose all relevant information" (at para 23). Nevertheless, the court concluded that the right of an accused to full disclosure by the Crown is an adjunct of the right to make full answer and defence, and that disclosure is not, in and of itself, a constitutionally protected right. In the view of the Court of Appeal, it was only when nondisclosure was motivated by an intention on the part of the Crown to deprive the accused of a fair trial would an abusive process arise. The Court of Appeal concluded that the trial judge erred in failing to inquire into the "materiality" of the nondisclosed information. The Court of Appeal ordered a new trial, a decision that was appealed to the Supreme Court of Canada by the defence.

The Supreme Court reviewed the Court of Appeal's thoughtful approach to the production guidelines of a complainant's medical and therapeutic records, the principal issue in the case from a mental health point of view. The Supreme Court distinguished between the Crown's obligation to disclose private records that are already in its possession and the production of records in the possession of third parties, that is, health care and mental health professionals. The Supreme Court further upheld the decision of the BC Court of Appeal overturning the stay of proceedings.

The Supreme Court of Canada decision in *R v O'Connor* emphasized the value of privacy in our society, noting that section 7 of the Canadian Charter of Rights and Freedoms includes a right to privacy. It thus crafted a two-stage procedure for the production of records based on the Court of Appeal decision (see table 8.1). Noting that it is the responsibility of the accused to demonstrate that the use of state power to compel production is justified in a free and democratic society, the

Table 8.1 Deciding the application for disclosure of records

Step	Criteria	Process
Stage 1: Production to the judge		
Written application to the judge		• Identify the record, guardian of record, grounds for production
Subpoena guardian of record		• Notify guardian that an application has been made • Record not brought before the court at this stage
In camera hearing as to whether to require the production of the records to the judge	• Need to make full answer and defence • Probative value • Nature and extent of privacy expectation • Whether based on discriminatory bias • Potential prejudice to dignity and right to privacy • Society's interest in reporting a sexual offence • Encouraging treatment for complainants • Integrity of the trial process	• Parties may call evidence • Complainant and guardian of records are not compellable witnesses
Stage 2: Disclosure to the defence		
Judge reviews the records and decides whether to disclose the record to the accused The judge may impose any conditions that they see fit	• Need to make full answer and defence • Probative value • Nature and extent of privacy expectation • Whether based on discriminatory bias • Potential prejudice to dignity and right to privacy • Society's interest in reporting a sexual offence • Encouraging treatment for complainants • Integrity of the trial process	• A decision may be made in the absence of parties or with the aid of an in camera hearing • May include conditions such as redacting portions of the record; no copies to be made; to be examined only at the court offices; any other conditions the judge sees fit • Written decisions may be appealed by accused or the Crown

previous onus was reversed, and the accused must now satisfy the judge that the information is likely to be relevant. Defence counsel must bring a written application to the trial judge prior to jury selection, setting out the specific grounds for production, and subpoena the guardian of the records, that is, the mental health professional. At this stage, the threshold is set to prevent the defence from engaging in "speculative, fanciful, disruptive, unmeritorious, obstructive and time-consuming requests for production" (R v O'Connor, 1995, at para 24), without imposing an onerous burden upon the accused. The court noted that placing a higher burden on the first stage of the procedure would place the accused in the difficult situation of having to argue about the relevance of this information without knowing the nature of the information. It cautioned against putting an accused in a "catch-22" situation.

In the second stage, the records are made available to the court, that is to the judge, who then examines the records to determine whether they should be made available to the accused. The judge determines whether the negative effects of a production order upon the privacy rights of the complainants outweigh its relevance to the ability of the accused to make full answer and defence. This is a higher test of relevance than in the firs stage in that the judge must be satisfied that there is a reasonable possibility that the information is logically probative to an issue at trial or to the competence of a witness to testify. It is only in the second stage that the competing rights of the privacy of the complainant enter into the analysis. In considering whether to compel disclosure of records, the judge must consider 1) whether it is necessary for the accused to make full answer and defence, 2) the probative value of the record balanced against the complainant's reasonable expectation of privacy, 3) whether disclosure is premised upon any discriminatory assumption or stereotype, and 4) the potential prejudice to the complainant's dignity, privacy, or security that would be occasioned by production of the record.

In coming to this decision, the Supreme Court listed a number of ways in which information in third-party records might be relevant in sexual assault cases:

1. They may contain information concerning the unfolding of events
2. They may reveal the use of therapy that influences the complai - ant's memory of the alleged events
3. They may contain information that bears on the complainant's credibility, including factors such as the quality of their perception of events at the time and their memory since. (R v O'Connor, 1995)

The court also noted that counselling or therapy notes might be of questionable value in the truth-seeking process, citing a previous case

(*R v Osolin*, 1993). First, the court noted that therapy and counselling records are hearsay. In addition, as was argued in *R v Mills* (discussed below), they are not made with a view to truth-seeking and, therefore, may not be reliably transcribed and, of course, are not given under oath (*R v Mills*, 1999). The court further noted that there is a risk that statements in counselling records could be taken out of context in a trial situation.

The court also considered whether complainants and third-party record holders should have standing. A companion case, *A. (LL) v B (A)* (1995), introduced the concept that complainants and third-party record holders should have standing to make submissions in the hearing. In this case, A (LL) sought counselling from the Sexual Assault Centre of the Plummer Memorial Hospital in Sault Ste. Marie. Her alleged assailant, who had been charged with sexual interference, served subpoenas on the centre, requesting all records be brought to court. The Crown filed a motion to quash the subpoenas, which the judge denied. Upon appeal to the Supreme Court, it was held that records concerning the complainant could be available to the accused, but that third parties (in this case, the Sexual Assault Centre) had standing to make an appeal as they would be directly affected by a production order (*A (LL) v B (A)*, 1995). This is considered an important reconceptualization of the role of complainants and third parties in criminal cases (Koshan, 2002; Neufeld, 1995).

An additional issue was whether counselling records should be subject to inclusion in a special category of "class privilege," similar to solicitor-client or spousal privilege. In some US jurisdictions, there is a statutory privilege for communications between counsellors and sexual assault complainants in criminal trials (Koshan, 2002). It was noted, however, that it is preferable to determine privilege on a case-by-case basis.

The court rejected other factors that were introduced by interveners in the case and included in the judgment of the minority: "the extent to which production of records of this nature would frustrate society's interest in encouraging reporting sexual offences and the acquisition of treatment by victims" (*R v O'Connor*, 1995). The majority felt that this matter would be argued regarding admissibility at a later stage.

Bill C-46

While the Supreme Court decisions in *R v O'Connor* and *A (LL) v B (A)* attempted to craft a procedure for balancing the privacy interests of complainants against the accused's right to make full answer and defence, they "predictably ... shocked and angered advocates for sexual assault victims ... [and] characterized the accused's ability to access emotion-based counselling records of the victim as another rape in itself" (Neufeld, 1995, p. 354). Critics suggested that the rulings would intimidate women, undermine their support networks, and ultimately discourage them from pursuing legal action – essentially forcing them to make a choice between either reporting sexual assaults or seeking treatment to deal with the effects of sexual assault. Six months later, Allan Rock, federal minister of justice and attorney general of Canada, introduced Bill C-46, amending the Criminal Code with respect to addressing the issue of access to records for complainants in sexual assault investigations (Department of Justice, 1995). In the preamble to this bill, Parliament expressed grave concern over the prevalence of sexual violence against women and children, suggesting that equal participation of women and children in society was impacted by conditions that undermined their rights and security. Secondly, it was stated that Parliament aimed to encourage the reporting of incidents of sexual violence and abuse and supported the prosecution of offences within a framework of laws that are consistent with the principles of fundamental justice as they affect both complainants and accused persons. It acknowledged that the routine production of personal information could deter victims of sexual violence from reporting offences to the police and also prevent them from seeking necessary treatment. In addition, it recognized that the compelled production of records and the process for protecting them would detrimentally affect those providing services to victims of sexual violence (Regehr, Glancy, & Bradford, 2000).

Paralleling the procedure established in *O'Connor*, Parliament set up a two-stage process (see table 8.1): production to the judge and disclosure to the accused (Marshall, 2004). One of the most significan changes introduced by Bill C-46 was that the two-stage test for production would apply to all records pertaining to sexual assault victims, including those in the hands of third parties, such as therapists, as well as those in the possession of the Crown. It also set a higher threshold for access to complainant records. The "likely relevant" standard was supplemented by a requirement that the production would have to be "deemed necessary in the interests of justice." In addition, when ruling on a production order, Bill C-46 added three considerations for the judge, in addition to those identified in *R v O'Connor*: 1) society's interest in encouraging reporting of sexual offences, 2) society's interest in encouraging the complainants in sexual offences to seek treatment, and 3) the effect of the determination on the integrity of the trial process. The legislation specifically noted that vague suspicions or broad generalizations would not suffice as reasons to compel disclosure. They listed a number of examples of issues that were not sufficient for disclosure (see table 8.2).

Figure 8.1 Deciding the application for disclosure of records

STEP	CRITERIA	PROCESS

STAGE 1

STEP 1
WRITTEN APPLICATION TO JUDGE

Identify the record, guardian of record, grounds for production

STEP 2
SUBPOENA GUARDIAN OF RECORD

Notify guardian that an application has been made

Record not brought to court at this stage

STEP 3
IN CAMERA HEARING AS TO WHETHER TO REQUIRE PRODUCTION OF THE RECORDS TO JUDGE

Make full answer and defence

Probative value

Nature and extent of privacy expectation

Based on discriminatory bias?

Potential prejudice to dignity and right of privacy

Societal interest in reporting sexual offense

Encouraging treatment for complainants

Integrity of the trial process

Parties may call evidence

Complainant and guardian of records not compellable witnesses

STAGE 2

STEP 4
JUDGE REVIEWS RECORDS AND DECIDES WHETHER TO DISCLOSE RECORD TO THE ACCUSED

Decision may be made in absence of parties or with aid of in camera hearing

STEP 5
JUDGE MAY IMPOSE ANY CONDITIONS THAT THEY SEE FIT

May include conditions such as: redacting portions of the record, no copies to be made, to be examined only at court offices, or any other conditions the judge sees fit

Table 8.2 Insufficient reasons for disclosure as specified in Bill C-46

That the record:
1. Exists
2. Relates to medical or psychiatric treatment, therapy or counselling
3. Relates to the incident that is the subject matter or the proceedings
4. May disclose a prior inconsistent statement by the complainant or witness
5. May relate to the credibility of the complainant
6. May relate to the reliability of the testimony merely because the complainant has received psychiatric treatment
7. May reveal allegations of sexual abuse of the complainant by a person other than the accused
8. Relates to the sexual activity of the complainant with any person including the accused
9. Relates to the presence or absence of another recent complaint
10. Relates to the complainant's sexual reputation

R v Mills

Within a few short months of its passage, Bill C-46 was overturned by three Superior Court judges (*G (A) v R (RJ)*, 1997; *R v Lee*, 1997; *R v Mills*, 1999). In *R v Mills*, Brian Mills was charged with sexual assault and unlawful sexual touching of a 13-year-old girl. According to the original complaint, the offence involved placing his hands in her pockets. The accused waived his right to a preliminary inquiry. On the day of the trial, over a year later, the Crown provided the accused with a second statement dated one week prior, alleging more serious actions. The case was adjourned, and sometime later counsel for the accused applied to have a new preliminary inquiry. At this stage defence counsel sought disclosure of all therapeutic records and notes relating to the complainant, contending that the counselling process may have contributed to a change in her story. The trial judge decided that the trial could not proceed until they dealt with the production of third-party records.

   In dealing with this issue, the judge advised the parties that Bill C-46 had been proclaimed into force four days prior. As a result of this, the Criminal Code was amended to include sections 278.1 to 278.91. Counsel for the accused gave notice that he intended to argue that the new amendments violated the Canadian Charter of Rights and Freedoms. The trial judge held that the constitutional challenge could go ahead and granted full standing to the complainant and to the attorney general of Canada. The judge then concluded that the new Criminal Code provisions infringed upon sections 7 and 11(d) of the Charter. The Court of Appeal of Alberta Court of Queen's Bench subsequently upheld the decision of the trial judge, determining that since the Supreme Court had so carefully crafted a procedure in *O'Connor*, any points of law not accepted in that decision would render the new legislation constitutionally invalid. Counsel argued that these changes altered the balance between privacy rights of the complainant and the rights of an accused to make full answer and defence, so carefully considered in *R v O'Connor* (1995).

After hearing the *Mills* case and others, the Supreme Court of Canada held that sections 278.1 to 278.91 of the Criminal Code were constitutional, upholding Bill C-46 in its entirety. The court emphasized that it was within the rights of Parliament to build upon the decision the court crafted in *R v O'Connor*. It was stated that courts have adopted "a posture of respect" (at para 56) toward Parliament and that the relationship between the courts and the legislature should be one of dialogue. In particular, the ruling noted that courts do not hold a monopoly on the promotion of rights and freedoms; rather, Parliament has the ability to act as an ally for vulnerable groups, especially in the context of sexual violence. The court acknowledged the pervasiveness of sexual violence and the unfortunate history of treatment of victims of sexual violence by society and by our judicial system; Parliament could be understood to be recognizing "horizontal" equality concerns, where women's inequality results from acts of other individuals and groups rather than the state.

The court noted that Parliament, in its process of consultation, which occurred prior to and subsequent to *O'Connor*, had more information at its disposal than did the Supreme Court. For instance, it quoted a study by Busby (1999) that reviewed all recorded cases involving applications for record disclosure in sexual violence cases during the 16 months between the decision in *R v O'Connor* and the passage of Bill C-46 and the 12 months following the passage of the bill. Approximately half of the records sought involved counselling; 40 per cent sought child welfare or medical records. Other records sought included those from schools, adoption agencies, probation and correctional services, criminal injuries compensation, victim services, and substance abuse services. The author concluded that the guidelines set out in *O'Connor* did not protect the rights of vulnerable groups. In the final analysis, disclosure of records was successful in 50 per cent of cases both before and after the passage of Bill C-46, indicating a possible consistency in judicial approach regardless of legislative changes. It was suggested that women with lengthy psychiatric histories were more vulnerable, owing to a greater volume of information available on them in various records (Busby, 1999). It could be argued that this information could be used to attack their credibility and that, therefore, the procedures discriminated against the disadvantaged group whose health records may include elements that negatively impact them and are not relevant to the matter at hand.

The court identified three competing principles: full answer and defence, privacy, and equality. It noted that no single one of these principles is absolute and capable of trumping the others. The accused's right to liberty under the Canadian Charter of Rights and Freedoms (1982) may be jeopardized by unjust imprisonment. Conversely, section 8 of the Charter protects the right to privacy. There is, therefore, the need to balance the accused's right to make full answer and defence against the possibility of unreasonable search and seizure of the complainant's records. Both these rights are fundamental to the administration of justice and must be considered within the context of each individual case. However, the court underlined that the principles of fundamental justice embrace more than the rights of the accused. It, therefore, suggested that the judgment be made "from the point of view of fairness in the eyes of the community and the complainant" and not just the accused (*R v E (AW)*, 1993, cited in *R v Mills*, 1999, at para 72).

In considering the submission of the Canadian Psychiatric Association, which held the role of the intervener in the case, the court emphasized that the "therapeutic relationship is one characterized by trust, an element of which is confidentialit . Therefore, the protection of the complainant's reasonable expectation of privacy in her therapeutic relationship protects the therapeutic relationship" (*R v Mills*, 1999). The court considered the impact of disclosure on both a complainant's willingness to report a crime or accept counselling and the security of the person, which is, in and of itself, a Charter right. In balancing the accused's right to make full answer and defence and the complainant's right to privacy, the court noted that, in this procedure, the accused would have a right only to records that are relevant, but not those that are irrelevant.

One major change arising from *Mills* is that records that are already in possession of the Crown are subject to the same procedures as new records for which the defence is seeking disclosure. Contrary to previous decisions (*R v O'Connor*, 1995; *R v Stinchcombe*, 1991), the court concluded that the complainant has not completely waived a reasonable expectation of privacy records for records already in the possession of the Crown unless this is explicitly undertaken. Chief Justice Lamer dissented on this issue, arguing that there should be a different standard of relevance for records already in the possession of the Crown. He posited that the appropriate procedure to use was one determined in a previous Supreme Court decision, *R v Stinchcombe* (1991) (the case of a lawyer charged with fraud and breach of trust); this is a procedure in which the Crown can argue against the production of records on the basis of relevance.

Critiques and Context

The *Mills* decision garnered considerable criticism. Defence counsel suggested that the "rights of the accused were simply washed away by a massive lobby of women's and victims' groups" (as cited in Makin, 1999). Several academic commentators made similar suggestions. Queen's University law professor Don Stuart, criticizing the reasoning behind the decision, called the judgment "more politically correct than we have seen the court in a long time" (as cited in Makin, 1999). Osgoode professor Jamie Cameron opined, "I have to wonder what other rights of the accused established over the past 10 years are going to be rolled back by the McLachlin court" (as cited in Makin, 1999). Koshan (2002) instead suggested that the legislative process involved in the development of these sections of the Code involved a democratic process and had been subject to public consultations with groups representing a range of interests. Koshan, therefore, concluded that the court was correct in recognizing this important factor when deciding how much deference to accord to Parliament. Other criticisms focused on the broad discretion given to trial judges to interpret the provisions in any manner to which they were inclined. Despite the fact that the Supreme Court of Canada stated that the disclosure procedure should be done in a manner consistent with Charter principles, it also noted that the trial judge need not engage in a conclusive and in-depth evaluation of each of the factors set out in the legislation. Although judges were now asked to make a decision that is consistent with the phrase "in the interests of justice," it remained unclear whether this standard gives any more clarity than a balancing of the privacy rights of the complainants and of the accused's right to full answer and defence.

   R v O'Connor, *R v Mills*, and other cases pertaining to access to counselling records occurred at a time when attention was focused on Indigenous peoples whose lives were affected by the residential school system, as well as on victims of sexual sexual violence. A report of Aboriginal Affairs and Northern Development Canada (2018) notes that some 150,000 Indigenous children were removed and separated from their families and communities and placed in residential schools and while most of the schools ceased to operate in the mid-1970s, the last federally run school did not close until the late 1990s. Bishop O'Connor's 1990 charges, related to offences occurring at a residential school at which he was the principal, came at a time when public attention and outrage regarding the issue of residential schools were on the rise. In the aftermath of the arrest of Bishop O'Connor, Canada's Roman Catholic bishops called for a national conference "to plot their strategic response to allegations of physical, emotional and sexual abuse at church-run Indian [*sic*] residential schools" (Roberts, 1991). In Manitoba, the site of 13 residential schools in which allegations of sexual abuse had been raised, the Assembly of Manitoba Chiefs accused the Catholic Church of damage control and of attempting to cover up abuse. Grand Chief Phil Fontaine, who had recently disclosed his own history of abuse at a residential school, called for full disclosure. The Church spokesman indicated in response that it did not deny that incidents of abuse occurred in residential schools. Nevertheless, he stated, "We don't believe in disclosure in front of TV cameras. That's disclosure that leads to political agendas" (as cited in Roberts, 1991).

The initial *O'Connor* trial occurred in the midst of this attention. The courtroom was filled over capacity with members of individuals from Indigenous communities seeking recognition for their experiences in the residential school system. The 1992 stay of proceedings *in R v O'Connor* was met with great consternation by many and was described as follows: "The bad news is, of course, that O'Connor walked, that the native community was handed yet another kick in the head from the Canadian justice system" (Cockburn, 1993).

Concomitantly, attention was focused on all victims of sexual violence in the criminal justice system. The Supreme Court of Canada in *R v Mills* (1999) referred to a long-standing "dialogue" between the courts and the legislature that had been occurring since the late 1970s regarding the relative rights of the accused and the complainant in cases of sexual violence. However, as Koshan (2002) has suggested, the voices of equality-seeking and anti-violence groups were also a central part of the discussion. Parliament responded to these concerns in 1977 when legislative changes determined that a complainant's sexual history was admissible solely at the discretion of the judge. Five years later, in 1983, the so-called rape shield act came into force, which not only forbade the admissibility of information about a complainant's previous sexual history but also eliminated spousal immunity in cases of sexual violence (Powell, 1997). In 1991, the Supreme Court of Canada struck down the rape shield law, declaring it unconstitutional in that it undermined the right to a fair trial. The following year, Justice Minister Kim Campbell brought forward Bill C-49, which re-enacted restrictions on sexual history evidence – albeit in weakened form – forbidding the raising of evidence of prior sexual activity without the explicit approval of the court and established a process for determining admissibility (Gotell, 2002, 2008). The trial of Bishop O'Connor was, thus, the next stage in a long struggle regarding the rights of the accused versus the rights of the complainant in the criminal justice system's attempts to deal with sexual violence.

A coalition of women's groups came together as intervenors in *R v O'Connor*; these groups included the Aboriginal Women's Council, the Canadian Association of Sexual Assault Centres, the Disabled Women's Network Canada, and the Women's Legal Education and Action Fund (LEAF). The Canadian Mental Health Association, which sought to have absolute privilege extended to sexual assault counselling records, was also granted intervenor status. The factum delivered by LEAF stated:

> Applications for the production rely upon and reinforce biased attitudes about women that are rooted in faulty stereotypes and deeply embedded myths about women and sexual assault. They also seek to exploit defamatory characterizations of counsellors as corrupt obstructers of justice ... [they] represent discriminatory treatment of women and children complainants setting them apart from other witnesses ... [and] draw upon groundless suspicion that women's reports of sexual violence are uniquely likely to be fabricated. (LEAF, 1999, p. 8)

Rape crisis centres and transition houses in Ontario and British Columbia began shredding their therapy session notes rather than turn them over (Bindman, 1995). As a result, a Windsor judge stayed a gross indecency charge against a former teacher because the relevant records held by a sexual assault crisis centre were destroyed (*R v Carosella*, 1997). In this case, a complainant went to a sexual assault crisis centre for counselling regarding an incident of historic sexual abuse that had occurred in 1964 when she was a student of the accused. A social worker interviewed the complainant, having informed the complainant that anything she said could be subpoenaed to court. The centre received government funding and entered into an agreement that required it to develop a close liaison with justice agencies and also to maintain all material under the centre's control as confidential and secure. Prior to the commencement of trial, the accused applied for the production of these records. The complainant and the Crown consented to this procedure. Subsequently, it was discovered that the notes had been destroyed, pursuant to the centre's policy of "shredding any files with police involvement." The trial judge found that the notes were relevant and material and would more likely than not assist the accused. He concluded that the destruction of the records had deprived the accused of the Charter right to make full answer and defence. The trial judge, therefore, ordered a stay of proceedings. The Ontario Court of Appeal set aside the order, reasoning that the evidence must disclose more than a mere risk to a Charter right.

The Supreme Court, in hearing a further appeal, stated that the accused is not required to show that the conduct of the defence is prejudiced. The court noted that, since the complainant and the Crown had waived privilege, this material would likely have been produced under the *R v Stinchcombe* regime and also under the *O'Connor* procedures. The court reasoned that denial of the right to disclosure of this material is a breach of the accused's right to make full answer and defence, without an additional showing of demonstrable prejudice. The court, therefore, found that the trial judge did not err in staying the proceedings, as the prejudice would cause damage to the integrity of the judicial system if the prosecution were continued (*R v Carosella*, 1997). Conversely, a BC judge allowed a trial to proceed despite the fact that a women's shelter had destroyed relevant records. Federal Minister of Justice Allan Rock thus announced, "There's a degree of urgency, and there's a degree of scope of this problem that requires legislative intervention" (as cited in Bindman, 1995).

British law professor Jennifer Temkin suggested that the main strategy employed by defence attorneys in sexual violence trials is to seek to undermine complainants, to attack and preferably destroy their credibility. In order to do this, the defence seeks access to records compiled by doctors, counsellors, therapists, and social workers (Temkin, 2002). Defence lawyer Alan Gold suggested that counselling records can be "crucial in proving that a fragmented account by a vulnerable or suggestible complainant had been bolstered by overzealous counsellors … We are talking about a kind of indoctrination where a therapist encourages a belief in a victim, hardening the memories or filling in the blanks" (as cited in Makin, 1995). Yet Temkin, in comparing practices throughout the English-speaking world, heralded Canada's approach, post-*Mills*, as an example of fairness to the rest of the world.

Implications for Forensic Mental Health Practice

Issues related to disclosure of mental health treatment records have profound effects on the practice of forensic mental health professionals. Clearly, many mental health professionals are likely to be involved in the assessment, treatment, and therapy of individuals who may, at some stage, become complainants in a sexual assault case. Thus, first and foremost, clients must be fully informed of the limits to confidentiality if their issues may at some point become a part of a judicial process. Second, clinical records should be prepared in a manner that anticipates the possible production of the records. Third, if records are subpoenaed for the courts, mental health professionals have an obligation to respond to the courts while simultaneously ensuring that they are upholding their professional responsibilities with respect to client rights to confidentiality. Finally, forensic mental health professionals may be involved in applications and subsequent hearings regarding the production of records.

Addressing Confidentiality

Dealing with the first issue, a variety of groups representing mental health professions were involved in both government consultations and the Supreme Court case of *R v Mills*. The court specifically referred to the submissions of the interveners and emphasized the centrality of confidentiality to the therapeutic relationship. Confidentiality as a central aspect of the provision of health and mental health services is also embedded in the right to privacy that is articulated in the Universal Declaration of Human Rights (United Nations, 1948) and in the codes of ethics of all mental health professions. Nevertheless, the Supreme Court rulings and changes to the Criminal Code of Canada make it clear that there are circumstances in which production orders may be issued for clinical records and other records relating to victims of sexual violence.

At the beginning of treatment, and possibly at the beginning of each session, the client or patient should be reminded that anything they say could possibly be produced in court. This conversation should be part of the informed consent process, and the client or patient should be allowed to ask questions about this and discuss the implications with the practitioner prior to beginning therapy. The mental health professional may want to advise the client that there are certain topics that should not be discussed in the therapy situation. For instance, the therapist may want to tell the client or patient that they should not discuss the exact details of a case that is likely to appear before the courts.

Therapies that are specifically intended to recover memories of previous trauma present particular difficulties. Therapists who undertake this type of therapy may be at particular risk of ensuing problems in court. This might also be true of therapies that involve hypnosis or other techniques that might be subject to later scrutiny in court. Feldthusen (1996), in discussing *O'Connor*, laments that innovative therapies, such as those intended to recover memory, may be most affected by this decision. It is for history to judge whether this is a positive or negative unintended sequela. We would again emphasize that the client or patient should be fully informed as a part of the consent to such procedures.

Record Keeping

The court system has recognized that therapeutic records are written in fraught contexts and are potentially unreliable as factual accounts of an event and, of course, are not given under oath. Although their limitations are recognized, and they are not to be treated as affidavits, clinical notes can become highly influential in a court process. Therefore, in this day and age, clinical notes should always be recorded with the view that they may become part of a legal process and should be subject to the same thought processes, care, and attention as one would expect a lawyer to provide when drawing up a contract.

In particular, practitioners should be mindful about their note taking when treating someone who has suffered recent trauma. The therapist should be careful to record or summarize what the patient or client has said accurately, according to standards of the specific profession. If it is thought necessary to transcribe exactly what the patient or client has disclosed, then quotation marks should be used. If, on the other hand, the therapist intends to summarize a long conversation, then this should be included in the written note. For example, one might record "X discussed at length a difficult relationship with Y, which ended badly on 31 December." Specific details regarding the offence should not be recorded as they are not being documented in the same manner as those compiled by the police or others in the criminal justice system, and may appear to contradict the complainant's story. Therapists should not include personal reflections that suggest that they are in a position to judge the veracity of the individual's story.

Therapists should also be careful about hastily written shorthand notes that may be open to misinterpretation later. For instance, the therapist may write "Feels guilty that Y may be convicted." It would be better to write a more complete description of what the patient or client actually said. In the aforementioned example, a fuller note may say, "Feels guilty for lying to mother about how they were getting home and realizes if they had been honest, mother might have picked them up and driven them home, so they could avoid walking through the dark park."

Responding to a Production Order

In addition to the ethical confidentiality obligations, mental health professionals are subject to legislation specific to confidentiality and privacy that govern the collection, maintenance, use, and disclosure of information. Canada has two federal privacy laws: the Privacy Act and the Personal Information Protection and Electronic Documents Act. The Privacy Act, which took effect in 1983, imposes obligations on federal government departments and agencies to respect privacy rights by limiting the collection, use, and disclosure of personal information. The Personal Information Protection and Electronic Documents Act sets out ground rules for how private-sector organizations may collect, use, or disclose personal information in the course of commercial activities. The provinces and territories have also enacted legislation governing the collection, use, and disclosure of personal information. These acts specify the circumstances under which practitioners may grant access to or disclose information to the individual from whom it was collected or to third parties. Further, mental health professionals should be aware that they may also be subject to various provincial statutes governing confidentiality, access, use, and disclosure in their specific areas of practice, including provincial education acts, child and family services acts, hospital acts, and mental health acts (Solomon & Visser, 2005).

Upon receiving a subpoena for production of records, mental health professionals should not be tempted to alter or destroy notes to avoid being involved in the legal arena. As we have discussed above, in one specific situation, this led to a case of sexual assault being stayed because it breached an accused's right to full answer and defence (*R v Carosella*, 1997). Destroying or altering notes may result in attenuating the legal process, as well as disciplinary actions from professional organizations and licensing bodies. Professionals should review the guidelines for responding to subpoenas if they exist in their organizations and, as necessary, seek legal counsel.

Professionals whose records are subject to subpoena have standing in criminal proceedings and a right to object to the order to produce confidential files. In those criminal cases involving sexual assault or similar charges where the accused has applied to a judge for the production of clinical records, seven days' notice of the application must be served on the prosecutor, complainant or witness, and the record holder. An in camera hearing is held at which the record keeper may appear and make submissions. Following this, a judge may order production of the record if they deem it necessary in the interests of justice. If the judge orders production of the record, they have the discretion to impose conditions in order to ensure, to the greatest extent possible, the privacy of the complainant or witness. These conditions can include the following: that the record be edited as directed by the judge, that a copy of the record rather than the original be produced, that the record be viewed only at the offices of the court and the contents not be disclosed, and that names and addresses regarding any person be severed from the record. Submissions by the mental health professional who is the guardian of the records may influence the nature of these conditions.

Despite the fact that subpoenas represent both a significant risk to the privacy of the client and an inconvenience to the mental health professional who is receiving it, serious sanctions can be imposed by the courts if a subpoena is ignored. However, a subpoena is not a licence to breach client confidentialit , and it does not grant the mental health practitioner permission to speak to a lawyer, police office , or anyone else about the content of the records or any aspect of the client's treatment. The therapist should also inform the patient or client that they are entitled to be a party in an *O'Connor* hearing and may wish to retain their own specialist counsel. Legal aid will generally fund this and reimburse counsel.

Participating as an Expert in a Production Hearing

Finally, mental health professionals may be retained by counsel in regard to an application for the production of records. As we have discussed above, defence counsel, having subpoenaed the guardian of the records, will write an application supporting their argument that third-party records are likely relevant to the credibility or reliability of a complainant, relevant to the competence of a witness, and necessary in the interests of justice. The forensic mental health professional may be asked to review certain documents, including police statements, transcripts of preliminary hearings, or other information already in the possession of retaining counsel in order to advise counsel whether there are mental health reasons or diagnoses that are likely relevant to the case at hand. In some cases, certain records may have been produced but not a complete record. For instance, there may be a summary of a course of therapy, but not the complete therapy notes; only by obtaining the complete record can it be seen that the therapist used hypnosis, which may be relevant to a theory of the defence.

Additionally, a mental health professional may be able to cast some light on the reliability of a complainant. For instance, a complainant with an acquired brain injury may have severe memory problems. It is not for the mental health professional to say that this person would make something up or tell lies, but it may be important for the court to know that this person may not be able to accurately relate to the court what happened at a specific time. Other diagnoses that may be considered relevant include a diagnosis of schizophrenia or delusional disorder involving erotomanic delusions about the accused, or a previous diagnosis of bipolar disorder involving a manic phase with symptoms of hypersexuality and disinhibition. It will be up to the court to decide whether this is likely relevant to the accused's Charter right to make a full answer and defence. We should note at this stage that reliability, as defined above, is different from credibility, which is defined as the veracity or truthfulness of a witness. As in every case, the forensic mental health professional should give an honest and objective opinion to the retaining party. For the forensic mental health professional, the ethical obligations of truth-telling and respect for persons override duty to serve the interests of the client or patient.

Summary

Clients and patients visiting mental health professionals expect that their information will not be revealed to others without their consent. In a study reported by the Canadian Medical Association (1999), the same year as the *R v Mills* decision, the public rated confidentiality of personal health information as second only to that of financial information. Similarly, 81 per cent of Canadians assumed that their medical information was entirely confidential and privileged (Schneider, 1996). Professional organizations generally mandate confidentiality issues in their ethical guidelines. For instance, the Canadian Medical Association ethical guidelines specifically state that it is the ethical duty of physicians to protect the personal health information of their patients (Canadian Medical Association, 2004). Similarly, the Ontario College of Social Workers and Social Service Workers (2005) provides a privacy toolkit to guide their members through this process.

Despite the universality of these guidelines, developing legislation and case law has incrementally eroded the once sacrosanct shibboleth of absolute confidentialit . This has led to a number of mandatory and discretionary directives from the courts to breach confidentiality (for a history, see Glancy, Regehr, & Bryant, 1998a, 1998b; Glancy, Regehr, Bryant, & Schneider, 1999). As a result of these developments in legislation and case law, forensic mental health professionals must be aware of and exercise their obligations with respect to maintaining records in a manner that will not negatively impact their clients or patients, ensure that individuals in treatment are aware of the limits to confidentialit , and be prepared to respond to a production order. Forensic mental health professionals who are called upon to provide an assessment and opinion in a production hearing must be aware of the law and the context in which their opinion is sought and provide an objective view.

Table 8.3 Key points regarding disclosure of records

R v O'Connor	
Establishment of a two-stage process	• Production to the judge • Disclosure to the defence
Scope	• Third-party records
Considerations for disclosure	• Necessary for the accused to make full answer and defence • The probative value of the record balanced against the complainant's reasonable expectation of privacy • Whether disclosure is premised upon any discriminatory assumption or stereotype • Potential prejudice to the complainant's dignity, privacy, or security
Bill C-46	
Scope	• The two-stage process also applies to all records
Three additional considerations for disclosure	• Society's interest in encouraging reporting of sexual offences • Society's interest in encouraging the obtaining of treatment by complainants of sexual offences • Effect of the determination on the integrity of the trial process
R v Mills	
Role of the courts	• Must maintain a posture of respect toward Parliament
Scope	• Includes records already in possession of the Crown
Implications for practice	
Addressing confidentiality	• Warning about possible limits to confidentiality if the case will be before the courts • Therapies intended to assist with recovering memories may be questioned by the court
Preparation of records	• Accurately summarize what the client has said • Avoid details of the offence • Do not speculate as to the veracity of statements
Responding to court orders	• Do not destroy records • Contact legal counsel • Determine organizational policies • Be aware of the right to be a party to the proceeding • Inform the client that they can be a party to a hearing regarding record production • Not a licence to breach confidentiality
Participating as an expert in hearings regarding the production of records	• Consider factors that may impact the credibility and/or reliability of a witness • Consider the relevance of the information to the court process • Provide an objective opinion

9 Duty to Warn and Protect

Smith v Jones

> [Michael Stephen Leopold], a 37-year-old labourer, was charged in 1996 after attacking a prostitute in an alley. After pleading guilty, he was taken into custody in December 1997 to await sentencing. But for a year, while he was out on $10,000 bail and the psychiatrist fought to release his report, Leopold wandered the streets of Vancouver's downtown east side, his mind brimming with fantasies of rape, abduction, and murder. (Hume, 1999)

Mr. Leopold (a.k.a. Mr. Jones) was charged with aggravated sexual assault on 18 September 1996 in relation to an attack on a local sex trade worker. It was alleged that Mr. Leopold had assaulted and attempted to tie up a woman with whom he had paid sex. The victim successfully attracted the attention of passersby; her assailant fled but was later identified by his licence plate number. Mr. Leopold's lawyer, Leslie Mackoff, referred him to a Vancouver-based forensic psychiatrist, known by the pseudonym Dr. Smith (Owens, 1999), to assist in the preparation of the defence or, in the event of a guilty plea, submissions on sentencing (*Smith v Jones*, 1999). Mr. Leopold was advised by his lawyer that the assessment was privileged in the same manner as were discussions with his lawyer.

In the course of a forensic psychiatric examination conducted on 30 July 1997, the psychiatrist became concerned that Mr. Leopold would carry out his sexually sadistic fantasies to kidnap, rape, and kill prostitutes. The accused reported previous encounters in which he hired sex trade workers and engaged in sexually sadistic behaviours. He reported specifically selecting women who were drug addicted and vulnerable, as they were more willing to endure pain and injury for money (O'Shaughnessy, Glancy, & Bradford, 1999). Mr. Leopold indicated that he began to have elaborate fantasies of torturing, raping, and murdering women. Further, he had recently decided to act on these fantasies and to kill and bury the potential victim in an isolated mountainous region near the city. He indicated he had made a number of preparations, including taking vacation time, purchasing items to restrain the potential victim, and preparing his home for the purposes of forcible confinement and torture. The concerns of the assessing psychiatrist were later reported in the press as follows:

> The psychiatrist said Leopold intended to kidnap the woman and turn her into a sex slave. "[Leopold] explained to me that his plan was to kill the woman by strangling her, and to then place her body into a utility trailer he had, and drive her to the bush area near Hope," the psychiatrist states in the affidavit
>
> "He said he had arranged time off from his employment and intended to use the logging roads near Hope to dispose of the body. He said that before burying the body, he planned to shoot her in the face with a shotgun, to prevent identification.
>
> The psychiatrist states that Leopold's fantasies escalated, becoming more and more violent.
>
> "He said he enjoyed the fantasy of power and that over time he became bored with these fantasies and then progressed to thoughts of raping specific women he had seen in high school, or on the street, or other specific locations ... by his late teens, he had developed an active repertoire of sexually sadistic fantasies which would include abduction, restraint, and transportation to a secluded location where he would rape the victim."
>
> Leopold told the psychiatrist he'd acted out some of his fantasies with prostitutes. "His fantasies effectively involve kidnapping and restraining a vulnerable individual who is smaller, keeping her for a number of days while he sexually assaults her and tortures her, and then killing her and disposing of the body."
>
> "In my opinion, I considered him to be a dangerous individual in that he would, more likely than not, act on these fantasies unless he had sufficient t eatment." (Hume, 1999)

The doctor brought his concerns to defence counsel, who requested that he keep this information and his views confidential under solicitor-client privilege. The psychiatrist, concerned about the safety of members of the public, commenced action to allow for disclosure. What followed was an unprecedented case regarding the scope of solicitor-client privilege and the manner in which it extends to experts retained by the defence.

Initially, the psychiatrist filed an affidavit with the court. Justice Henderson ruled in December 1997

> that the public safety exception to the law of solicitor–client privilege and doctor–patient confidentiality released [the psychiatrist] from his duties of confidentiality. He went on to rule that [the psychiatrist] was under a duty to disclose to the police and the Crown both the statements made by [the accused] and his opinion based upon them. (*Smith v Jones*, 1999, p. 473)

Mr. Leopold appealed to the BC Court of Appeal, which changed the mandatory reporting order to one permitting the psychiatrist to disclose to the police. Upon further appeal, the Supreme Court of Canada ruled that danger of serious harm to the public overrules solicitor-client privilege, the highest privilege recognized by the courts. As such, forensic mental health professionals now share the duty to warn and protect with other health care professionals.

The Court of Appeal imposed what was described in the press as an "unusually oppressive publication ban" (Owens, 1999) on the case. The Supreme Court of Canada noted that as solicitor-client privilege was being claimed for the doctor's report, the names of the parties were replaced by pseudonyms (Dr. Smith and Mr. Jones) until the outcome was determined. Although the Supreme Court eventually lifted the publication ban, the case is known as *Smith v Jones*, which is how we will now refer to the case in our discussion.

Context

The time and place in which *Smith v Jones* occurred is a critical feature of this case. During the 1990s, attention was focused on the plight of women in Vancouver's Downtown Eastside neighbourhood. One website focused on missing women describes the environment as follows:

> Vancouver's Downtown Eastside is the poorest neighbourhood in British Columbia – in all of Canada, for that matter. No other slum or

ghetto in the country matches the squalor of this 10-block urban waste-land, with its rundown hotels and pawn shops, stained and fractured sidewalks, gutters and alleyways littered with garbage, used condoms and discarded hypodermic needles. Downtown Eastside has another name as well, used commonly by residents and the police who clean up after them. They call the district "Low Track," and it fits … Low Track is the heart of British Columbia's rock-bottom drug scene … Most of Low Track's female addicts support their habits via prostitution, trolling the streets night and day, haunted creatures rendered skeletal by what one Seattle Times reporter has dubbed "the Jenny Crack diet" … But there were other dangers on the street, as well. Three years before Expo '86 opened its gates, prostitutes began to vanish from Low Track. ("Vancouver Eastside," 2016)

News of women disappearing from Vancouver's Eastside made the international press. *The Guardian*, published in the UK, reported that over the next two decades, "more than 60 women, mainly working in the sex trade, many from the Aboriginal community, would vanish" ("The Disappeared," 2005). Robert Pickton, notorious serial killer of women in Vancouver's sex trade, first became known to police in 1997, after Wendy Lynn Eistetter was stabbed during a rave at his pig farm. It was later learned that

The frequent parties at Piggy's Palace drew female drug addicts like a magnet. They knew they could get a fix there … "That farm was the dregs of the earth," one prostitute from Downtown Eastside has said. "It was a hellhole … Police had known about the farm for some time, but nothing had changed." ("The Disappeared," 2005)

In 2001, Vancouver police formed the Missing Women's Task Force, launching an investigation into the disappearances of 54 women known to be missing from the area. Three months later, Robert Pick-ton was charged with two counts of first-deg ee murder; he was later linked to the deaths of at least 33 women ("Missing Women Timeline," 2012; Fournier, 2011).

Thus, at the time in which the psychiatrist interviewed Mr. Leopold, the time that the British Columbia courts made their rulings, and the time in which the Supreme Court of Canada heard *Smith v Jones*, concerns were high about the disappearance and assumed murder of Vancouver women working in the sex trade, but the killer had not been identified or app ehended.

Supreme Court Decision in *Smith v Jones*

The Supreme Court of Canada in *Smith v Jones* (1999) concluded:

> The solicitor–client privilege is a principle of fundamental importance to the administration of justice. It is the highest privilege recognized by the courts. However, despite its importance, the privilege is not absolute and remains subject to limited exceptions, including the public safety exception.
>
> Three factors should be taken into consideration in determining whether public safety outweighs solicitor–client privilege:
> 1. Is there a clear risk to an identifiable person or g oup of persons?
> 2. Is there a risk of serious bodily harm or death?
> 3. Is the danger imminent? (p. 457)

The court went on to specify that each of these factors must be defined and weighed within their particular context. It may be that, at times, the identifiable group is less clear, but the threat of harm is particularly compelling in terms of seriousness and imminence, thereby making it appropriate to lift confidentialit .

In the particular case at hand, *Smith v Jones*, the court considered that the accused was reported to have a paraphilic disorder (sexual sadism) and drug abuse, had clearly identified a group of victims (sex trade workers in a particular area), and had a clearly defined plan for initiating bodily harm and murder. As such, the court concluded that the combination of all these elements met the criteria for clarity and seriousness. With respect to imminence, the court considered that the accused had breached his bail and was continuing to visit the Eastside area, which resulted in a sense of urgency to address the issue (*Smith v Jones*, 1999). While the court was unanimous on the fact that information should be released, there was a division with respect to the scope of information to be released. The majority opinion was that all information should be released, whereas the minority felt that only the conclusion that the accused posed a danger to prostitutes in a particular area should be released (O'Shaughnessy et al., 1999).

Tarasoff v Regents of the University of California

In coming to its ruling in *Smith v Jones*, the Supreme Court of Canada considered a number of cases from other jurisdictions. The concept of duty to warn and protect others has a long tradition in the United

States, where it was highlighted and clarified by the famous *Tarasoff* decision (*Tarasoff v Regents of the University of California*, 1976).

Prosenjit Poddar, an international graduate student at University of California Berkeley, told his treating psychologist that he intended to kill Tatiana Tarasoff, and, some time later, proceeded to commit the murder. Mr. Poddar and Ms. Tarasoff met at folk-dancing classes at the International House in the fall of 1968. They spent time together on a weekly basis over the fall, and on New Year's Eve, they shared a kiss, which Mr. Poddar understood to indicate a serious relationship. Ms. Tarasoff attempted to dissuade him of this view, which resulted in an emotional crisis for Mr. Poddar. He reportedly became depressed, weeping and speaking disjointedly. He spoke to friends alternatively about loving Ms. Tarasoff, wanting to kill her, and wanting to blow up her room. He met on occasion with Ms. Tarasoff and recorded their conversations, replaying them in an attempt to understand why she did not love him. In the summer of 1969, Ms. Tarasoff left the country to go to Brazil. While Mr. Poddar appeared to improve somewhat, he agreed, on the urging of friends, to seek help from Cowell Memorial Hospital, which is associated with the university.

In his ninth session with psychologist Lawrence Moore, Mr. Poddar confided that he intended to commit murder. The therapist, concluding that Mr. Poddar was dangerous, contacted the campus police and requested Mr. Poddar be taken to hospital for a 72-hour detention. Mr. Poddar was questioned by police in an apartment he shared with Ms. Tarasoff's younger brother, but as they determined that Mr. Poddar had changed his attitude, they left him with a warning. Cowell Memorial Hospital took no further action to protect Ms. Tarasoff. In October, Ms. Tarasoff returned from Brazil. Mr. Poddar went to her home, shot her with a pellet gun and stabbed her to death (Buckner & Firestone, 2000). He then phoned the city police and told them he thought he had killed someone.

Ms. Tarasoff's parents filed wrongful death suits against the university and the therapists, alleging a failure to warn them that Mr. Poddar represented a grave danger to their daughter. The court found that the police had failed to warn Ms. Tarasoff but nevertheless released them from liability. On appeal in 1974, the California Supreme Court, despite defence arguments that the duty to warn violated the accepted ethical obligation to maintain confidentialit , ruled in the plaintiff's favour. The court concluded that "the doctor bears a duty to use reasonable care to give threatened persons such warnings as are essential to avert danger arising from the patient's condition" and the "protective privilege ends when public peril begins" (*Tarasoff v Regents of the University of California*, 1974, p. 347). The California Supreme Court reheard in the case in 1976. At this time, the court further stated

> When a therapist determines, or pursuant to the standards of his profession should determine, that his patient presents a serious danger of violence to another, he incurs an obligation to use reasonable care to protect the intended victim against such danger. The discharge of this duty may require the therapist to take one or more steps depending on the nature of the case. Thus, it may call for him to warn the intended victim or if it is likely, to apprise the victim of a danger, to notify the police, or take whatever steps are reasonably necessary under the circumstances. (*Tarasoff v Regents of the University of California*, 1976, p. 340)

Tarasoff thus expanded the duty of care of health to include third parties, well beyond the earlier common law duties to patients (Buckner & Firestone, 2000). This was later codified by amendments to the California Civil Code (1985) that, because of efforts of the California Psychiatric Association, limited the *Tarasoff* liability to a "serious threat" against a "reasonably identified victim." While the *Tarasoff* decision, requiring a duty to warn and protect third parties, did not apply in Canadian jurisdictions, it was generally assumed that Canadian courts would offer a similar decision should the issue arise.

Wenden v Trikha

Fifteen years after *Tarasoff*, the first Canadian precedent-setting case regarding duty to warn was decided: *Wenden v Trikha*. The case involves a voluntarily admitted psychiatric patient, Anil Trikha, who left the Royal Alexandra Hospital in Alberta without the knowledge of hospital staff, drove his car in a dangerous and erratic manner at an excessive rate of speed, and collided with the vehicle of Johanna Wenden (*Wenden v Trikha*, 1991). Prior to the accident, Mr. Trikha's car was in the parking lot of the hospital unbeknownst to hospital staff; they did not see any keys among his possessions and were uncertain how he managed to start the car and leave. Mr. Trikha was under close supervision, with checks every 15 minutes; however, it was reported that he appeared to be calm, and there was no indication that he had any intention of harming others.

The accident caused by Mr. Trikha tragically resulted in severe injury to Ms. Wenden, and she eventually lost custody of her children because she was unable to care for them. Her family commenced action against the hospital and the psychiatrist, claiming that they owed her a duty of care and were in breach of that duty by reason of the manner in which they had cared for the patient. Action against both the hospital and doctor was dismissed because it was determined that there was no indication that the patient presented a risk to others, and there was no previous relationship between the injured party and the patient. This finding was later confirmed by the Alberta Court of Appeal. However, the judge suggested that both hospitals and psychiatrists who become aware that a patient presents a serious danger to others owe a duty to warn and protect such a person or persons if a requisite proximity of relationship exists between them (*Wenden v Trikha* [1993]).

While this decision formed the basis of a common law duty to warn, mental health practitioners continued to question their responsibilities, as no provincial or federal statutes (except in Quebec) required or permitted therapists to report clients who threatened to seriously harm a member of the public (Carlisle, 1996). Breaching confidentia-ity in this manner might, therefore, have resulted in disciplinary action by licensing bodies and exemplified that lack of consistency between ethical codes and common law (Regehr & Kanani, 2010). *Smith v Jones* clarified the issue

Pittman Estate v Bain

A further example of the contradiction between common law and legislation in Canada was exemplified in a case that considered the duty to warn in the context of the risk that HIV-infected people present to intimate partners. While US case law placed an affirmative duty on physicians to break physician-patient confidences and warn those exposed to harm of contagious disease (Spillane, 1989), health care providers in Ontario, for instance, had been prohibited from disclosing the HIV status of their patients to anyone but the medical officer of health without patients' consent, even if they believed that their patients presented a significant risk of infection to a contact (Casswell, 1989; Flanagan, 1988). The 1994 Ontario decision in *Pittman Estate v Bain* challenged this directive regarding confidentiality.

Kenneth Pittman underwent cardiac surgery at Toronto General Hospital (TGH) in 1984, during which he received a transfusion of cryoprecipitate, a blood derivative that helped stop bleeding. As a result of the transfusion, he was infected with HIV and subsequently died of AIDS-related pneumonia in March 1990. In 1987, when testing became available, the Canadian Red Cross Society determined the original blood donor was HIV positive and traced the potentially tainted blood to TGH. In 1989, the hospital determined that Mr. Pittman was a recipient, and notified his family physician, Dr. Bain. Dr. Bain, who was concerned about his patient's physical and mental health, elected not to inform him, as he believed that Mr. Pittman and his wife were not engaging in intercourse and, therefore, she was not at risk. Mrs. Pittman, however, learned in September 1990 that she had contracted HIV from her husband. The family sued Dr. Bain, the Canadian Red Cross, and TGH. The court determined that the plaintiffs had failed to establish negligence for the Red Cross or for TGH. However, Dr. Bain was found negligent of his duty to protect. In finding this, the court considered that the Discipline Committee of the College of Physicians and Surgeons had found Dr. Bain guilty of professional misconduct for failing to maintain the standard of practice but noted that it did not carry much weight in common law. The court found that "Dr. Bain's decision to withhold information from Mr. Pittman, while no doubt motivated by a misplaced desire to save Mr. Pittman from anxiety, caused damage to both Mr. and Mrs. Pittman" (*Pittman Estate v Bain*, 1994). It was reasoned that Mr. Pittman might have received treatment to address the risk of fatal pneumonia, and they would have taken measures to avoid the infection of Mrs. Pittman.

Ahmed v Stefaniu

In an unprecedented move, the Ontario Court of Appeal ruled in 2006 that Toronto psychiatrist Rodica Stefaniu was civilly liable for a brutal 1997 murder committed by William Johannes, a patient whom she had released from Humber Memorial Hospital weeks before (*Ahmed v Stefaniu*, 2006). The murder and case were described by the press as follows:

> Gripped by a floridly psychotic rage, Mr. Johannes stabbed his sister – Roslyn Knipe – 60 times before cutting out one of her lungs in the belief that she was possessed by the devil … The Ontario Court of Appeal stated firmly that there was solid evidence that, but for Dr. Stefaniu's decision to release Mr. Johannes, his 39-year-old sister would not have been killed. (Makin, 2006)

Mr. Johannes, who had a history of psychiatric admissions, began to deteriorate in the summer of 1996, demonstrating bizarre and aggressive behaviours and paranoid ideation. On 25 September 1996, his sister, Roslyn Knipe, with whom he resided, contacted her family practitioner and informed him that Mr. Johannes had threatened to hurt her if she did not prove that she was "on his side" within two weeks. The police were informed, and Mr. Johannes was taken to the hospital and admitted involuntarily, pursuant to a Form 1 under the Mental Health Act of Ontario. The physician found that he was likely to cause serious bodily harm to another person, and he was also declared not capable of consenting to treatment (Glancy & Glancy, 2009). Mr. Johannes appealed his involuntary hospitalization to the Consent and Capacity Review Board, which concluded:

> The board is of the opinion that at this time, without treatment, there is a likelihood that the patient if he left hospital would continue to deteriorate to the point where the likelihood that he will cause serious bodily harm to another person. He would simply lose control due to anger and frustration. (*Ahmed v Stefaniu*, 2006, p. 3)

During his time in hospital, Mr. Johannes further deteriorated, remaining delusional and paranoid and behaving in an aggressive manner, striking other patients and threatening medical staff. He became known as an extremely difficult patient (Makin, 2007); indeed, it was recorded that during his stay in the hospital, physical restraints were used on him on 25 different occasions. He would wander around naked and habitually sat next to the nursing station preaching loudly. At one point, he launched a rebellion, encouraging other patients to refuse their medication. The staff were anxious to discharge him, some believing that he had a manipulative personality disorder. A number of consultations were arranged, suggesting a division of opinion regarding his diagnosis. At least two of the consultants suggested he was faking some of his symptoms and acting out in a manner suggestive of a personality disorder. Nevertheless, the general impression over the course of his hospital stay was that he became less threatening and that there was a general trend of improvement in his behaviour (Glancy & Glancy, 2009).

On the evening of 4 December 1996, Dr. Stefaniu assessed the patient and described him as appropriate, cooperative, and having no signs or symptoms of paranoia or psychosis. Mr. Johannes informed the doctor that he had no intention of harming himself or anybody else and that he had faked his illness, although she later testified that she did not believe him. She concluded that he probably did not meet the criteria for an involuntary patient at that time and she decided to meet with him the next day for further discussion. Acting on her opinion that he no longer met the criteria to be detained in hospital as an involuntary patient, Dr. Stefaniu changed his status from involuntary to voluntary under the Mental Health Act. He refused to remain in hospital as a voluntarily patient, declined to continue outpatient care, and was, therefore, discharged from the hospital. He moved back into his sister's apartment, where he resided with her and her two small daughters.

Forty-seven days after his discharge, on 21 January 1997, Mr. Johannes attended the emergency department of a different hospital and was assessed by a psychiatrist. It was concluded that Johannes was not a danger to himself or others and, therefore, he did not meet the criteria for involuntary admission. The very next day, he attended yet another hospital emergency department, where he was seen by an emergency department resident who once more concluded that he did not meet the criteria for involuntary admission under the Mental Health Act (Willems & Robertson, 2007). No issue was taken at trial as to the standard of these assessments.

On 24 January 1997, William Johannes killed his sister in her apartment and was subsequently found NCR-MD and ordered to a maximum-security psychiatric hospital. Two experts called by the plaintiff testified that Dr. Stefaniu failed to meet the standard of care expected of a psychiatrist in the circumstances. In the ensuing civil trial, two experts called by the defence testified that the doctor acted in an honest and intelligent manner and that she met the standard required in her management of the patient. Nevertheless, Dr. Stefaniu was found negligent in that she failed to meet the standard of care of a psychiatrist practising in a general inpatient psychiatric unit in a community hospital when she made the decision to change Mr. Johannes' status to that of an involuntary patient. The court awarded the plaintiff damages in the amount of $172,000. The verdict was appealed and dismissed by the Ontario Court of Appeal with the conclusion that the verdict of the jury was not unreasonable (*Ahmed v Stefaniu*, 2006).

One of the issues that has caused concern in this ruling is the apparent contradiction between the requirement for psychiatrists to detain individuals on an involuntary basis for an indeterminate period of time if they may present a risk to others, and the imperative to reform mental health services, continuing the move from hospital-based care to community-based care. Deinstitutionalization movements have significantly reduced the numbers of psychiatric beds. For instance, in Ontario, the influential Graham Report set the target that by 2003, the number of psychiatric beds in Ontario should be 30 per 100,000 population, down from 219 per 100,000 population in 1965 and 58 in 1992 (Regehr & Glancy, 2014). This target was established despite evidence from the United States and other jurisdictions that there is a direct link between deinstitutionalization, homelessness, and the percentage of individuals with mental health problems in correctional facilities (Harcourt, 2005; Lamb & Bachrach, 2001; Lamb & Weinberger, 2001). Thus, both a philosophical and practical dilemma is presented to mental health professionals faced with the decision to detain an individual considered dangerous.

A recent case exemplifies some of the possible challenges and deleterious effects that can arise from exercising a duty to warn (some details have been altered to protect confidentiality) (Glancy, Glancy, Felthous, & Chaimowitz, 2015). In this case, a 13-year-old youth was seeing a child and youth worker regarding depression, deliberate self-harm, and occasional drug abuse subsequent to being bullied at school. The youth expressed fantasies to the therapist of kidnapping the bullies, taking them somewhere isolated (although at age 13, the youth could not drive), tying them up, and killing them if the harassment continued during the new school year, which was scheduled to begin in two weeks. The therapist reported this at a team meeting with the supervising psychiatrist, who was not the attending psychiatrist for the youth. The psychiatrist directed the therapist to inform the police. The police arrested the patient and laid a charge of threatening. Subsequently, the patient was detained in a youth detention centre wherein the youth was sexually assaulted. The police also informed the schoolmates, the bullies, and their families of the threat. The criminal case was adjourned for one year. In this space of time, the youth had to change schools, the family had to relocate, and a new therapist had to be found.

The salutary warning that comes from this case is that informing the police can have serious effects. In this case, other measures might have preceded this action. For instance, a consultation between the treating psychiatrist and the supervising psychiatrist might have clarified the risk and its imminence. Admitting the youth to an inpatient unit may have given the team more time for a thorough risk assessment, as well as further consultation. A period of inpatient treatment may have mitigated the risk. Had these options been considered, the youth would have been much better served. In this particular case, the psychiatrist was successfully sued and, owing to the fact that she likely had not met the standard of care, the case was settled out of court.

Implications for Forensic Mental Health Practice

In the United States, *Tarasoff v Regents of the University of California* (1974/1976) established for mental health professionals a positive duty to warn and protect the public if there is reason to believe that a patient presents a threat to others). Canadian cases have now determined that a similar duty to protect exists in Canada (*Pittman Estate v Bain*, 1994; *Wenden v Trikha*, 1993). Indeed, this duty is so compelling that it even overrides the solicitor-client privilege that binds a forensic mental health professional (*Smith v Jones*, 1999). A duty to warn and protect exists 1) in the event that a risk to a clearly identifiable person or group of persons is determined; 2) when the risk of harm includes severe bodily injury, death, or serious psychological harm; and 3) when there is an element of imminence, creating a sense of urgency. The duty requires the practitioner to inform the intended victim, the police, the courts, or others regarding the risk of harm; it almost always results in a breach of confidentiality. The duty to protect implies a broader range of actions, including detaining or treating the individual, that may or may not involve breaching confidentiality (Chaimowitz, Glancy, & Blackburn, 2000).

Failure to effectively exercise these duties can result in liability for the mental health professional as evidenced in several Canadian cases (*Ahmed v Stefaniu*, 2006; *Pittman Estate v Bain*, 1994). Canadian law requires four essential components to prove professional negligence: 1) the defendant must owe the plaintiff a duty of care; 2) the defendant must have breached this standard of care; 3) the plaintiff has suffered an injury or loss; and 4) the defendant's conduct has been the actual and legal cause of the plaintiff's injury (Picard & Robertson, 2007). Thus, the greatest protection for the mental health practitioner is familiarity with guidelines offered by their professional bodies on issues of confide - tiality and duty to protect and on adherence to current standards of practice.

As a first step, the Canadian Psychiatric Association position paper on the duty to protect (Chaimowitz & Glancy, 2002) recommends that all patients should be warned about limits to confidentiality in the informed consent process. While concerns have been raised that such an approach might undermine trust in the therapeutic relationship, shift the burden of responsibility onto the patient, and dissuade them from sharing violent impulses with clinicians (Chaimowitz et al., 2000), it is fully consistent with the consensus statement of Ontario's Medical Expert Panel on Duty to Inform (Ferris et al., 1998). A further concern is determining what information should be transmitted once a duty to warn has been established. While there are no easy answers to this question, it is suggested that sharing the least amount of information required to produce the intended result should be transmitted to the authorities or to the victims.

Appelbaum (1985) indicates that, in the decade that followed the *Tarasoff* decision, court decisions that considered the duty to warn and protect applied a three-part approach: 1) assessing dangerousness through gathering data and determining the level of risk; 2) selecting a course of action which may include hospitalization, transfer to a more secure setting, or intensifying treatment; and 3) implementing and monitoring. In the Canadian context, Truscott and Crook (1993) suggest that limiting liability related to the duty to warn and protect involves careful documentation regarding information gathered and communicated, consultation with professional colleagues and evidence of professional consensus, and actions taken. They also note the importance of ensuring that all threats are recorded verbatim. Data that should be taken into account include the context and manner in which the threat is made, history of violence, relationship and access to the threatened person(s), the opportunity to act on the threat (for instance, access to means), exacerbating factors (substance use, relational issues), and response to treatment. In addition, where possible, the individual should be engaged in the process to the degree possible (Chaimowitz et al., 2000; Truscott & Crook, 1993). For instances in which the threat is clear, the plan specific and concrete, and the method available, the Ontario Medical Expert Panel on Duty to Inform advises notifying police immediately and, where appropriate, notifying the potential victim (Ferris et al., 1998).

Risk assessment measures should be considered to augment the assessment and consultation process. The American Psychiatric Association *Resource Document on Violence Risk Assessment* is an excellent guide to the use of various approaches to risk assessment (Buchanan, Binder, Norko, & Swartz, 2012, 2015). This document notes that actuarial instruments, such as the *Violence Risk Assessment Guide* (VRAG), formalize the approach to examining correlates to violence risk. Structured professional judgment tools such as the HCR-20 serve as an *aide-memoire* and encourage clinicians to consider the relevance of a number of variables while simultaneously taking into account the context and unique variables presented by the case (Buchanan et al., 2012). In addition, Chaimowitz and Glancy (2002) present a threat assessment algorithm to guide the clinical decision-making that has been used in the *Canadian Psychiatric Association Guidelines*, a modification of which can be found in figu e 9.1. This algorithm includes the consideration of the degree to which the risk of harm to others is the result of a serious mental illness, in which case actions under the relevant mental health legislation, such as voluntary or involuntary hospitalization and treatment, can present options.

Figure 9.1 Assessing threat and duty to warn and protect

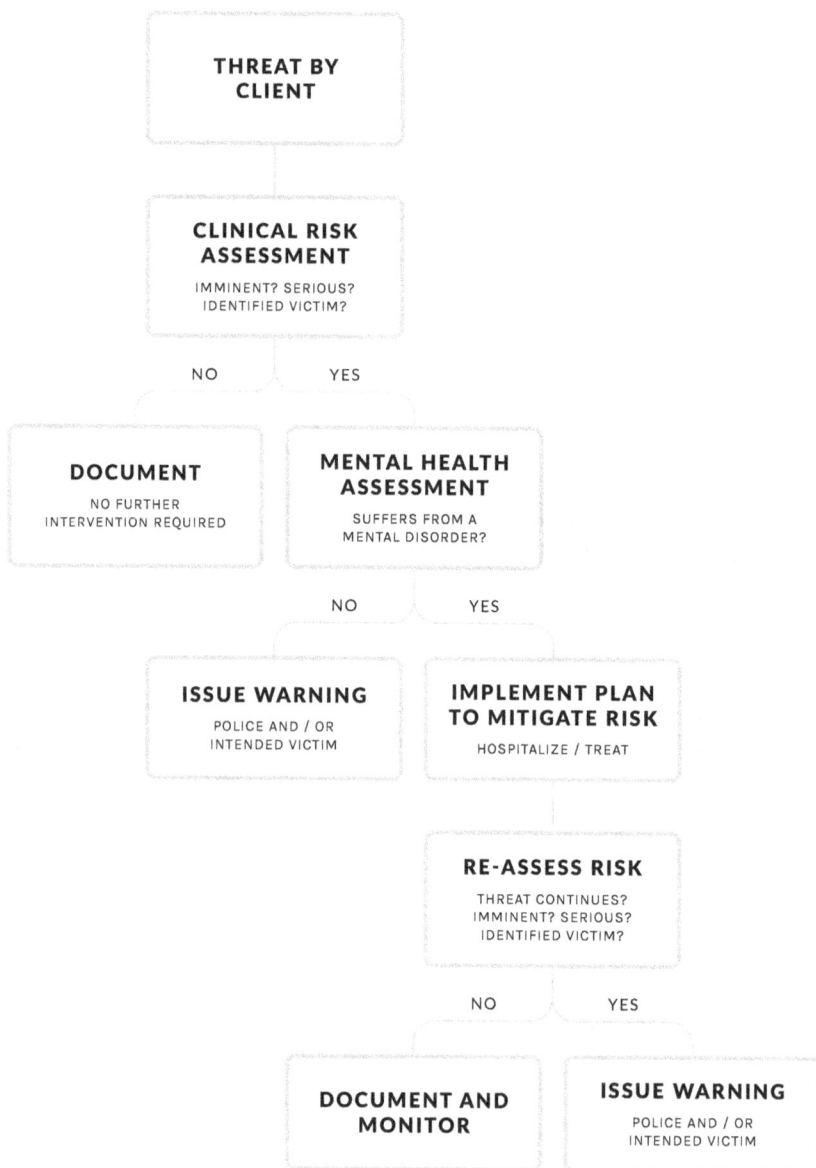

THREAT BY CLIENT

CLINICAL RISK ASSESSMENT
IMMINENT? SERIOUS?
IDENTIFIED VICTIM?

NO   YES

DOCUMENT
NO FURTHER
INTERVENTION REQUIRED

MENTAL HEALTH ASSESSMENT
SUFFERS FROM A
MENTAL DISORDER?

NO   YES

ISSUE WARNING
POLICE AND / OR
INTENDED VICTIM

IMPLEMENT PLAN TO MITIGATE RISK
HOSPITALIZE / TREAT

RE-ASSESS RISK
THREAT CONTINUES?
IMMINENT? SERIOUS?
IDENTIFIED VICTIM?

NO   YES

DOCUMENT AND MONITOR

ISSUE WARNING
POLICE AND / OR
INTENDED VICTIM

Source: Adapted from Chaimowitz & Glancy (2002)

Summary

The nature of a duty to protect the public has been argued in psychiatric and legal circles for some time. The definitive case begins with the *Tarasoff* decisions (*Tarasoff v Regents of the University of California*, 1974/1976). In *Tarasoff I* (1974), it became law that therapists had a duty *to warn* potential victims of violence about foreseeably dangerous patients. In *Tarasoff II* (1976), the therapist is mandated to have an obligation to use reasonable care *to protect* an intended victim from danger. Canada had been a little slower to come to some conclusions about these matters. However, in *Wenden v Trikha* (1993), while the court did not find liability in this particular case, it found that the hospital may have been liable if it had been possible to identify a victim. This case opened the door to future litigation in this area.

Later, in *Smith v Jones*, a psychiatrist assessed a client who had been referred by a lawyer for a defence psycho-legal assessment. The accused told the psychiatrist that he had elaborate plans to kidnap a prostitute, and then torture and murder her. The psychiatrist sought to disclose the information for the safety of the public. The case was fast-tracked to the Supreme Court of Canada, which concluded that if a patient or client makes a serious threat of imminent harm to a third party, then the mental health practitioner is obliged to take steps to warn and protect the third party provided there is a threat of serious harm to an identified person or group and the threat is imminent. This was later reinforced by the case of *Ahmed v Stefaniu* (2006), which held the psychiatrist liable for failure to protect. The Supreme Court in *Smith v Jones* declined to outline the steps necessary to warn or protect potential victims, leaving this to assessment on an individual case basis. This led to the development of a Canadian Psychiatric Association position paper on the duty to protect (Chaimowitz & Glancy, 2002). In the end, forensic mental health professionals must exercise their duty to warn and protect through careful assessment, definitive action, and continued assessment of their interventions.

Table 9.1 Key points regarding duty to warn and protect

Tarasoff v Regents of the University of California (1974/1976)	
Tarasoff I (1974) The duty to warn	• The professional bears a duty of care to *warn* threatened persons of possible danger arising from a patient's condition • "Protective privilege ends when public peril begins"
Tarasoff II (1976)	• The professional has an obligation to use reasonable care to *protect* the intended victim
Wenden v Trikha (1993)	
Duty to warn and protect in Canada	• If a patient presents a serious danger to others, hospitals and professionals owe a duty to warn and protect if a requisite proximity of relationship exists
Pittman Estate v Bain (1994)	
Duty to warn and protect with respect to HIV transmission	• A physician is responsible for informing patients of the risk of harming others due to transmission of HIV infection
Smith v Jones (1999)	
Solicitor-client privilege and doctor-patient confidentiality	• Public safety overrules solicitor-client privilege and doctor-patient confidentiality • Three factors should be taken into consideration in determining whether public safety outweighs solicitor-client privilege: 1. Is there a clear risk to an identifiable person or group of persons? 2. Is there a risk of serious bodily harm or death? 3. Is the danger imminent?
Ahmed v Stefaniu (2006)	
Standard of care	• Professionals who do not successfully protect third parties may be found to have not reached the standard of care and may be found liable
Implications for practice	
Informed consent	• All patients should be warned about the limits to confidentiality
Duty to warn and protect	• Assess dangerousness (may involve the use of actuarial or structured professional judgment tools) • Select course of action (may involve hospitalization, treatment, warning of potential victims, notification of police) • Implement course of action and continue to monitor and assess dangerousness

10 Consent to Treatment

Starson v Swayze

The headline in the *Toronto Star* on 16 December 2001, read: "Mentally ill genius fights for the right to refuse treatment" (Tyler, 2001a). The story began as follows:

> "I was born on Friday the 13th, so I can't say I am lucky," Scott Starson says in an understatement of vast proportions. Dressed in a pinstripe suit and pumpkin-coloured turtleneck, he sits in the barren visitor's lounge of Ontario's most secure psychiatric hospital … Between bites of cheeseburger, he makes the following observations:
>
> His lawyer, Anita Szigeti, has "problems" because she will only live another 1,155 years.
>
> Comic Don Rickles is "pissed off" at him for standing up Joan Rivers in Toronto last summer. Starson believes he is married to the comedienne but says he also plans to marry actress Joan Collins in the "world's first scientific wedding" on July 4, 2003. Then, he will have "13 scientifi wives."
>
> He was sent to the Oak Ridge division of the Penetanguishene Mental Health Centre by Mumbles, a blue macaw. Mumbles' brain is the "force of all intelligence in the universe," but, more importantly, Mumbles is "my son." (Tyler, 2001a)

Born Scott Jeffrey Schutzman in January 1956 in Brooklyn, Mr. Starson legally changed his name to Professor Starson in 1993 because, according to his mother, Jeanne Stevens, "He actually believed he was the son of the stars" (Tibbetts, 2003). Ms. Stevens described her son as the quintessential American boy, inquisitive and demonstrating an early aptitude in science and math. Yet, she is also quick to dispute reports that he was "advanced at birth" or able to converse in English at the age of six months (Tyler, 2001a). He graduated from Ryerson Polytechnic Institute (which became Ryerson University in 1993) in control engineering and obtained a sales job in the Toronto branch of an American engineering firm. He was described by friends as high energy, needing little sleep, a daredevil on the ski slopes, impeccably groomed, and having head-turning good looks resembling the actor Tom Selleck.

Then it all began to change. Mr. Schutzman (as he was known then), the firm's top salesman in North America, became erratic, his hyperactivity switching at times to outbursts of shouting and unexplained laughter. At first, others believed that he was taking drugs, but his continued success at sales caused superiors to ignore troubling behaviour. However, he later began to show up at work in an unkempt state, too dishevelled to see clients, and one day in 1985 called his college friend and colleague Frank Cianciotta, referring to him as Captain Kirk and asking him to issue him mission orders. Mr. Cianciotta went to his friend's home and was so concerned about his state that he called the police, who brought him to the Clarke Institute of Psychiatry for assessment. Shortly thereafter, he lost his job. "His career was over. He was 29 years old" (O'Neill & Fischer, 2005).

Between 1985 and 1998, Mr. Starson was arrested over 10 times for mischief, trespassing, harassing phone calls, and disturbing the peace and was charged a dozen times for making death threats. He was admitted 15 different times to psychiatric institutions by order of the court (O'Neill & Fischer, 2005). At one point, he was questioned by the RCMP and US Secret Services for making threatening phone calls to US President George W. Bush (Tibbetts, 2003). He also repeatedly harassed comedienne Joan Rivers: on one occasion this resulted in his being arrested and confined to Manhattan's Bellevue Hospital, and on another his being arrested at a Boca Raton bookstore and sentenced to 178 days in jail (Tyler, 2001a). Then in July 1998, having returned to Toronto, Mr. Starson's landlord called police indicating the Mr. Starson had made threats toward him. He similarly threatened the police officer who responded to the call. Mr. Starson was charged with two counts of uttering threats. While he was initially found unfit to stand trial, he was treated on a compulsory basis and became fit. He was then found not criminal responsible due to mental disorder (NCR-MD), was placed under the jurisdiction of the Ontario Consent and Capacity Review Board, and ordered to a secure mental health facility (Gray & O'Reilly, 2009). Thus began the odyssey of his series of appeals, which ultimately led him to the Supreme Court of Canada.

Throughout the series of legal proceedings, Mr. Starson's advanced intellectual ability was often purported. He was referred to as a physics prodigy (Tyler, 2001b), and was compared to Beethoven, Sir Isaac Newton, and Nobel prize–winning scientist John Nash of *A Beautiful Mind* fame. It was repeatedly suggested that Mr. Starson was accepted as a peer by some of the world's leading physicists (Tibbetts, 2003). Pierre Noyes, former director of the Linear Accelerator Center at Stanford University, described Mr. Starson's thinking as 10 years ahead of its time (Tyler, 2001b). He is quoted as saying, "He had some far-out ideas [including] being in contact with aliens. I'm enough of a believer … that they might be in contact for all I know. It's a long shot, but I'm sure not to rule it out." (as cited in O'Neill & Fischer, 2005). Professor Noyes further stated, "He's certainly brilliant and some of the ideas he has may prove to be correct" (as cited in Tibbetts, 2003). In 1991, Noyes used some of Mr. Starson's ideas in a scientific paper and credited him with co-authorship (Noyes & Starson, 1991). The paper has since been cited four times, three of these citations by Noyes himself.

Others disputed his genius. Friends were reported to be astonished by "the heroic picture of the guy who pestered them," someone whom they described as smart but no genius (O'Neill & Fischer, 2005). Professor emeritus of physics John Moffat of the University of Toronto described Mr. Starson as a nuisance and as "one of the disturbing people with whom he had an unwanted association in the 1980s and 1990s" (as cited in O'Neill & Fischer, 2005). Nobel prize–winning physicist Brian Josephson concluded, after numerous calls over a period of years, that "what [Mr. Starson is] saying doesn't make any sense" (as cited in Tyler, 2001a).

Building on the theme of wronged genius, Kirk Makin (2003) of the *Globe and Mail* stated, "His life reads like a blended plot summary from the films *A Beautiful Mind* and *One Flew Over the Cuckoo's Nest.*" Yet each of the news reports describing his genius in physics includes side mentions of disordered thought, indicative of his mental condition. In an interview with Canadian Press, he spoke compellingly of his research and ideas for inventions from personal nuclear reactors to laser shavers. Then he casually mentioned "Pope Paul works for me now" … and described his wedding plans to Joan Rivers, whom he has never met, and suggested that Pierre Elliott Trudeau was killed by an alien (Bailey, 2003).

Mr. Starson's mother, Jeanne Stevens, had throughout this process attempted to convince the courts that her son, whom she described as a man of great potential who is suffering without medication, required treatment (Makin, 2003; Tyler, 2001b). Ms. Stevens repeatedly told others that she was upset that she has not been permitted to participate in proceedings and indicated that she was "heartsick" and "devasted" over the judgment allowing her son to refuse treatment (Bailey, 2003) and that the ruling was, in essence, a life sentence for her son (Tibbetts, 2003).

> I'm very angry with the Supreme Court. I wish each one of them understood what it was like to have a son like Scott, who is so talented and so brilliant and has so much to offer and then to take his life away, which is what they've just done. Without his medication now, he will have lucid moments, but he will be institutionalized for the rest of his life. (as cited in "Physicist Wins Right," 2003)

> He thinks he's superman. He thinks he is the most brilliant person in the world. I adore my son, the man that is my son. He is truly such a good-natured, gentle, fascinating, beautiful person, but his illness has destroyed me. It's been devastating. (as cited in Tyler, 2001b)

Ms. Stevens indicated that her son's mental health had been steadily deteriorating, and he had been unable to write a paper since 1996 (Tibbetts, 2003).

Supreme Court Decision in *Starson v Swayze*

The issue considered by the Supreme Court of Canada was "whether the Ontario Consent and Capacity Review Board acted unreasonably in finding that Scott Jeffery Schultzman (who prefers to be called "Professor Starson" or simply "Starson") [to be] incapable by reason of mental illness of consenting to treatment under the Health Care Consent Act, 1996" (*Starson v Swayze*, 2003, p. 727). In the case, Mr. Starson compellingly testified,

> I know the effects [of the drugs] and what they want to achieve is to slow down my brain, basically, and slow down my brain means I can't do what I've been trying to do, or what I have been doing for the 30 years and will be successful in doing," said Mr. Schultzman [Starson]. "And that would just be like worse than death." (as cited in Bricker, 2001)

The Supreme Court was split 6–3 on the issue of whether the Consent and Capacity Review Board had properly applied the law. The majority ruling of the court was that the board's decision regarding Mr. Starson's incapacity was unreasonable, and that the board misapplied the statutory test. Specificall , the court determined that the board mistakenly considered Mr. Starson's best interest, rather than his capacity to decide whether or not he wished to take medication for his illness. Mr. Justice Major wrote:

> The enforced injection of mind-altering drugs against the respondent's will is highly offensive to his dignity and autonomy and is to be avoided unless it is demonstrated that he lacked capacity to make his own decision.
>
> As a result of its focus on the respondent's best interests, the Board disregarded clear evidence of his capacity. Professor Starson acknowledged that he suffered from a mental condition and appreciated the purpose of the proposed medication and the possible benefits suggested by doctors. He had tried other treatments in the past to no avail. The evidence did not suggest that enforced treatment was likely to improve his condition. Professor Starson preferred his altered state to what he viewed as the boredom of normalcy. (*Starson v Swayze*, 2003, p. 766)

Of particular note in the case was the strength of the dissenting view, written by Chief Justice McLachlin. In her submission, she indicated that she agreed with the majority decision written by Mr. Justice Major that the "test for capacity requires more than mere intellectual ability" (*Starson v Swayze*, 2003, p. 727). Nevertheless, she concluded that

> The Board had before it ample evidence to support the conclusion the Professor Starson, while he might have been highly intelligent, was unable, because of his delusional state, to understand the information relevant to treatment or to appreciate the benefits of the proposed newer medications; to appreciate the likelihood of deterioration without treatment; and to appreciate his future prospects under the Review Board, absent treatment. The Board's conclusion was firmly anchored in the evidence and cannot be characterized as unreasonable. (p. 750) …
>
> I conclude that the Board applied the law correctly … I would allow the appeal and restore the Board's decision. (p. 753)

Evidence considered with respect to Mr. Starson's ability to understand included the testimony of psychiatrist Paul Posner, who indicated that

Mr. Starson believed that the antipsychotic Haldol was a toxic agent used by psychiatrists to kill people as part of a religion (Amdur, 2003). Madame Justice McLachlin concluded that expert testimony suggested that Mr. Starson could have made an enormous contribution to society but is now lost in a psychotic world. Three years later, Chief Justice McLachlin referred in a speech to the fact that Starson was still hospitalized, noting the cruel paradox that his right to refuse treatment resulted in his loss of liberty as he remained a danger and could not be released.

Mr. Starson's lawyer, Anita Szigeti, heralded the ruling as a victory for the rights of those with serious mental illness stating:

> The significance of this ruling relates to our right to refuse any kind of treatment. It involves safeguarding the rights of capable individuals to refuse all kinds of intervention, even when they appear to be in our best interest ... The ruling will ensure that the kind of paternalistic approach which has been rampant toward people with mental health problems is going to have to stop. (as cited in Makin, 2003)

Former member of the Ontario Criminal Code Review Board and professor emeritus of law Ian Hunter countered that the decision reflected "rights-mad Canada where the blind regularly lead the blind and inmates rule the madhouse" (as cited in Hunter, 2003). Mental health professionals concurred. In an article in the *National Post*, Dr. Richard O'Reilly (2004), professor of psychiatry at the University of Western Ontario (now Western University) questioned "How can a civilized society confine an individual because of the symptoms of his illness and the throw away the only key to his freedom – treatment with anti-psychotic medication?" In an op-ed in the *Waterloo Record*, Quebec social worker Reuel Amdur (2003) suggested that everyone loses:

> As a result of this unfortunate decision, everyone loses except the lawyers. Schutzman-Starson loses any chance of improvement. Doctors, their hands tied by such decisions and forced to spend hours and days trying to get treatment for unwilling patients in the face of overwhelming obstacles, are apt to forgo the battle and simply abide by the mad wishes of such "competent" patients ... Scarce medical resources are squandered in endless legal wrangling. And then there is the loss to the patient, in the case under discussion, a once brilliant man in the field of physics.

At the time of the Supreme Court case, Mr. Starson was a patient in the secure forensic unit at the Royal Ottawa Hospital (ROH). Following the ruling, his case returned to the Ontario Criminal Code Review

Board for disposition. As predicted by Dr. John Bradford, clinical director of forensic psychiatry at the ROH, he was not released into the community owing to his untreated mental illness and his lengthy record of uttering death threats, but was rather returned to secure custody.

Postscript on *Starson v Swayze*

Two years after the Supreme Court ruling in *Starson v Swayze*, the *Ottawa Citizen* carried a story indicating that the Ontario Consent and Capacity Review Board had ordered treatment for Mr. Starson on the consent of his mother. He had refused all hospital food and fluids for a period of months in response to auditory hallucinations that convinced him that the hospital was trying to poison him. His weight had dropped to 118 pounds, a mere shadow of his former bulky 6'1" self. He lacked the physical strength to walk short distances. One reporter noted that "His dazzling model looks are gone. A front tooth recently fell out and seven others are in dire straits. His complexion is sallow. His clothes hang loosely on his bony frame" (O'Neill & Fischer, 2005). His younger brother Brad had severed ties with him. Friends had stopped taking calls and changed their phone numbers. At his 2007 annual review by the board, it was noted that Mr. Starson had significantly improved since beginning medication two years earlier and he was discharged to the community. Over the next two years, he had periods of decompensation and re-hospitalization and then returned to the community following treatment (Gray & O'Reilly, 2009).

In 2013, the following appeared in an article in the *National Post*:

> In his first interview since being conditionally discharged from the criminal justice system, 15 years after being found not criminally responsible for death threats, the man whose Supreme Court case established the legal right to refuse medication said he is healthy and happy, "fantastic, plus, plus, plus, and other superlatives."
>
> Professor Starson says he is 17 billion years old, immortal, engaged to Joan Rivers, and about to publish ground breaking physics research about the speed of light, the mass of the Earth, and the temperature of the universe, which he worked out in his apartment in northwest Toronto.
>
> He is taking anti-psychotic drugs – this is effectively the condition of his discharge – but the grandiose delusions remain, symptomatic of a lifelong mental illness that has been variously diagnosed as bipolar or schizo-affective disorder. And as the Ontario Court of Appeal has held in

a new ruling, he continues to post a "significant threat to the safety of the public," due to his "extremely intimidating behaviour." (Brean, 2013)

The article further stated that Mr. Starson requested an absolute discharge from the Court of Appeal, but instead, it upheld a summer 2013 decision of the Ontario Criminal Code Review Board that required weekly meetings at the Centre for Addiction and Mental Health. The article noted that the board's chair had concerns about the continuing implications of the Supreme Court ruling.

> Michael Bay, who chaired Ontario's Consent and Capacity Board when it decided Starson was incapable of consenting to treatment, said the Starson case did not change the law, but rather reflected a cultural shift. Where once a doctor's judgment was seen as paramount, even to the point of infallibility, Starson's case heralded the rise of patient autonomy ... Once there were plenty of beds available, and too many people were being held and treated against their will. Now there are not enough beds, and families struggle to get their loved ones treated, Mr. Bay said. (Brean, 2013)

As of 2018, Mr. Starson's LinkedIn page identified his current position as "CEO, Director & President of the UNIVERSE and EARTH."

Context

The case of *Starson v Swayze* occurred at a time of societal tension between those who believed that an individual's right to determine whether or not they will accept treatment was paramount and those who sought to ensure that individuals in the midst of a mental health crisis were not abandoned by society. Strong opinions were expressed and continue to be expressed on both sides of the issue.

One nexus of tension was between those who had been directly affected by mental health struggles, both individuals and their families, and the mental health system. The psychiatric survivors' movement had gained momentum and secured the right for those affected by mental illness to participate in hospital governance decisions and public policy development (Reville & Church, 2012). Survivor groups focused on abuses they endured as a result of involuntary admission and involuntary treatment (including electronconvulsive therapy and use of medications) (Capponi, 1992) and argued for their abolition. Politician and psychiatric survivor David Reville worked with survivor-advocate Pat Capponi and others to build grassroots movements to highlight the plight of those who found themselves in the psychiatric system and to fight for their right to choose independently whether or not they would be hospitalized and treated (Reville & Church, 2012).

Others, such as Hershel Hardin (1993), a member of the Vancouver Civil Liberties Association and a parent of a person with schizophrenia, contended that civil liberties are not respected when people are denied involuntary treatment and left as prisoners of their illnesses. He fought for the right of families to ensure that their ill loved ones received treatment. Indeed, the Schizophrenia Society of Canada, a family-based support organization, along with the Centre for Addiction and Mental Health, was an intervener in the case of *Starson v Swayze,*. Hardin (1993) stated:

> Anti-treatment advocates seem content to sacrifice a few lives here and there to uphold an abstract doctrine. Their intent, if noble, has a chilly, Stalinist justification – the odd tragedy along the way is warranted to ensure the greater good … How can so much degradation and death – so much inhumanity be justified in the name of civil liberties?

More recently, Erin Hawkes wrote in an editorial about her struggle with schizophrenia and her experience with involuntary admission. She described the auditory hallucinations telling her to die and her delusions that she must commit suicide to fulfil a deep purpose. She concluded, "being involuntarily hospitalized and medicated against my will saved me from my suicidal self" (as cited in Hawkes, 2012).

A second nexus of tension was, and continues to be, between civil rights lawyers and the mental health professionals, particularly on the question of what constitutes the best interest of a patient (Sklar, 2007). In *Starson v Swayze*, mental health professionals were frequently referred to as "paternalistic." Legal counsels who did not take a rights advocacy position were similarly open to critique. In a keynote address published in the *Windsor Review of Legal and Social Issues*, A.A. Dhir (2008) stated:

> from my own experience and from anecdotal evidence, patients' counsel can sometimes substitute engaged lawyering with paternalism and can fall into the trap of conflating the presence of mental disability with incapacity. With clinicians and adjudicators exhibiting the same tendency, we are left with the possibility of a sort of nightmare state where antiquated, sanist notions are left untested by rigorous advocacy. (p. 109)

These tensions were clearly played out in the many years of appeals, review boards, and ultimately the Supreme Court decision in *Starson v*

Swayze. They are also played out in the continuously evolving nature of health care consent legislation.

Healthcare Consent Legislation

In *Starson v Swayze*, the Supreme Court was expressly interpreting Ontario provincial legislation on consent and capacity. Nevertheless, for the Supreme Court of Canada to agree to hear a case, it must be persuaded that the case is of national importance (Szigeti, 2019). Every province now has consent legislation that makes it clear that a health care professional cannot administer treatment to an individual without valid consent (see table 10.1), although British Columbia does provide for capable persons who are hospitalized to be treated without consent. Nevertheless, this provision may not survive a challenge following *Starson* (Szigeti, 2019). As one example, the Consent to Treatment and Health Care Directives Act (1988) of Prince Edward Island states:

> Every patient who is capable of giving or refusing consent to treatment has the right
> (a) to give consent or to refuse consent on any grounds, including moral or religious grounds, even if the refusal will result in death;
> (b) to select a particular form of treatment from among those proposed by a health practitioner on any grounds, including moral or religious grounds;
> (c) to be assisted by an associate; and
> (d) to be involved to the greatest degree practicable in case planning and decision-making. (c. 10, s. 4)

The Ontario Health Care Consent Act, 1996, specifically referenced in the Supreme Court ruling, "aims to provide a complete codification of the common law requirements for obtaining informed consent" and the principles for assessing competency (Hiltz & Szigeti, 2005, (p. 163). In order to have the capacity to consent, an individual must be able to understand and appreciate the information that is relevant to the decision that must be made (Regehr, Kanani, McFadden, & Saini, 2015). The act states that a person is capable of consenting to treatment if

1. the person is able to understand the information that is relevant to making a decision about the treatment; and
2. able to appreciate the reasonably foreseeable consequences of a decision or lack of decision. (s. 4(1))

Table 10.1   Provincial health care consent legislation

Alberta	• Adult Guardianship and Trusteeship Act, SA 2008, c. A-4.2 • Personal Directives Act, RSA 2000, c. P-6 • Mental Health Act, RSA 2000, c. M-13
British Columbia	• Adult Guardianship Act, RSBC 1996, c. 6 • The Health Care (Consent) and Care Facility (Admission) Act, RSBC 1996, c. 181 • Representation Agreement Act, RSBC 1996, c. 405 • Mental Health Act, RSBC 1996, c. 288
Manitoba	• Health Care Directives Act, CCSM c. H27 • Vulnerable Persons Living with a Mental Disability Act, CCSM c. V90 • The Public Health Act, CCSM c P210 • Mental Health Act, CCSM c. M110
New Brunswick	• Infirm Persons Act, R.S.N.B. 2000, c. I-8 • Medical Consent of Minors Act, SNB 1976, c M-6.1 • Advance Health Care Directives Act, RSN. 2016, c. 46 • Mental Health Act, RSNB 1973, c. M-10
Newfoundland and Labrador	• Advance Health Care Directives Act, SNL 1995, c. A-4.1 • Mental Health Care and Treatment Act, SNL 2006, c. M-9.1 • Mental Health Act, RSNL 1990, c. M-9
Northwest Territories	• Personal Directives Act, SNWT 2005, c. 16 • Guardianship and Trusteeship Act, SNWT 1994, c. 29 • Mental Health Act, RSNWT 1988, c. M-10
Nova Scotia	• An Act Respecting Representative Decision-making, SNS 2017, c. 4 • Hospitals Act, RSNS 1989, c. 208 • Involuntary Psychiatric Treatment Act, SNS 2005, c. 42 • Medical Consent Act, RSNS 1989, c. 279 • Personal Directives Act, SNS.2008, c. 8
Nunavut	• Guardianship and Trusteeship Act, SNWT (Nu) 1994, c. 29 • Mental Health Act, RSNWT (Nu) 1988, c. M-10
Ontario	• Health Care Consent Act, 1996, SO 1996, c. 2, Sch A • Mental Health Act, RSO 1990, c. M.7
Prince Edward Island	• Consent to Treatment and Health Care Directives Act, RSPEI 1988, c. C-17.2 • Mental Health Act, RSPEI 1988, c. M-6.1 • Adult Protection Act, RSPEI 1988, c. A-5
Quebec	• Civil Code of Quebec, CQLR c. CCQ-1991 • Public Curator Act, CQLR c. C-81 • Act respecting health services and social services, CQLR c. S-4.2 • Act respecting end-of-life care, RSQ c. S-32.0001
Saskatchewan	• The Health Care Directives and Substitute Health Care Decision Makers Act, 2015, SS 2015, c. H-0.002
Yukon	• Health Act, SY 1989–90 • Care Consent Act, SY 2003 c. 21, Sch. B • Decision-Making Support and Protection to Adults Act, SY 2003, c. 21 • Mental Health Act, RSY 2002, c. 150

A person is not capable of consenting if they fail either test component: ability to understand or ability to appreciate the consequences. The act carries a presumption of capacity unless there are reasonable grounds to believe that the person is incapable. It is clear that refusal to accept treatment is not incapacity; neither is the refusal to engage in discussion regarding the proposed treatment.

Capacity is decision-specific; it relates to a specific treatment proposed at a specific time under specific circumstances. A person may be capable of consenting to some treatments but incapable of consenting to others. For example, a person may be capable of consenting to a procedure such as blood work but not to cardiac surgery. In addition, consent is fluid. A person may also be capable of consenting to a particular treatment at one time but not capable of consenting to the same treatment at another time.

Once consent is provided, it can be withdrawn. As stated in a decision of the Supreme Court of Canada: "an individual's right to determine what medical procedures will be accepted must include the right to stop the procedure" (*Ciarlariello v Schacter*, 1993, at para 43). If consent has been withdrawn, medical staff are obligated to stop the procedure, although they must ensure that they do so at a stage where the patient's safety is not in jeopardy. Any treatment provided without consent may result in criminal charges of assault or civil actions of negligence or battery (the unlawful application of force to another person) (Morris, Ferguson, & Dykeman, 1999; Rozovsky, 2003). No intent to harm is necessary for a finding of battery; the lack of consent to the named intervention will be sufficient to establish the liability of the practitioner.

If a health care practitioner determines that an individual is not capable of providing consent to treatment, this must be communicated to the patient. In the case of psychiatric patients in Ontario, this must be in done by providing the required form under the Ontario Health Care Consent Act, and a rights adviser must be notified. The rights adviser will ensure that the patient is aware that they may appeal to the Consent and Capacity Review Board for a review and will provide assistance in obtaining legal counsel (Hiltz & Szigeti, 2005).

Where a patient is not capable of consenting, or refusing consent, to treatment, a substitute decision-maker must be identified to make decisions on the incapable patient's behalf. The process for obtaining a substitute decision-maker and for determining who is legally able to act as a substitute decision-maker is defined by legislation in most provinces and territories. For instance, the Health Care (Consent) and Care Facility (Admission) Act of British Columbia sets out a list of substitute decision-makers, and health care providers must select the first one who qualifies. The Ontario Health Care Consent Act outlines a hierarchical list of those who may act as substitute decision-makers: a statutory or court-ordered guardian ranks the highest, followed by a power of attorney for personal care, and a representative appointed by the Consent and Capacity Board to make health care decisions.

Implications for Forensic Mental Health Practice

Informed consent to treatment is founded on the principle that individuals have the right to make their own health decisions. In most cases, the role of the health care professional is to provide appropriate information and advice. The patient can choose to accept the advice, and ultimately the treatment recommended, or refuse it. For the forensic mental health professional, additional aspects of consent include determining the capacity to consent and preparing to address issues of consent before consent and capacity review boards and the courts. The Canadian Psychiatric Association position paper makes the following statements regarding the ethical imperative for informed consent (Neilson & Chaimowitz, 2015):

- Practitioners must be thoroughly familiar with the elements of consent and the legal and procedural aspects of consent
- Informed consent is reliant on the sharing of information
- Autonomous decisions of capable patients, including the right to accept or reject treatment, must be respected
- Treatment wishes of incapable patients, as they were expressed before the patient became incapable, should be ascertained
- In some circumstances, respect for autonomy may need to be balanced with ethical obligations of beneficence, non-malevolence, and serving justice

In order for the patient to be properly informed, information must be made available regarding all the relevant risks and benefits of treatment, as well as the risks of having no treatment. Clearly, in any treatment decision, there is a vast array of possible outcomes, some highly unlikely; disclosure of each and every one could result in information overload and impair the patient's ability to make a decision. In *Reibl v Hughes* (1980), the Supreme Court of Canada stated that practitioners have a duty to disclose "all material risks." In addition, the legislation in some jurisdictions defines specific information required to be disclosed, including the nature of the treatment, the expected benefits, the material risks, the material side effects, alternative courses of action, and the likely consequences of not having the treatment.

However, in some situations, an individual may be harmed by receiving the full scope and depth of disclosure as outlined above. In *Reibl v Hughes* (1980), Chief Justice Laskin of the Supreme Court stated:

> It may be the case that a particular patient may, because of emotional factors, be unable to cope with facts relevant to recommended surgery or treatment and the doctor may, in such a case, be justified in withholding or generalizing information as to which he would otherwise be required to be more specific. (p. 13)

Therefore, if a health care provider believes the person's mental health would be compromised or emotional state would be significantly affected, the professional may limit the information provided to the patient. Dickens (2002) cautioned, however, that this does not imply that the obligation to provide information is erased. Health care professionals may need to consider alternative means to ensure that information is conveyed to the patient in a manner that is less distressing.

Neilson and Chaimowitz (2015), building on the work of Roznovsky (2003), discuss the provision of information that is useful for a patient to consider in making a decision. When describing the recommended treatment, specific information should be included as to the nature of the treatment, the mode of delivery, who will be performing the treatment, and the frequency and length of treatment. Next, patients should be informed of the evidence supporting, or not supporting, the treatment and any reasonable alternatives that may exist. It is important to note possible impacts on the patient's lifestyle, such as sexual dysfunction, contraindications for driving, and any cost considerations. Finally, the person should be informed of the consequences of refusing treatment. However, even if the consequences of refusal are dire in the view of the health care professional, *Starson v Swayze* has clearly established that this view does not impact a determination of capacity.

In order to satisfy the requirement of voluntariness, an individual's decision to consent or refuse consent must be free of coercion or undue influence. Such influence is generally considered to include financial incentives, unnecessary fear, or influence created by the therapeutic alliance between the patient and the health care provider (Regehr & Antle, 1997). In forensic mental health practice, other factors also limit the voluntary nature of consent, as was evidenced in *Starson v Swayze*, in which treatment refusal resulted in Mr. Starson's continued confinement in a secure mental health facility owing to the concern that his illness contributed to his being dangerous to others.

The Canadian Medical Protective Association (CMPA) (2018) advises that in all cases it is important to for practitioners to take notes about discussions regarding consent. The notes should contain major risks discussed, minor but important risks mentioned, any questions that the patient asked, answers given, the patient's apparent understanding of information provided, and any handout materials provided. The CMPA further advises that while a consent form is not in and of itself consent, it can be a useful addition to the dialogue with the patient.

Determining Capacity to Consent

Formal capacity assessments are completed by specially trained professionals who may include psychologists, psychiatrists, or social workers. The components of capacity to consent are comprehension, free choice, and reliability (Sorrentino, 2014). The first element, comprehension, refers to the patient's factual understanding of their condition, including the nature and expected course of the illness and the risks and benefits of treatment. The patient should also be able to demonstrate coherent and logical thought processes and the ability to manipulate information. Free choice can be limited by a number of external factors as discussed above, but from the perspective of capacity assessment, it may also be limited by unrealistic fears or expectations about treatment or by other impaired mental processes. Reliability refers to the consistency of the patient's choice over time (Sorrentino, 2014). The Mini-Mental State Examination has not been found to discriminate capacity status well, although it does correlate with clinical views of capacity at the high and low end of the scale (Kim & Caine, 2002). However, the MacArthur Competence Tool for Treatment (Mac-CAT-T) (Appelbaum & Grisso, 1995; Grisso & Appelbaum, 1995) can be used in combination with clinical interviews to produce highly reliable judgments (Cairns et al., 2005). Once capacity to consent has been determined, the action steps are outlined in figure 10.1.

Presenting to a Consent and Capacity Review Board

Health practice lawyer Karen Frelick (2003) notes that while consent and capacity review boards were intended to be navigated primarily by lay persons, the courts are approaching them in a legalistic manner and are adopting a standard of correctness in interpreting the law. She advises that the court decision in *Starson v Swayze* highlights the need for clear and cogent evidence when challenging the presumption of capacity of an individual before the Consent and Capacity Review

Figure 10.1 Action steps in consent

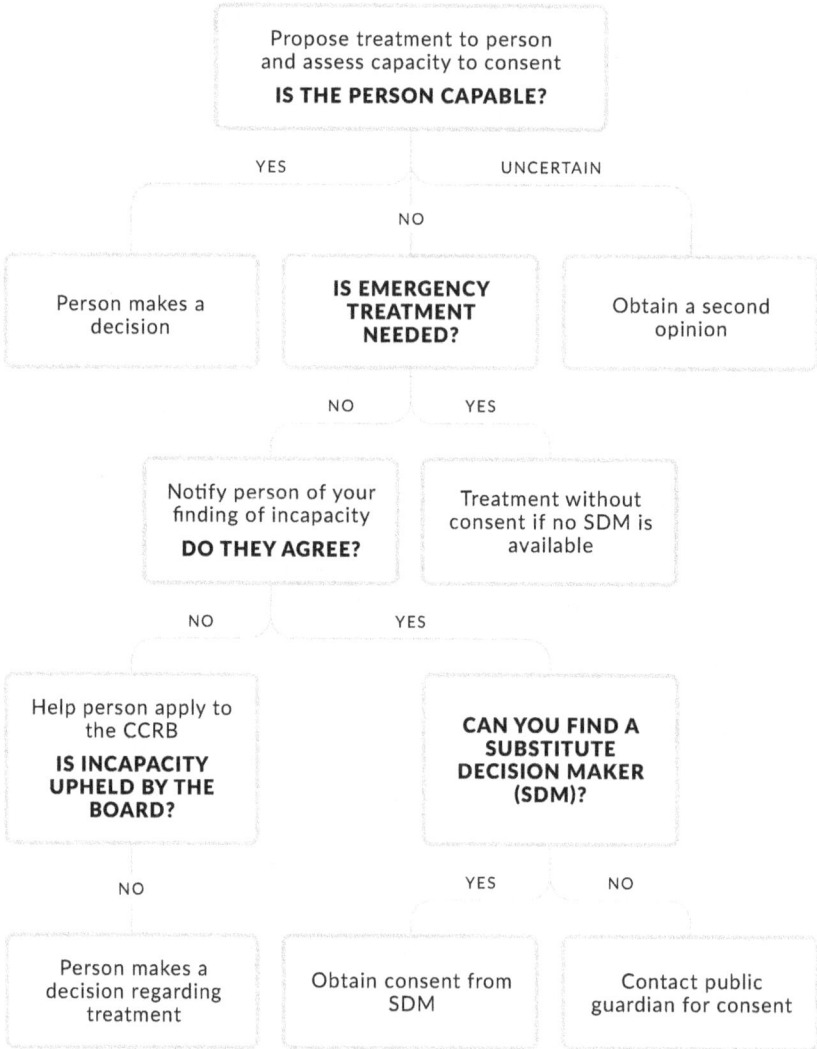

Propose treatment to person
and assess capacity to consent
IS THE PERSON CAPABLE?

YES   UNCERTAIN

NO

Person makes a
decision

**IS EMERGENCY
TREATMENT
NEEDED?**

Obtain a second
opinion

NO   YES

Notify person of your
finding of incapacity
DO THEY AGREE?

Treatment without
consent if no SDM is
available

NO   YES

Help person apply to
the CCRB
**IS INCAPACITY
UPHELD BY THE
BOARD?**

**CAN YOU FIND A
SUBSTITUTE
DECISION MAKER
(SDM)?**

NO   YES   NO

Person makes a
decision regarding
treatment

Obtain consent from
SDM

Contact public
guardian for consent

Source: Tremblay et al. (2007)

Table 10.2   Key points regarding consent to treatment

Starson v Swayze (2003)

Capacity to consent	• Patient must be able to understand the information relevant to making a decision regarding treatment • Patient must be able to appreciate the reasonably forseeable consequences of the decision whether to accept or not accept treatment
Understanding	• Patient may be fully aware of the manifestations of the illness even if they do yet not accept the diagnosis
Appreciating	• Capacity is not influenced by whether the patient's decision regarding treatment is not viewed by others to be in the patient's best interest

Consent and capacity legislation

	• Each province and territory has legislation that establishes that health care professionals cannot administer treatment without valid consent

Ontario Health Care Consent Act

Presumption of capacity	• A person is presumed to be capable of consenting or refusing treatment unless they fail to either understand or appreciate the nature and consequences of the illness, treatment, or lack of treatment
Incapable of consenting	• The patient is advised • Substitute decision-maker can make decisions • The patient can appeal to the Consent and Capacity Review Board and the courts

Implications for practice

Autonomy	• Respect for the autonomy of capable individuals to make decisions about their own health care
Elements of consent	• A person must have the capacity to consent • Consent must be informed; information provided about the risks and benefits of treatment or no treatment • Consent must be voluntary and free from overt or implied consequences for non-consent
Determining the capacity to consent	• Comprehension of risks and benefits • Free choice is not limited by unrealistic fears or expectations • Reliability and consistency of patient's choice over time
Presenting at Consent and Capacity Review Board	• Clear and cogent evidence when challenging the presumption of capacity • Caution in using statements that may be interpreted as paternalistic

---

Board. If the ruling of the board is challenged through judicial review, the court in most cases will be restricted to analysing the evidence that formed the board's record of proceedings. All supporting documents, such as clinical notes and medical records, therefore, need to be marked as evidence to ensure they can be considered in the review. Frelick further advises that mental health professionals should use caution in expressing concern or what might be interpreted as paternalistic statements, as these may undermine the argument.

Summary

In order to have the capacity to consent, people must be able to understand information that is provided to them and how that information applies to their specific situation. Controversy arises however over the concept of "understanding," an issue addressed by the Supreme Court of Canada in *Starson v Swayze* (2003). Scott Starson (born Scott Schutzman) challenged an Ontario Consent and Capacity Review Board decision, which ruled that he was incapable of refusing mental health treatment. Starson had been found not criminally responsible due to mental disorder of criminal charges related to uttering threats, and as a result, he was ordered to be confined at the Centre for Addiction and Mental Health. He did not believe that he suffered from bipolar affective disorder, despite repeated hospitalizations in Canada and the United States over an 18-year period. As a result, he refused all treatment while confined to hospital. The Supreme Court decision was split, but it nevertheless concluded that while Starson's decision may not have been rational, "unwise choices are permitted" under the law and people have the right to "act unreasonably."

The case of *Starson* highlights a particular challenge whereby individuals may have the right to refuse medication but, by virtue of the danger they present as a result of their illness, do not have the right to leave hospital and return to the community. Gutheil (1980) referred to this situation decades ago as "rotting with your rights on." Kress (2006), in exploring this issue, identifies that there is a group of patients who do not become treatment compliant until they are "substantially healthier than being barely not mentally ill or barely not dangerous" (p. 573). He similarly underscores the problem of restricting liberty through civil commitment while not compelling treatment.

For forensic mental health practitioners, three issues are critical for practice: understanding the legal and ethical parameters of informed consent, possessing the ability to perform capacity assessments, and possessing knowledge and skill regarding presenting data for a consent and capacity hearing.

Athey v Leonati

Jon Athey, a 43-year-old auto body mechanic and body shop manager for a Budget car rental location, suffered a series of unfortunate events in the year of 1991. In February of 1991, he was involved in a motor vehicle accident in which his vehicle was demolished as the result of both front- and rear-end collisions. He was duly taken to the hospital, where he was examined and then discharged. He participated in physiotherapy and chiropractic treatments, and was apparently on the way to recovery. In April of the same year, a semi-trailer truck crossed into his lane of traffic and hit his vehicle head-on. He did not lose consciousness and was able to walk away from the wrecked vehicle, apparently not severely injured. He continued to work full-time but did not perform any duties involving heavy labour (*Athey v Leonati*, 1996).

Mr. Athey had a history of minor back problems prior to 1991. Following the accidents, he attended physiotherapy and chiropractic treatments, and his condition gradually improved. On the suggestion of his physician, he began to resume his regular exercise regime at a local health club. One day, as he was stretching during his warm-up, he felt a "pop" in his back and immediately experienced a great deal of pain. He hobbled to the showers, was able to get dressed, and returned home. However, by the next morning, he was unable to move and was, therefore, transported to hospital, where he remained for three weeks. Mr. Athey was diagnosed as suffering from a herniated disc, and after a period of observation, it was decided that he required surgery. The outcome of the resulting surgery was described by his physician as "good, but not excellent" (*Athey v Leonati*, 1996). Upon discharge from the hospital, Mr. Athey obtained a manager position at another company where he would not have to perform heavy labour; however, his compensation was lower than what he earned at his previous employment.

Mr. Athey commenced legal action to obtain compensation for the damages he suffered as a result of the accidents. While this action involved two separate events, the complications in the case were reduced by the fact that both of the drivers who had crashed into Mr. Athey were represented by the same legal counsel and both the drivers conceded fault. Consequently, the case proceeded as though the two accidents were one (Klimchuk & Black, 1997). The trial judge noted that, although the drivers conceded that they were at fault for the accidents, they denied liability, arguing that the disc herniation was unrelated to the car accidents.

In considering the evidence, the trial judge ruled that the disc herniation was not the direct result of the injuries suffered in the two motor vehicle accidents but rather concluded that the motor vehicle accidents played a minor causative role. This minor role was considered to be 25 per cent of the total injury, attributing the other 75 per cent of the injury to be presumably caused by pre-existing back problems and the health club incident. Mr. Athey was awarded one-quarter of the damages, the total of which was assessed at $221,000. He appealed to the British Columbia Court of Appeal, which dismissed the appeal, and thus he further appealed to the Supreme Court of Canada. There was some surprise that Mr. Athey was granted leave to appeal to the Supreme Court, given that its role by statute is not to ensure justice in individual disputes, but rather to deal with errors committed in the justice system and with matters of national importance (McInnes, 1996).

Supreme Court Decision in *Athey v Leonati*

The key issue for the Supreme Court was whether the court had erred in its apportioning of the liability. That is, the trial judge ruled that although the accidents were not the sole cause of the disc herniation, they played a causal role and thus awarded 25 per cent of the total damages assessed. The Supreme Court determined in this case that:

> A defendant is liable for any injuries caused or contributed to by his or her negligence. The presence of other non-tortious causes does not reduce the extent of that liability. Loss cannot be apportioned according to the degree of causation where it is created by tortious and non-tortious causes. (*Athey v Leonati*, 1996, p. 459)

Tortious acts are wrongful acts causing physical, emotional, or financial harms to others. Torts take two forms: intentional and unintentional. Intentional torts are deliberate acts to injure another person such as assault, harassment, battery, and defamation, or deliberate acts that infringe on another person's rights such as false imprisonment, trespass, and fraud. Unintentional (or negligence) torts arise from failing to protect the safety of another person (Klar, 1991, 2013). Causes of injury or harm that do not arise from the wrongs committed by others are referred to as non-tortious. Tort law is a means of compensating individuals who have suffered damages as a result of the actions of others. Damages awarded by the courts in tort cases are restitutionary in nature, designed to place the victim in the position they would have been in should the tort not have occurred (Regehr, Kanani, McFadden, & Saini, 2015). The role of the courts is to determine causality and assess damages.

In the case of *Athey v Leonati*, the Supreme Court ruled that the general test of causation is the *but for* test. In this test, the plaintiff must show that the injury would not have occurred *but for* the negligence or tortious act of the defendant. In a judgment written by Mr. Justice Major, the court stated that where this test is unworkable, causation may be established where the defendant *materially contributed* to the injury. He explained that the law does not excuse a defendant from liability merely because "other causal factors which he or she is not responsible also help produce the harm" (*Athey v Leonati*, 1996, p. 459). As such, the court held that causation can be proven if the defendant's negligence was "a cause of the harm" (p. 459) (note the use of the words "a cause" not "the cause").

Mr. Justice Major maintained that apportionment between tortious and non-tortious causes is contrary to the principles of tort law in that the defendant should accept liability for *any* injury that they caused or to which they contributed. Rather confusingly, the court held that "separation of distinct divisible injuries is not truly apportionment; it is simply making each defendant liable only for the injury he or she has caused" (*Athey v Leonati*, 1996, p. 460). Apparently, separation is permitted where some of the injuries have tortious causes, and some have non-tortious causes. The court went on to say that the disc herniation was a "single indivisible injury," so "division was neither possible, nor appropriate." As such, the defendant is liable if the plaintiff can prove that the injuries caused or contributed to the disc herniation. In this regard, warming up at the gym was not a cause, but rather the effect, and as such "it was the injury" (p. 460).

There had been no suggestion of negligence on the part of Mr. Athey in contributing to his own injury.

The court determined that this appeal involves a straightforward application of the *thin skull rule* (described in greater detail below). In other words, even though Mr. Athey may have had a pre-existing disposition, the defendant must take the plaintiff as he finds him. In this case, the defendant's negligence exacerbated the existing condition, which manifested itself in a disc herniation. Therefore, the defendant is the cause of the disc herniation, and the defendant is fully liable for the full amount of damages.

Determining Causation

In order to establish causation, the plaintiff must prove that the defendant caused or contributed to the injury on a balance of probabilities, which is the civil standard. Generally speaking, the test for causation is the *but for* test. That is, the injury or loss would not have occurred *but for* the negligence or tortious act of the defendant. In some cases, this test does not easily flow from the facts, and thus courts in the United Kingdom have recognized that causation can be established when the defendant's negligence *materially contributed* to the occurrence of the injury (*Bonnington Castings Ltd v Wardlaw*, 1956; *McGhee v National Coal Board*, 1973). In order to establish that a factor has had a material contribution, it must be judged to be above the *de minimus* (minor or trivial) range.

In the British case of *McGhee v National Coal Board*, the plaintiff's employment involved emptying kilns in a brickyard. At the end of the work day, he would cycle home covered in dust and shower upon arrival. One day, he was required to empty a kiln that was apparently dustier and hotter than was customary, and subsequently, he developed dermatitis. It was determined that, because of the heat, he sweated more than usual and was, therefore, more vulnerable to irritation by a greater volume of dust than to which he was usually exposed. The court found that the National Coal Board was negligent in failing to provide showers, which would have reduced the time that his skin was exposed to the dust, decreasing the risk of dermatitis. It could not be proven scientifically that the provision of showers would have prevented the dermatitis. However, the possibility that he had not contracted dermatitis as a result of his exposure could not be ruled out. Consequently, the House of Lords held that if the defendant's action or omission materially contributed to the risk that Mr. McGee would develop dermatitis, then they were the cause in fact. "From a broad and practical viewpoint, I can see no substantial difference between saying that what the defendants did materially increased the risk of injury to the pursuer and saying what the defendant did made a material contribution to his injury" (as cited in Reid, Wilberforce, of Glaisdale, Kilbrandon, & Salmon, 1973, p. 475).

Relying on the decision of the House of Lords in *McGhee v National Coal Board*, the Supreme Court of Canada ruled in the case of *Snell v Farrell* (1990) that, while the plaintiff must prove that the tortious conduct caused or contributed to the injury, in terms of the evidentiary burden, a party's failure to corroborate or refute evidence allows the court to draw an inference as to the facts. In this case of alleged medical malpractice, the plaintiff lost vision in one eye following cataract surgery. The plaintiff, Ms. Snell, commenced legal action against her ophthalmologist, seeking compensation for her injury. Expert witnesses who reviewed the medical evidence regarding the surgery were unable to state with certainty the cause of the injury. In light of the fact that a definitive cause could not be established, the court defined that the test for causation is essentially a practical question of fact, one which can best be answered by ordinary common sense, and, therefore, it "need not be determined by scientific precision" (at para 30). It may be acknowledged that there are a number of background events that were necessary or were a cause of the injury, but the plaintiff does not have to establish that the negligence or tortious act was the sole cause of the injury. Indeed, the court ruled that there is no basis for reduction of liability because of the existence of other preconditions; as long as the defendant contributed by their negligence, they are liable.

Mr. Justice Major, writing in *Athey v Leonati* (1996), noted that most events are a result of a complex set of factors and, therefore, there will be a variety of causes contributing to any injury or disability. As such, plaintiffs would rarely receive full compensation even after proving the defendant caused the injury. He believed that such an outcome is contrary to the position entrenched in law and stated that there is no reason to depart from this. He noted that, even though it was argued that there was justification for apportionment between tortious and non-tortious causes, this could not be allowed because the plaintiff would not have been placed in the present position but for the negligence of the defendants. Therefore, the apportionment between tortious and non-tortious causes is contrary to the principles of tort law. Apportionment can only be allowed if there is more than one defendant who has been proven to have committed a tortious act. An example of this is an Australian case cited by McInnes (1996). In this case, Mr. Chapman drove negligently, which resulted in his being thrown from the car and rendered unconscious. Dr. Cherry stopped at the scene to help him, but while doing so, was struck by a car negligently driven by Mr. Hearse. Dr. Cherry was killed while acting as a Good Samaritan. Both parties, Chapman and Hearse, were found to have been negligent in their driving and were held partially responsible. In such a case, the plaintiff may recover damages from either defendant or from both (McInnes, 1996).

Damages

The crucial issue in *Athey v Leonati* was the argument that, given that Mr. Athey had previous back problems, he was predisposed to disc herniation, and he, therefore, had a *crumbling skull* (described below). If this was determined to be the case, "the defendant need not put the plaintiff in a position better than his or her original position" (p. 472) and damages awarded could be reduced. However, the Supreme Court did not make a finding of any measurable risk that the disc herniation would have occurred without the accident, and there was, therefore, no basis to reduce the award to Mr. Athey using a crumbling skull argument.

The Crumbling Skull and the Thin Skull

The *thin skull* rule applies to the metaphorical situation wherein a person who has a particularly thin skull, but is otherwise functioning normally, receives a hit to the head, which would have little effect on a normal person, but shatters the skull of this particular person. The construct arose from a 1901 case of the UK High Court King's Bench, in which a pregnant woman working in her husband's pub was hit by a horse and cart that crashed through the building. She developed nervous shock, and nine days later, gave birth prematurely to a child with developmental problems. In awarding damages, the judge concluded:

> If a man is negligently run over or otherwise negligently injured in his body, it is no answer to the sufferer's claim for damages that he would have suffered less injury, or no injury at all, if he had not had an unusually thin skull or an unusually weak heart. (*Dulieu v White and Sons*, 1901, p. 679)

Thus, the person who inflicted the injury is fully liable for the unexpectedly serious consequences of their actions. In other words, they have to take their victim as they find them. In *Athey v Leonati*, it so happened that Jon Athey had a particularly weak spinal column; thus, when he was hit by the defendants, he suffered unexpectedly serious consequences. The defendants, therefore, had to take Mr. Athey as they found him, weak spinal column and all.

In the case of a *crumbling skull*, the plaintiff has a condition that predates the negligence or act. Again, as in the thin skull, the defendant is liable for any injuries caused by their wrongdoing. However, the defendant need not compensate the plaintiff for any debilitating effects of the pre-existing condition that they would have experienced anyway. That is, if it is likely that this pre-existing condition would have deteriorated to such an extent that the plaintiff would be experiencing the same symptoms or lack of function, even without a defendant's negligence, then this can be considered in reducing the overall award.

A Supreme Court of British Columbia ruling differentiated between the thin skull – in which an individual is in a stable condition before the accident, and presumably, were it not for the accident, would remain so – and an individual with a crumbling skull (*Shaw v Clark*, 1986). In the concept of the crumbling skull, the hypothetical person, whether having a thin skull or thick skull, is not stable before the accident, but rather has an ongoing condition or predisposition that results in deterioration, and the accident accelerates the process of that deterioration. The defendant then, as determined in a ruling of the Ontario Court of Appeal, is only liable to restore the plaintiff to the state or condition related to the negligence, that is, where the individual would have been had it not been for the hit on the head (*Graham v Rourke*, 1990). This then represents a future-looking exercise, taking into account the prognosis of the victim's condition or illness, and the task is to predict their probable disability. It suggests that individuals are responsible for meeting the exigencies of their own lives (McInnes, 1996). In *Athey v Leonati* (1996), the Supreme Court clearly made the point that the defendant need not compensate the plaintiff for any debilitating effects of the pre-existing condition that the plaintiff would have experienced anyway. In a subsequent case, the Supreme Court of Canada affirmed that the defendant need not put the plaintiff in a position better than they would have been if they had not incurred the injury (*B (KL) v British Columbia*, 2003).

Recently, the BC Court of Appeal ordered a new trial in a personal injury case, finding that the use of the phrase "crumbling skull" is rarely helpful (*Gordon v Ahn*, 2017). In this case, the plaintiff was injured in a car accident in which she suffered injuries and reported becoming depressed as a result. The trial judge concluded that her depression "existed because of her deteriorating relationship with her mother but worsened due to the accident and pain she suffered." However, the judge concluded that the crumbling skull doctrine applied to the plaintiff's emotional and psychological condition at the time of the accident, therefore reducing her damages. The Court of Appeal allowed the appeal. In the finding, the Court of Appeal noted that the plaintiff did not actually qualify under the crumbling skull doctrine. In other words, although she had had some earlier relationship problems, there was no expert opinion suggesting that she would probably or inevitably develop major depression. It was, however, noted that if the court had at their disposal a detailed consideration of her mental health before and after the accident, as well as a prognostication as to her future functioning, then this would have guided the court (*Gordon v Ahn*, 2017). One may argue that it was unduly harsh of the court to determine on the basis of this one case that this doctrine is rarely helpful, since it can be defined operationally, as we have discussed above, and if sufficient analysis is applied, it would appear to be a useful legal concept.

Critiques

Critiques of the Supreme Court ruling and tort law respecting damages fall into two broad categories: concerns regarding the manner in which damages are apportioned and concerns that the manner in which damages are viewed and compensated creates perverse incentives and undermines personal responsibility and fortitude.

Apportioning of Damages

Injuries or harms with multiple causations are particularly challenging for the court. The apportioning of damages requires a balancing of tortious and non-tortious causes, and determining whether non-tortious causes, once established, are vulnerabilities that would have led to deterioration without the wrongful event, or whether the individual would have remained stable (see figure 11.1). Such determinations are open to considerable judicial discretion, based on the weighting of evidence provided. They are also based on the manner in which the issue is framed. Waddams (1998), in addressing this issue in the Supreme Court decision of *Athey v Leonati*, asserts that the interpretation depended on the way in which the trial judge expressed her conclusion. He argued that if the trial judge intended to say that Mr. Athey's pre-accident back condition was fragile but stable, and would not have likely caused him any further trouble, then this would be a thin skull case. If, however, the trial judge meant to say that it was likely that the herniated disc would have occurred even if the accidents had not happened, then this would be a crumbling skull case. Waddams (1998) believes that this is what

Figure 11.1 Scenarios differentiating the thin skull and the crumbling skull

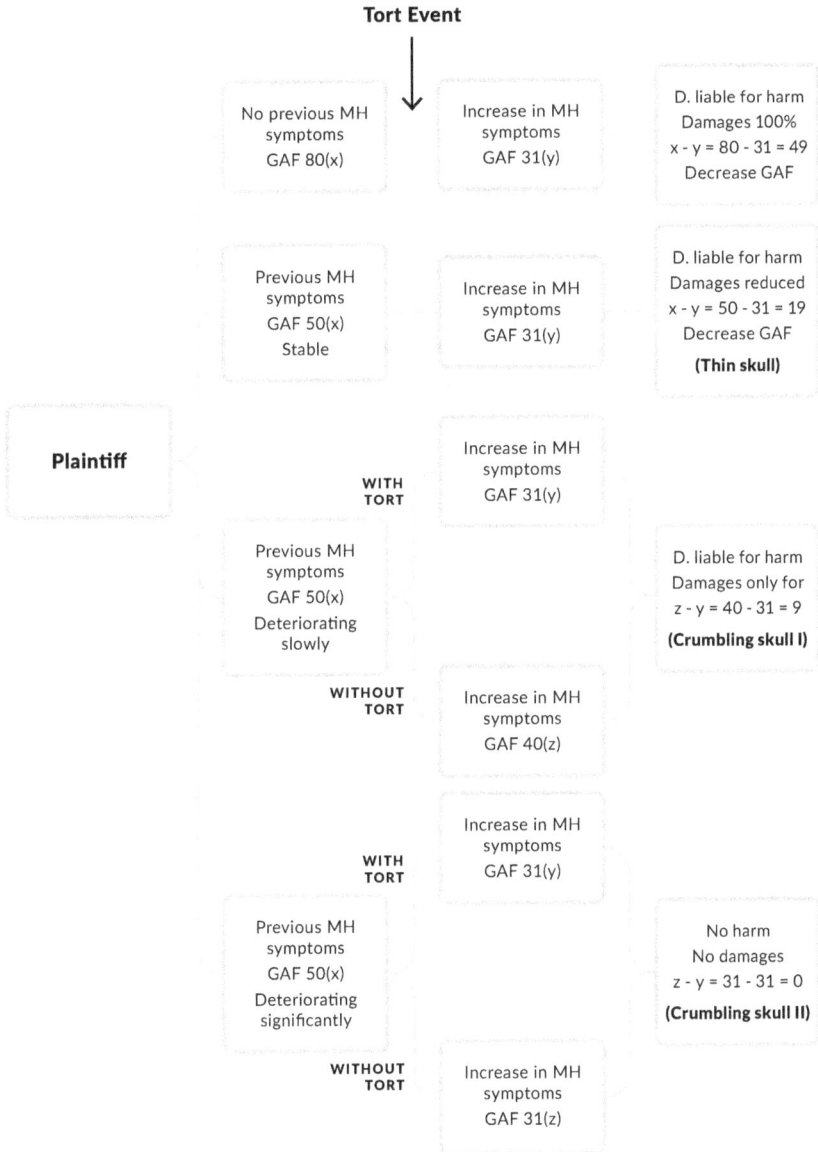

Tort Event

No previous MH symptoms GAF 80(x)

Increase in MH symptoms GAF 31(y)

D. liable for harm Damages 100% x - y = 80 - 31 = 49 Decrease GAF

Previous MH symptoms GAF 50(x) Stable

Increase in MH symptoms GAF 31(y)

D. liable for harm Damages reduced x - y = 50 - 31 = 19 Decrease GAF **(Thin skull)**

Plaintiff

WITH TORT

Increase in MH symptoms GAF 31(y)

Previous MH symptoms GAF 50(x) Deteriorating slowly

D. liable for harm Damages only for z - y = 40 - 31 = 9 **(Crumbling skull I)**

WITHOUT TORT

Increase in MH symptoms GAF 40(z)

WITH TORT

Increase in MH symptoms GAF 31(y)

Previous MH symptoms GAF 50(x) Deteriorating significantly

No harm No damages z - y = 31 - 31 = 0 **(Crumbling skull II)**

WITHOUT TORT

Increase in MH symptoms GAF 31(z)

the judge probably intended, and thus questioned the merit in compelling an all-or-nothing decision regarding causation. The court identified what were referred to as "competing causes" in the case of *Athey v Leonati*. The trial judge concluded that the injuries in the accidents contributed to some degree to the subsequent herniation, but played a minor causal role, which she assessed to be 25 per cent. The Supreme Court concluded that 25 per cent falls outside the de minimis range and is thus a material contribution, leading to a finding to full liability.

Other authors are also critical of the Supreme Court judgment with respect to apportionment. Klimchuk and Black (1997) note that the Supreme Court's conclusion was based on both the *but for test* and the *material contribution test*, and also note that, at the same time, the Supreme Court characterized these tests as disjunctive and mutually exclusive. Consequently, they assert that it was not necessary for the Supreme Court to consider the material causation test and note that it is generally accepted that the courts consider a pre-existing medical condition by adjusting the assessment of damages. Klimchuk and Black (1997) conjecture that in the case of *Athey*, an adjustment should have been made based on the fact that his previous back problems would likely have resulted in ongoing pain and may have interfered with his ability to continue performing manual labour for much longer. They state that "while the defendants were 100% causally responsible for injuring the plaintiff's back, they should not be held liable for the difference between a bad back and the back Athey had when he came to trial, since Athey did not have a good back to begin with" (pp. 172–3). In other words, the trial judge made the mistake of taking evidence that would normally be considered at this stage of damage assessment and regarding it as relative to the question of causation.

Misalignment of Incentives

In an article entitled "Eggshell Economics," Calandrillo and Buehler (2013) discuss social implications of the thin skull (or *eggshell skull*, as it is sometimes called) plaintiff rule. They argue that this doctrine misaligns incentives in socially undesirable ways. They argue that offering compensation for the full extent of injuries decreases the motivations of individuals to protect themselves against losses or injury. They propose that this rule should be replaced by a foreseeability rule, wherein tortfeasors are only liable for the reasonably foreseeable scope of a plaintiff's injuries. Others argue that the thin skull approach incentivizes "plaintiffs to allege that present outrageous behaviour" is exacerbated by previous conditions (Eden, 2001).

A further case before the Supreme Court of Canada indeed considered these issues: *Mustapha v Culligan of Canada Ltd.* (2008). The case involved a plaintiff who saw a dead fly in a bottle of drinking water, and subsequently developed a phobia, anxiety, and depression, and became dysfunctional. The Supreme Court held that he did not have "fortitude," suggesting that it was not foreseeable that a person would develop this unusual and severe mental disorder in response to a relatively trivial harm. Although the thin skull rule is generally applied to damages, it does not account for situations where it was unforeseeable that an ordinary individual would be harmed by the defendant's conduct, as in this case.

Applications in Cases of Sexual Violence

As indicated earlier, the thin skull plaintiff rule has a relatively long tradition in cases of physical injury. However, the thin skull rule has more recently been applied with respect to victims of sexual assault and harassment who have previously suffered from sexual abuse (Rose, Wallace, & Piccard, 2010). In these situations, parties may argue that a person traumatized in childhood who is subjected to further trauma as an adult may suffer more severe psychological effects. An early example of this was the North Carolina case of *Poole v Copland* (1998), in which a woman sued her former co-worker and her employer for sexual harassment. The plaintiff asserted that as a result of the harassment, she experienced flashbacks of repressed child sexual abuse. A thin skull argument was advanced based on her previous abuse and the fact that she suffered from a dissociative disorder. The court allowed her to recover the full amount of her damages as her susceptibility contributed to emotional distress from the wrongdoing (Eden, 2001).

In a recent Canadian case (*Corfield v Shaw*, 2011), the trial judge used the analysis from *Athey* in arriving at the judgment. The plaintiff in this case, Ms. Corfield, was an apprentice at a small, family-owned plumbing business. She alleged that her supervisor sexually assaulted her on a number of occasions. Upon revealing this to the owner, she quit work and commenced legal action claiming psychological and emotional harm as a result of the assaults. Ms. Corfield was acknowledged to have been the victim of childhood sexual abuse. Her stepfather had pleaded guilty to sexual touching and intercourse when Ms. Corfield was between the ages of 13 and 17. She also acknowledged that she experienced emotional and psychological distress following her childhood abuse but indicated that she was well on the way to recovery.

The defendant asserted that Ms. Corfield would have continued to suffer from the effects of childhood abuse with or without the additional assaults. In supporting this statement, it was noted that Ms. Corfield' childhood abuse was significantly more severe in nature than the harassment and assaults that were currently being alleged; she found another job within two weeks of leaving the firm, a job which she held continuously for more than five years, and despite opportunities to do so, Ms. Corfield did not readily attend counselling after the most recent assaults. The judge referred to a report of a psychologist whom Ms. Corfield saw for approximately four counselling sessions; the psychologist noted that Ms Corfield was moderately depressed, mildly anxious, and suffered from post-traumatic stress disorder. The psychologist opined that the "history of childhood abuse and neglect could, and probably does, make her more vulnerable to experience a more intense emotional affect from stressful events" (*Corfield v Shaw*, 2011, p. 94).

The judge found that the injuries from the assault and from the childhood abuse are indivisible. The judge then quoted *Athey* regarding the crumbling skull doctrine. It was noted that Ms. Corfield continued to suffer some symptoms from the childhood abuse prior to the assaults, and this was confirmed by her mother. The judge concluded that as she was still struggling with emotional issues from her childhood abuse, there was a measurable risk that would have detrimentally affected her in the future, and as such this was a "classic example of the crumbling skull situation" (*Corfield v Shaw*, 2011, p. 107). The judge, therefore, awarded an amount that represented Ms. Corfield's loss and damage as a result of the later assaults and reduced this by a percentage to take into account her original position, that is, suffering some psychological effects from childhood abuse.

Implications for Forensic Mental Health Practice

Mental health professionals are involved in tort law when they are retained to assess a plaintiff's psychological damages, most commonly in cases involving motor vehicle accidents, sexual assaults, and discrimination or harassment in the workplace. As noted in the *Practice Guideline for the Forensic Assessment* of the American Academy of Psychiatry and the Law (2005), this can be a difficult exercise and requires careful assessment (Glancy et al., 2015). In particular, the evaluator should strive for honesty and objectivity (American Academy of Psychiatry and the Law, 2005) and should, as discussed in chapter 2, consider any possible sources of perceived or actual conflict of interest that may result in allegations of bias. One impairment to this objectivity is if a treating mental health professional becomes the evaluator. In civil litigation, unlike in criminal litigation, the court sometimes does wish to hear from the treating therapist. However, in the United States and Canada, ethics guidelines for forensic psychiatrists suggest that every effort should be made to avoid this situation, and therapists should instead refer the case to an independent evaluator (American Association of Psychiatry and the Law, 2005; Canadian Academy of Psychiatry and the Law, 2018).

The task of the evaluator is to measure or quantify the psychological damages and to link any damages to impairments in functioning. Some aspects of the assessment are the same as those described for a forensic assessment for insanity, described in chapter 3 these include obtaining referral information, collateral information, and consent. Some elements of the assessment are similar, but slightly modified; these include determining the nature of the precipitant and considering the possibility of malingering. Other aspects are unique; these include determining the immediate, short-term, and long-term effects of the event. These tasks are listed in table 11.2. The evaluator should also be aware of the types and categories of damages, such as future wage loss claims, if the plaintiff is unable to work (Gold, Anfang, & Drukteinis, 2008); compensation for pain and suffering; and future care costs.

All data considered in the assessment, including the interview, that may form the basis for a legal opinion should be recorded. This process may be aided by accurate verbatim note-taking or by making an audio or video recording the interview, with the understanding that any notes or audio or video recordings may be requested by the court and become part of the legal record. Audio or video recordings are obviously the most accurate methods of recording the interview and as such may enhance the credibility of the testimony, although the use of such recordings is not standard procedure in Canada. The American Academy of Psychiatry and the Law discusses the pros and cons of video recording and concludes that the use of such recordings has a lot to commend it and is allowable, although it is not standard procedure in the United States (AAPL, 1999; Glancy et al., 2015).

Precipitating Event

It is important to carefully record a detailed description of the alleged precipitating factors and their time frame. This record may include the duration and degree of exposure to any alleged trauma and the evaluee's response to a traumatic event. Information should be obtained through direct interviews and the collection of collateral information. This material might include previous medical records and counselling records, as well as interviews with spouses or significant others, family members, friends, or colleagues.

Table 11.1 Evaluating impacts of event or wrongdoing

	Social functioning	Occupational functioning	Psychological functioning
Immediate effects (up to one month)			
Medium term effects (one month–one year)			
Long-term effects (over one year)			

Effects of the Precipitating Event

The evaluation should include a detailed history regarding the impact, if any, of the alleged wrongdoing in three areas of functioning: psychological functioning, social functioning, and occupational functioning. It is helpful to ask open-ended questions regarding three arbitrary time periods: the immediate time after the injury (the first few minutes up to one month), the medium term (one month to one year after the injury), and the long-term (one year and onwards after the injury) (see table 11.1). Having reviewed collateral information, the interviewer may need to see the evaluee again and ask them to explain, in their own words, any discrepancies that arise. This should be done in a non-confrontative manner; the evaluator should explain that they merely want to understand how these apparent discrepancies arose.

Social Impact

Evaluation of social functioning contributes to understanding the non-pecuniary (loss of enjoyment in life) sequelae to injury, in other words, how the injury may have affected the evaluee's day-to-day life. This evaluation might include a detailed account of how the evaluee spends each day from beginning to end, including how they manage the activities of daily living, such as cleaning, shopping, cooking, paying bills, and attending to personal needs. This level of activity would need to be compared to that prior to the injury. Other forms of social activity to be included in the assessment are interpersonal relationships, hobbies and other pastimes, vacations, and attendance at religious institutions and social functions. The evaluee should be canvassed for other psychosocial stressors that may affect their current state and level of functioning. These might include interpersonal problems, separations, family problems, or exposure to other traumatic incidents.

Table 11.2   Forensic assessment for personal injury

Obtain referral information	• Determine if the case falls within an area of expertise
Explain the limits of confidentiality	• Evaluation will be sent to retaining party • Evaluation is not for treatment • Evaluation is subject to disclosure in court • Evaluee has right to decline to answer
Obtain collateral information	• Medical, psychiatric, counselling, and other records • Interviews with others
Precipitating event	• Duration and degree of exposure • Evaluee's perception of the event
Social impacts	• Activities of daily living • Leisure activities • Relationships
Occupational impacts	• Detailed occupational history • Current work and income • Previous work and income • Problems encountered in the workplace • Attendance at work and perceived barriers to return to work
Psychological impacts	• Previous trauma history • Previous mental health, emotional, and medical history • Concurrent life stressors
Consider malingering	• Use standardized tests • Be aware of possible motivations and gains • Be alert to distortions, under-, and over-reporting of symptoms
Opinion and report	• Determine any change in social, occupational, and psychological functioning • Consider the contribution of a "thin skull" or "crumbling skull" • Establish nexus between event and symptoms • Suggest treatments that may ameliorate impact

Occupational Impact

An occupational history may be of great importance. This history should commence with the person's first employment and include all subsequent jobs held. The collection of this information is necessary to assess the level of occupational functioning since the injury and guides the evaluator in forming an opinion about whether there has been any specific change. This history might include attempts to return to work. Some specific issues to be addressed are listed in table 11.2.

Psychological Impact

The evaluator should specifically ask about previous mental health history, eliciting a full personal history and family history of mental disorder, in order to determine any biological, psychological, or social factors that may have contributed to the evaluee's current mental health functioning. The medical history may include consideration of medical illnesses that can mimic psychological dysfunction or lead to psychological symptoms. In particular, neurological diseases, such as multiple sclerosis, neurocognitive disorders, or seizure disorders, may be relevant. Endocrinological disorders such as diabetes or thyroid conditions may also cause psychiatric symptoms. Where possible, mental health, counselling, and medical records should be obtained, supplemented by collateral information from family and friends. Finally, it is important to record the evaluee's use of substances. Heavy use of alcohol, street drugs, or even medications can mimic or exacerbate a variety of social and mental health problems. Sometimes, the presence of a substance use disorder can only be discovered by questioning colleagues, family, or friends of the evaluee.

The evaluation would be incomplete without accurate information about any previous traumas that the evaluee may have encountered throughout their life. The nature of previous trauma exposures, the impact of previous exposures, and any treatments that the evaluee may have undertaken add valuable information to the eventual opinion. This information might include a history of psychological, psychosocial, and psychotherapeutic treatments. Important areas for assessment include adherence to treatment and a history of which treatments have and have not been helpful.

It may be helpful to also include the results of standardized tests. Some tests require the level of expertise of a psychologist, but others can be interpreted and administered, with the assistance of the test manual, by other mental health professionals. Some tests, such as the Hare Psychopathy Checklist, require specific training and should not be used absent this training. Physical examinations, clinical testing, and imaging may be required for certain cases. Generally speaking, referrals can be made for these specialist examinations if they are thought to be helpful in formulating the case and answering the specific legal questions

Consider Malingering

The evaluator should be alert to any distortions in diagnosis due to an over- or under-reporting of symptoms (Piel, 2012) and also to any signs of possible malingering (Hoffman & O'Shaughnessy, 2013). Drukteinis (2018) identifies the pitfalls of self-report in the assessment of psychiatric disability. He advises the importance of corroboration of observations made by the evaluator and collateral sources, including medical and psychiatric records, employment files, and tax returns. Psychometric testing, such as PTSD rating scales, can be of assistance, as are tools specifically designed to assess malingering (Weiss & Watson, 2018). Other people in the individual's life may also provide corroborating data, but as they may also be invested in the disability or damages claim, they could possibly distort information in support of the claim. Thus, the evaluator should consider alternative explanations for the claim that may assist the court in determining damages (Drukteinis, 2018).

Opinion and Report

If a mental health professional is retained by a lawyer to assess causality and damages in a case of psychic injury, the lawyer will generally request that the findings and opinion be presented in the form of a final written report. The report will explain the basis of the expert's opinion and the logical processes that led to that opinion. The structure of a mental health report varies according to jurisdiction, and is influenced by guidelines, legislation, and local custom. Buchanan and Norko (2011) propose a generic structure for a forensic report and discuss and demonstrate how this structure can be used in the various types of work forensic mental health professionals are called upon to do, including assessments for psychic injury.

The opinion section is the final conclusion of the report and the element of the report that will be most carefully scrutinized. Therefore, the language of each word of the opinion requires careful consideration. The forensic mental health professional may choose to use the language that the courts use, for instance, in the use of terms such as "thin skull" or "crumbling skull," but in doing so they must be fully aware of the implications of these complicated terms. Others may want to deliberately avoid the use of legal language and use purely mental health terms, which can be interpreted by the lawyers as they see fit. In either event, it is incumbent to delineate the contribution of all predisposing and precipitating factors using a biopsychosocial model.

The opinion section should attempt to address only the specifi psycho-legal question that the lawyer requested to be addressed. If the question is not addressed, there should be an explanation as to the reason for this omission, confirming that this is a considered decision and not an oversight. The opinion section should not include new data, as all of the data upon which the opinion is based should be in the body of the report. In some jurisdictions, the opinion is recorded at the very beginning of the report; in others, the opinion is situated at the end.

A common pitfall in forensic mental health reports is failing to establish a nexus between the injury and the presenting symptoms. Simply recording symptoms, reporting test results, or even making a diagnosis does not equate to causation. Typically, the mental health professional is asked to assess and describe the evaluee's level of disability and their symptoms, which can help the court to decide upon damages. Gerbasi (2004) cautions the mental health professional to be alert to the issues of somatization, pre-existing conditions, personality disorders, and the over- or under-reporting of symptoms. The mental health professional may also consider whether the litigation itself may be affecting the level of symptomatology (Drukteinis, 2018).

Differentiating the Thin Skull and the Crumbling Skull

Figure 11.1 provides a graphic illustration of the way in which the thin skull and the crumbling skull may be differentiated. In this illustration, the Global Assessment of Functioning scale (GAF) from the DSM-IV is used to describe changes in functioning. Any other equivalent measure could be used. For instance, the DSM-5 (American Psychiatric Association, 2013) refers to the World Health Organization's Disability Assessment Schedule (WHO-DAS), which has greater reliability and may be used for this purpose. The illustration has four scenarios, each with different features and outcomes: the average plaintiff; the thin skull plaintiff; the crumbling skull plaintiff, whose deterioration has been accelerated by the wrongdoing; and the crumbling skull plaintiff, for whom the wrongdoing has not accelerated the deterioration.

Summary

Tort law is the civil law process by which the courts can assess and award damages to an individual who has suffered physical, emotional, or financial harms as a result of the deliberate wrongdoing or negligence of another person. In doing so, the court must determine that a wrongful act has occurred and that injuries or harms have been sustained as

Table 11.3   Scenarios differentiating the thin skull and the crumbling skull

Scenario 1: The average plaintiff

Prior condition	• No mental health symptoms • Normal social, psychological, and occupational functioning • No more than slight impairment • GAF score 80 (X)
Condition following tort	• Marked mental health symptoms • Major impairment in several areas, e.g., school, family relations, judgment, thinking, or mood • GAF score 31 (Y)
Outcome	• The defendant is liable for all harms • Damages are assessed at 100% • Damages are 80–31 = 49

Scenario 2: The thin skull plaintiff

Prior condition	• Mild to moderate mental health symptoms • Moderate functional difficulties • Relatively stable • GAF score 50
Condition following tort	• Increased mental health symptoms • Major impairment in functioning • GAF score 31
Outcome	• The defendant is liable for all harms • Damages assessed at 100% • Damages are 50–31 = 19

Scenario 3: The crumbling skull A

Prior condition	• Mild to moderate mental health symptoms • Moderate functional difficulties • Gradually and incrementally deteriorating • GAF score 50
Condition following the tort	• Increase in mental health symptoms • Major impairment in functioning • GAF score 31
Estimation of current condition had tort not occurred	• Deterioration expected • Increased mental health symptoms and reduced functioning but less severe if no tort • Estimated GAF score 40
Outcome	• Damages only for restoring the plaintiff to position without the tort • Damages are 40–31 = 9

Scenario 4: The crumbling skull B

Prior condition	• Mild to moderate mental health symptoms • Moderate functional difficulties • Gradually and incrementally deteriorating • GAF score 50

(continued)

Table 11.3 (*continued*)

Condition following the tort	• Increase in mental health symptoms • Major impairment in functioning • GAF score 31
Estimation of current condition had tort not occurred	• Significant deterioration expected • Likely same condition if tort had not occurred • Estimated GAF score 31
Outcome	• No harm or damages • Damages are 31–31 = 0

Table 11.4   Key points regarding assessing damages

Athey v Leonati (1996)

Apportioning responsibility	• The defendant is liable for any injuries caused or contributed to by negligence or tortious act • Presence of non-tortious (not due to wrongdoing) causes does not reduce liability
But for test	• The plaintiff must show that injury would not have occurred but for the actions or negligence of the defendant
Material contribution	• A contribution to the injury that is above de minimis (minor or trivial) range
Key concepts	
Thin skull	• Pre-existing condition or vulnerability • Stable before the wrongdoing • The person who inflicted injury is fully liable for unexpected serious consequences
Crumbling skull	• Pre-existing condition or vulnerability • Condition results in ongoing deterioration • Defendant liable for restoring the individual to where they would have been without the tort
Implications for practice	
Primary objectives of the assessment	• To quantify damages • To assess nexus between event and symptoms • To suggest treatments that ameliorate impacts
Aspects of the forensic assessment	• Limits of confidentiality • Precipitating event • Social, occupational, and psychological impacts • Prior vulnerabilities • Consideration of possible malingering • Opinion
Considerations	• Perceptions of conflict of interest or bias • Differentiating between thin skull or crumbling skull

a result of the tort, and then determine the degree of harm, apportion responsibility, and award damages accordingly. First, the plaintiff must demonstrate that the injury would not have occurred but for the actions or negligence of the defendant. Next, or in the alternative, the court must appraise that the actions of the defendant made a material contribution to the harm experienced. This is often a difficult task because injuries or harms frequently have multiple contributing factors. Some of these factors are inherent in the individual as pre-existing conditions. Thus, the courts must determine if the pre-existing condition was stable and would not have resulted in the symptoms observed in the plaintiff if the wrongdoing had not occurred (thin skull). However, if the pre-existing condition would likely have resulted in some deterioration even without the wrongdoing (a crumbling skull), the damages attributed to the defendant are consequently reduced. Mental health professionals are frequently called upon to assist with this determination. In such cases, the mental health professional must provide a comprehensive assessment that helps the court to determine the social, psychological, and occupational effects of the wrongdoing. The opinion offered by the professional must quantify damages, assess the nexus between the event and the symptoms, help differentiate between the thin skull and the crumbling skull, and suggest treatments that may ameliorate the impacts.

References

1. Landmark Cases

American Psychological Association. (2018). *Specialty guidelines for forensic psychology*. Retrieved from http://www.apa.org/practice/guidelines/forensic-psychology.aspx.

Athey v Leonati, [1996] 3 SCR 458, 140 DLR (4th) 235.

Bill C-30, *An Act to amend the Criminal Code (mental disorder) and to amend the National Defence Act and the Young Offenders Act in consequence thereof*, 3rd Sess, 34th Parl, 1991 (as passed by the House of Commons November 21, 1991).

Bow Valley Husky (Bermuda) Ltd. v Saint John Shipbuilding Ltd, [1997] 3 SCR 1210, 153 DLR (4th) 385.

Canadian Charter of Rights and Freedoms, Part I of the Constitution Act 1982, being Schedule B to the Canada Act 1982 (UK), 1982, c. 11.

Canadian Federation of Students. (2018). Gender-based violence. Retrieved from http://cfsontario.ca/campaigns/gender-based-violence/.

Cardozo, B.N. (1921). *The nature of the judicial process*. New Haven, CT: Yale University Press.

Civil Marriage Act, SC 2005, c 33.

Constitutional Act of 1791 (UK) 31 Geo III, c 31 (UK), reprinted in RSC 1985, Appendix II, No 3.

Courts of Nova Scotia. (2004). A history of the Supreme Court. Retrieved from http://courts.ns.ca/History_of_Courts/history_site.htm.

Criminal Code, RSC 1985, c C-46.*Criminal Code, 1892*, SC 1892, c 29. Department of Justice Canada. (2015). Canada's system of justice. Retrieved from https://www.justice.gc.ca/eng/csj-sjc/index.html.

Department of Justice Canada. (2017). How courts are organized. Retrieved from http://www.justice.gc.ca/eng/csj-sjc/ccs-ajc/02.html.

Driedger, E. (1974). *Contruction of statutes*. Toronto: Butterworths.

Ferguson, D. (2009). *Ontario courtroom procedure*. Toronto: LexisNexis.

Gennaioli, N., & Shleifer, A. (2007). The evolution of common law. *Journal of Political Economy, 115*(1), 43–68.

Glancy, G., Regehr, C., & Bryant, A. (1998). Confidentiality in crisis: Part I – The duty to inform. *Canadian Journal of Psychiatry, 43*(10), 1001–5.

Grey v Pearson (1857), 10 ER 1216 (HL (Eng)).

Innocence Canada Foundation. (2018). About us. Retrieved from http://innocencecanada.com/about-us/.

Innocence Project. (2018). Innocence Project 25th anniversary. Retrieved from https://www.innocenceproject.org/.

Johnson, B. (1992, 9 November). Campus confidential: University courtship is like an arcade game in which the rules of confusing and hazard warnings loom at every turn. *Maclean's*.

Lefroy, A.H.F. (1914). *Leading cases in Canadian constitutional law*. Toronto: Carswell.

Macey, J.R. (1986). Promoting public-regarding legislation through statutory interpretation: An interest group model. *Columbia Law Review, 86*(2), 223–68.

Ontario Justice Education Network. (2006). *Cases that have changed society*. Retrieved from http://ojen.ca/en/resource/cases-that-have-changed-society.

Parkes, D. (2006). Precedent unbound – Contemporary approaches to precedent in Canada. *Manitoba Law Journal, 32*, 135.

Practice Statement (Judicial Precedent), [1966] 3 All ER 77, [1966] 1 WLR 1234, HL(E), (Lord Gardiner).

Presser, J., & Szigeti, A. (2017). Even and especially, the most reviled and despised: Justice Marc Rosenberg's commitment to access to justice and procedural fairness for the mentally disordered. In B. Berger, E. Cunliffe, & J. Stribopoulos (Eds), *To ensure that justice is done: Essays in memory of Marc Rosenberg*. Toronto: Canada Law Book.

Provincial Court of British Columbia. (2014). "History." Retrieved from http://www.provincialcourt.bc.ca/about-the-court/history.

Quebec Act, 1774 (UK), 14 Geo III, c 83 (UK), reprinted in RSC 1895, Appendix II, No 2.

R v Bouchard-Lebrun, 2011 SCC 58.

R v Chaulk, [1990] 3 SCR 1303, 62 CCC (3d) 193.

R v Daviault, [1994] 3 SCR 63, 118 DLR (4th) 469.

R v Ewanchuk, 1998 ABCA 52.

R v Ewanchuk, [1999] 1 SCR 330, 169 DLR (4th) 193.

R v M'Naghten, (1843) 8 ER 718, 10 Cl & Fin 200 (Central Crim Ct).

R v Mohan, [1994] 2 SCR 9, 114 DLR (4th) 419.

R v Neves, 2005 MBCA 112.

R v Oakes, [1986] 1 SCR 103, 26 DLR (4th) 200.

R v Oommen, [1994] 2 SCR 507, 155 AR 190.

R v Parks, [1992] 2 SCR 871, 95 DLR (4th) 27.

R v Salituro, [1991] 3 SCR 654, 68 CCC (3d) 289.

R v Stinchcombe, [1991] 3 SCR 326, 68 CCC (3d) 1.

R v Stone, [1999] 2 SCR 290, 173 DLR (4th) 66.

R v Swain, [1991] 1 SCR 933, 63 CCC (3d) 481.

R v Taylor (1992), 11 OR (3d) 323, 77 CCC (3d) 551 (CA).

Radin, M. (1930). Statutory interpretation. *Harvard Law Review, 43*(6), 863–85.

Reference re Same-Sex Marriage, 2004 SCC 79.

Regehr, C., & Kanani, K. (2010). *Essential law for social work practice in Canada*. Toronto: Oxford University Press.

Richards, M.J., & Kritzer, H.M. (2002). Jurisprudential regimes in Supreme Court decision making. *American Political Science Review, 96*(2), 305–20.

Schneider, R.D. (2009) *The lunatic and the lords*. Toronto: Irwin Law.

Segal, J.A., & Spaeth, H.J. (1996). The influence of sta e decisis on the votes of United States Supreme Court justices. *American Journal of Political Science*, 971–1003.

Smith v Jones, [1999] 1 SCR 455, 169 DLR (4th) 385.

Songer, D.R., & Lindquist, S.A. (1996). Not the whole story: The impact of justices' values on Supreme Court decision making. *American Journal of Political Science, 40*(4), 1049–63.

Starson v Swayze, 2003 SCC 32.

Sullivan, R. (2016). Statutory interpretation in Canada: The legacy of Elmer Driedger. Retrieved from https://kja321.files.wo dpress.com/2016/04 /statutory-interpretation-in-canada.pdf.

Winny, J.S. (2008). Stare decisis n Ontario law. *Advocates' Quarterly, 35*, 68.

Youth Criminal Justice Act, SC 2002, c. 1.

2. Expert Testimony

American Academy of Psychiatry and the Law. (1999). AAPL Task Force: Videotaping of forensic psychiatric evaluations. *Journal of the American Academy of Psychiatry and the Law, 27*, 345–8.

Abbott and Haliburton Co. v White Burgess Langille Inman, 2013 NSCA 66.

Abbott and Haliburton Co. v White Burgess Langille Inman, 2012 NSSC 210.

American Academy of Psychiatry and the Law. (2005). Ethical guidelines for the practice of forensic psychiatry. Retrieved from http://www.aapl.org /ethics.htm.

Appelbaum, P.S. (1997). A theory of ethics for forensic psychiatry. *Journal of the American Academy of Psychiatry and the Law Online, 25*(3), 233–47.

Belkin, L. (1988, 6 June). The law: Expert witness is unfazed by Dr. Death label. *New York Times*. Retrieved from http://www.nytimes.com/1988/06/10 /us/the-law-expert-witness-is-unfazed-by-dr-death-label.html.

Blumenthal, I. (2002). Shaken baby syndrome. *Postgraduate Medical Journal, 78*(926), 732–5.

Canadian Association of Psychiatry and the Law. (2018). *Ethical guidelines for the practice of forensic psychology.* Retrieved from http://www.capl-acpd .org/ethical-guidelines/.

Canadian Charter of Rights and Freedoms: Part I of the Constitution Act 1982, being Schedule B to the Canada Act 1982 (UK) c. 11.

Candilis, P.J. (2009). The revolution in forensic ethics: Narrative, compassion, and a robust professionalism. *Psychiatric Clinics, 32*(2), 423–35.

Chief Coroner for Ontario. (2005). Results of audit into tissue samples arising from homicide and criminally suspicious autopsies performed at the Hospital for Sick Children. Retrieved from http://www.mcscs.jus.gov.on.ca /english/publications/pubs.html.

College of Physicians and Surgeons of Ontario. (2011). News release: Discipline committee decisions. Retrieved from http://www.cpso.on.ca /whatsnew/news/default.aspx?id=4908

Daubert v Merrell Dow Pharmaceuticals, Inc, 118 S. Ct. 2786 (US 1993).

Deported doc faces immigration hearing. (2005, 18 August). *Bay Today.* Retrieved from https://www.baytoday.ca/local-news/deported -doc-faces-immigration-hearing-59170.

Discipline Committee, College of Physicians and Surgeons of Ontario. (1991). CPSO 56233.

Dr. Charles Smith: The man behind the public inquiry. (2009, 7 December). Canadian Broadcasting Corporation [News post]. Retrieved from http:// www.cbc.ca/canada/story/2009/12/07/f-charles-smith-goudge-inquiry .html.

Frye v United States, 293 F 1013 (DC Ct App 1923. Glancy, G., Ash, P., Bath, E., Buchanan, A., Fedoroff, P., Frierson, R. L., ... Knoll, J. (2015). AAPL Practice Guideline for the Forensic Assessment. *The Journal of the American Academy of Psychiatry and the Law, 43*(2 Suppl.), S3.

Glancy, G., & Bradford, J. (2007). The admissibility of expert evidence in Canada. *Journal of the American Academy of Psychiatry and the Law, 35*(2), 350–6.

Glancy, G., & Regehr, C. (2012). From schadenfreude to contemplation: Lessons for forensic experts. *Journal of the American Academy of Psychiatry and the Law Online, 40*(1), 81–8.

Glancy, G., & Saini, M. (2009). The confluence of evidence-based practice and *Daubert* within the fields of fo ensic psychiatry and the law. *Journal of the American Academy of Psychiatry and the Law Online, 37*(4), 438–41.

Goudge, S. (2008). *Inquiry into pediatric forensic pathology in Ontario report.* Retrieved from http://www.attorneygeneral.just.gov.on.ca/inquiries /goudest/report/index.html.

Gray, C. (1991). Healers who harm: Ontario college takes aim at physicians who abuse patients. *Canadian Medical Association Journal, 44*(10), 1298–1300.

Griffith, E.E. (2005). Personal narrative and an African-American perspective on medical ethics. *Journal of the American Academy of Psychiatry and the Law Online, 33*(3), 371–81.

Griffith, E.E., Stankovic, A., & Baranoski, M. (2010). Conceptualizing the forensic psychiatry report as performative narrative. *Journal of the American Academy of Psychiatry and the Law Online, 38*(1), 32–42.

Grove, W.M., & Barden, R.C. (1999). Protecting the integrity of the legal system: The admissibility of testimony from mental health experts under Daubert/Kumho analyses. *Psychology, Public Policy, and Law, 5*(1), 224.

Gutheil, T. G., & Simon, R.I. (1999). Attorneys' pressures on the expert witness: Early warning signs of endangered honesty, objectivity, and fair compensation. *Journal of the American Academy of Psychiatry and the Law Online, 27*(4), 546–53.

Harding, B., Risdon, R.A., & Krous, H.F. (2004). Shaken baby syndrome. *British Medical Journal, 328*, 720–1

Iacobucci, F., & Hamilton, G. (2010). The Goudge Inquiry and the role of medical expert witnesses. *Canadian Medical Association Journal, 182*(1), 53–6.

Imeson v Maryvale (Maryvale Adolescent and Family Services), 2018 ONCA 888.

Jones, A. (2016, 27 January). Former Ontario Liberal staffers due back in court Feb. 24 on charges in gas plant case [Television news report]. Retrieved from https://globalnews.ca/news/2479966/court-appearance-today-for-laura -miller-david-livingston-in-ontario-liberal-gas-plant-case/.

Leckie, S. (1997). Exclusionary rules in Canada and the United States. *Dalhousie Journal of Legal Studies, 6*, 263.

Levine, M. (1984). The adversary process and social science in the courts: *Barefoot v. Estelle. The Journal of Psychiatry & Law, 12*(2), 147–81.

Meintjes-Van Der Walt, L. (2011). Tracing trends: The impact of science and technology on the law of criminal evidence and procedure. *South African Law Journal, 128*(1), 147–71.

Mohan's deportation a question of when and where. (2005, 19 August). *Bay Today.* Retrieved from https://www.baytoday.ca/local-news /mohans-deportation-a-question-of-when-and-where-59165.

Norko, M.A. (2005). Commentary: Compassion at the core of forensic ethics. *Journal of the American Academy of Psychiatry and the Law Online, 33*(3), 386–9.

Ontario Rules of Civil Procedure, R.R.O. 1990, Reg 194.

Osborne, C. (2007). *Civil justice reform project.* https://www.attorneygeneral .jus.gov.on.ca/english/about/pubs/cjrp/.

Dr Grigson, Dr Death. (2004). Associated Press. Retrieved from http://www .chron.com/disp/story.mpl/metropolitan/2627280.html.

R v Abbey, [1982] 2 SCR 24, 138 DLR (3d) 202 *R v Lavallee*, [1990] 1 SCR 852, 55 CCC (3d) 97.

R c J-JL (1998), 130 CCC (3d) 541 (Qc CA).

R c J-JL (2000), SCC 51 at para 25.

R v Lavallee (1990), 52 Man. R (2d) 274, 44 CCC (3d) 113, (CA).

R v Livingston, 2017 ONCJ 645 at para 51.

R v Mohan (1992), 55 OAC 309, 8 OR (3d) 173 (CA).

R v Mohan, [1994] 2 SCR 9, 114 DLR (4th) 419.

R v Tang, 2015 ONCA 470.

R. v Turner, [1974] 60 Crim App, R 80.

Regehr, C., & Antle, B. (1997). Coercive influences: Informed consent in court mandated social work practice. *Social Work, 42*(3), 300–6.

Regehr, C., & Glancy, G. (1995). Battered woman syndrome defense in Canadian courts. *Canadian Journal of Psychiatry, 40*(3), 130–5.

Rosner, R. (2003). *Principles and practice of forensic psychiatry*: CRC Press.

Ross, S., & Rodriques, M. (2018). Clarity on participant experts – Imeson v. Maryvale. Retrieved from http://www.mondaq.com/canada/x/767252/trials+appeals+compensation/Clarity+On+Participant+Experts+Imeson+v+Maryvale.

Schuller, R.A. (1995). Expert evidence and hearsay. *Law and Human Behavior, 19*(4), 345–62.

Schwartz, A. (1996). Dogma of empiricism revisited: *Daubert v. Merrell Dow Pharmaceuticals, Inc.* and the need to resurrect the philosophical insight of Frye v. United States. *Harvard Journal of Law & Technology, 10*, 149.

Smith v Jones, [1999] 1 S.C.R. 455.

Strasburger, L.H., Gutheil, T.G., & Brodsky, A. (1997). On wearing two hats: Role conflict in serving as both psychotherapist and expert witness. *American Journal of Psychiatry, 154*(4), 448–56.

Tolson, M. (2004, 17 June). Effect of "Dr. Death" and his testimony lingers. *Houston Chronicle*. Retrieved from https://www.chron.com/news/houston-texas/article/Effect-of-Dr-Death-and-his-testimony-lingers-1960299.php.

UK Ministry of Justice. (2017). *Civil procedure rules: Practice direction 35 for expert and assessors*. Retrieved from https://www.justice.gov.uk/courts/procedure-rules/civil/pdf/practice_directions/pd_part35.pdf.

Utley, T. (2005, 15 July). How could an expert like Roy Meadow get it so terribly wrong? *The Telegraph*. Retrieved from https://www.telegraph.co.uk/comment/personal-view/3618377/How-could-an-expert-like-Roy-Meadow-get-it-so-terribly-wrong.html.

Westerhof v Gee Estate, 2013 ONSC 2093.

Westerhof v Gee Estate, 2015 ONCA 206 at para 60.

White Burgess Langille Inman v Abbott and Haliburton Co, 2015 SCC 23.

3. Insanity Defence

An Act for the Safe Custody of Insane Persons Charged with Offenses 1800 (UK), 39 & 40 Geo 3, c 94.

Allnutt, S., Samuels, A., & O'Driscoll, C. (2007). The insanity defence: From wild beasts to M'Naghten. *Australasian Psychiatry, 15*(4), 292–8.

American Psychiatric Association. (2013). *Diagnostic and Statistical Manual of Mental Disorders* (5th ed.) Washington, DC: Author.

Brown, D. (1989). *The genesis of the Canadian Criminal Code of 1892.* Toronto: University of Toronto Press.

Cooper v R, [1980] 1 SCR 1149, 110 DLR (3d) 46.

Criminal Code, 1892, SC 1892, c 29.

Dalby, J.T. (2006). The case of Daniel M cNaughton: Let's get the story straight. *American Journal of Forensic Psychiatry, 27*(4), 17.

Diamond, B.L. (1956). Isaac Ray and the trial of Daniel M'Naghten. *American Journal of Psychiatry, 112*(8), 651–6.

Dietz, P.E. (1996). The quest for excellence in forensic psychiatry. *Journal of the American Academy of Psychiatry and the Law Online, 24*(2), 153–63.

Duhaime. (2018). Duhaime's encyclopedia of law. Retrieved from http://www.duhaime.org/.

Durham v United States, 2 F 2d 862 (DC Cir 1954.

Giorgi-Guarnieri, D., Janofsky, J., Keram, E., Lawsky, S., Merideth, P., Mossman, D., … Zonona, H. (2002). AAPL practice guideline for forensic psychiatric evaluation of defendants raising the insanity defense. *Journal of the American Academy of Psychiatry and the Law, 30*(2) S3–S40.

Glancy, G., Ash, P., Bath, E., Buchanan, A., Fedoroff, P., Frierson, R. L., … Knoll, J. (2015). AAPL ractice guideline for the forensic assessment. *Journal of the American Academy of Psychiatry and the Law, 43*(2 Suppl.), S3.

Hall, J. (1963). The M'Naghten rules and proposed alternatives. *American Bar Association Journal, 49*, 960–4.

Janssen, S. (2004). Mental condition defences in supranational criminal law. *International Criminal Law Review, 4*(1), 83–98.

Kjeldsen v R, [1981] 2 SCR 617, 131 DLR (3d) 121.

Knoll, J., & Resnick, P. (2008). Insanity defense evaluations: Toward a model for evidence-based practice. *Brief Treatment and Crisis Intervention, 8*(1), 92.

McRuer, J., Desrochers, G., Kinnear, H., Jones, R., & Harris, J. (1956). Report of the Royal Commission on the Law of Insanity as a Defense in Criminal Cases. Hull, QC: Edmond Cloutier Queen's Printer and Controller of Stationery. Retrieved from http://publications.gc.ca/collections/collection_2014/bcp-pco/CP32-99-1956-eng.pdf.

Miller, R. (2003). Criminal competence. In R. Rosner (Ed.), *Principles and practice of forensic psychiatry* (2nd ed., pp. 182–6). London: Arnold, 186–212.

Moran, R. (1985a). The modern foundation for the insanity defense: The cases of James Hadfield (1800) and Daniel McNaughtan (1843). *The Annals of the American Academy of Political and Social Science, 477*(1), 31–42.

Moran, R. (1985b). The origin of insanity as a special verdict: The trial for treason of James Hadfield (1800). *Law and Society Review, 19*, 487–519.

Moran, R. (1986). The punitive uses of the insanity defense: The trial for treason of Edward Oxford (1840). *International Journal of Law and Psychiatry, 9*(2) 171–90.

Over the footlights. (1800). Retrieved from http://www.overthefootlights .co.uk/1800.pdf.

Quen, J.M. (1968). An historical view of the M'Naghten trial. *Bulletin of the History of Medicine, 42*(1), 43–51.

R v Barnier, [1980] 1 SCR 1124, 109 DLR (3d) 257.

R v Hadfield, (1800) 27 How St Tr 1281.

R v M'Naghten, (1843) 8 ER 718, 10 Cl & Fin 200 (Central Crim Ct).

R v Oommen, [1994] 2 SCR 507, 155 AR 190.

R v Swain, [1991] 1 SCR 933, 63 CCC (3d) 481.

Ray, I. (1853). *Treatise on the medical jurisprudence of insanity.* Boston: Little, Brown.

Roach, K. (2009). Foreword. In R. Schneider (Ed.), *The lunatic and the lords* (pp. vii–x). Toronto: Irwin Law.

Rogers, R., & Shuman, D.W. (2000). *Conducting insanity evaluations*: Guilford Press.

Rogers, R., Turner, R.E., Helfield, R., & Dickens, S. (1988). Fo ensic psychiatrists' and psychologists' understanding of insanity: Misguided expertise? *The Canadian Journal of Psychiatry, 33*(8), 691–5.

Rome Statute of the International Criminal Court, 17 July 1998, 2187 UNTS 90 (in force 1 July 2002).

Schneider, R. (2009). *The lunatic and the lords.* Toronto: Irwin Law.

Scott, C. (2018). Evaluation of criminal responsibility. In L. Gold & R. L. Frierson (Eds), *Textbook of Forensic Psychiatry* (pp. 281–96). Arlington, VA: APA Press.

Simon, R.J. (1983). The defense of insanity. *Journal of Psychiatry and the Law, 11,* 183.

Szasz, T.S. (1966). The insanity plea and the insanity verdict. *Temple Law Quarterly, 40,* 271.

Taylor, H. . (1950). The M'Naghten rule. *Syracuse Law Review, 2,* 349.

Vagrancy Act of 1744 (UK), 17 Geo 2, c 5.

4. Criminal Responsibility

Bagby, R.M. (1987). The effects of legislative reform on admission rates to psychiatric units of general hospitals. *International Journal of Law and Psychiatry, 10*(4), 383–94.

Bagby, R.M., & Thompson, J.S. (1991). Decision making in psychiatric civil commitment: An experimental analysis. *The American Journal of Psychiatry, 148*(1), 28.

Balachandra, K., Swaminath, S., & Litman, L. (2004). Impact of *Winko* on absolute discharges. *Journal of the American Academy of Psychiatry and the Law, 32*(2), 173–7.

Bill C-30, *An Act to amend the Criminal Code (mental disorder) and to amend the National Defence Act and the Young Offenders Act in consequence thereof,* 3rd Sess, 34th Parl, 1991 (as passed by the House of Commons November 21, 1991).

Bill C-54, *An Act to amend the Criminal Code and the National Defence Act (mental disorder) Not Criminally Responsible Reform Act,* 1st Sess, 41st Parl, 2013 (first eading in the Senate June 18, 2013) reintroduced and passed as Bill C-14, *An Act to amend the Criminal Code and the National Defence Act (mental disorder),* 2nd Sess 41st Parl, 2014 (assented to April 11, 2014).

Bindman, S. (1991a, 30 April). After more than a year of deliberation. *Ottawa Citizen.*

Bindman, S. (1991b, 1 May). High-tech test fails high court. *Ottawa Citizen.*

Bindman, S. (1991c, 3 May). The Insanity Decision; Court ends long wait for rights; government must rewrite law confining the criminally insane *Ottawa Citizen.* Retrieved from http://myaccess.library.utoronto.ca /login?url=https://search-proquest-com.myaccess.library.utoronto.ca /docview/239555640?accountid=14771.

Bindman, S. (1991d, 2 May). Owen Swain is sane and free again. *Can West News.* Retrieved from http://myaccess.library.utoronto.ca /login?url=https://search-proquest-com.myaccess.library.utoronto.ca /docview/460797511?accountid=14771.

Canadian Charter of Rights and Freedoms, Part I of the Constitution Act 1982, being Schedule B to the Canada Act 1982 (UK), 1982, c. 11.

Capponi, P. (1992). *Upstairs in the crazy house: The life of a psychiatric survivor.* Viking.

Charette, Y., Crocker, A.G., Seto, M.C., Salem, L., Nicholls, T.L., & Caulet, M. (2015). The National Trajectory Project of individuals found not criminally responsible on account of mental disorder in Canada. Part 4: Criminal recidivism. *Canadian Journal of Psychiatry, 60*(3), 127–34.

Claridge, T. (1986, 12 February). Man remains in mental institution after court upholds judge's ruling. *Globe and Mail.*

Craig, S. (1985, 2 September). Man worse off after acquittal due to insanity, court told. *Toronto Star.* Retrieved from http://myaccess.library.utoronto .ca/login?url=https://search-proquest-com.myaccess.library.utoronto.ca /docview/435339353?accountid=14771.

Crocker, A.G., Charette, Y., Seto, M.C., Nicholls, T.L., Côté, G., & Caulet, M. (2015). The National Trajectory Project of individuals found not criminally responsible on account of mental disorder in Canada. Part 3: Trajectories and outcomes through the forensic system. *Canadian Journal of Psychiatry, 60*(3), 117–26.

Crocker, A.G., Nicholls, T.L., Seto, M.C., Charette, Y., Côté, G., & Caulet, M. (2015). The National Trajectory Project of individuals found not criminally responsible on account of mental disorder in Canada. Part 2: The people behind the label. *Canadian Journal of Psychiatry, 60*(3), 106–16.

Crocker, A.G., Nicholls, T.L., Seto, M.C., Côté, G., Charette, Y., & Caulet, M. (2015). The National Trajectory Project of individuals found not criminally responsible on account of mental disorder in Canada. Part 1: Context and methods. *Canadian Journal of Psychiatry, 60*(3), 98–105.

Criminal Code, RSC 1985, c C-46.

Desmarais, S.L., Hucker, S., Brink, J., & De Freitas, K. (2008). A Canadian example of insanity defence reform: Accused found not criminally responsible before and after the *Winko* decision. *International Journal of Forensic Mental Health, 7*(1), 1–14.

Dupuis. T. (2013). *Bill C-54: An Act to amend the Criminal Code and National Defense Act* (mental disorder). Parliamentary Information and Research Service. Ottawa: Library of Parliament.

Glancy, G., & Bradford, J. (1999). Canadian landmark case: *Regina v. Swain*: Translating M'Naughton into twentieth century Canadian. *The Journal of the American Academy of Psychiatry and the Law, 27*(2), 301–7.

Kamba, L. (2013). The provincial and territorial review boards. In H. Bloom & R. Schneider (Eds), *Law and Mental Disorder: A Comprehensive and Practical Approach* (pp. 673–701). Toronto: Irwin Law.

Ketchum v Hislop (1984), 54 BCLR 327, 1984 CarswellBC 189 (SC)

Lacroix, R., O'Shaughnessy, R., McNiel, D.E., & Binder, R.L. (2017). Controversies concerning the Canadian Not Criminally Responsible Reform Act. *Journal of the American Academy of Psychiatry and the Law, 45*(1), 44–51.

Livingston, J.D., Wilson, D., Tien, G., & Bond, L. (2003). A follow-up study of persons found not criminally responsible on account of mental disorder in British Columbia. *Canadian Journal of Psychiatry, 48*(6), 408–15.

Lussa v Health Sciences Centre, 1983 CarswellMan 403, 5 CHRR D / 2203 (Man QB).

Makin, K. (1985, 9 May). Dispatching of criminally insane backed. *Globe and Mail.*

Makin, K. (1990, 20 February). Judgment reserved by Supreme Court on warrant challenge. *Globe and Mail.*

McGinty, E.E., Webster, D.W., & Barry, C.L. (2013). Effects of news media messages about mass shootings on attitudes toward persons with serious mental illness and public support for gun control policies. *American Journal of Psychiatry, 170*(5), 494–501.

McGinty, E.E., Webster, D.W., Jarlenski, M., & Barry, C.L. (2014). News media framing of serious mental illness and gun violence in the United States, 1997–2012. *American Journal of Public Health, 104*(3), 406–13.

McNeil, G. (1990, 20 February). Crown seeks acquittal of insane criminals; high court reviews legality of practice. *Ottawa Citizen.*

Nicholls, T.L., Crocker, A.G., Seto, M.C., Wilson, C.M., Charette, Y., & Côté, G. (2015). The National Trajectory Project of individuals found not criminally responsible on account of mental disorder. Part 5: How essential are gender-specific fo ensic psychiatric services? *Canadian Journal of Psychiatry, 60*(3), 135–45.

Lussa v Health Sciences Centre, 1983 CarswellMan 403, 5 CHRR D/2203 (Man QB).

Orwen, P. (1987, 26 May). Redefining justice for the mentally ill *Toronto Star*. Retrieved from http://myaccess.library.utoronto.ca/login?url=https://search-proquest-com.myaccess.library.utoronto.ca/docview/435557156?accountid=14771.

Payne, E. (1990, 7 April). Lieutenant-governor's warrants; system rapped after man found not guilty for reasons of insanity in second attack. *Ottawa Citizen*.

Pilon, M. (1999). *Mental disorder and Canadian criminal law*. Retrieved from http://www.publications.gc.ca/Collection-R/LoPBdP/BP/prb9922-e.htm#(8).

R v Schoenborn, 2017 BCSC 1556.

R v Swain (1986), 53 OR (2d) 609, 24 CCC (3d) 385 (CA).

R v Swain, 1985 CarswellOnt 2250, (Dist Ct J).

R v Swain, [1991] 1 SCR 933, 63 CCC (3d) 481.

R v Taylor (1992), 11 OR (3d) 323, 77 CCC (3d) 551 (CA).

Ranieri, Re, 2015 ONCA 444.

Safe Streets and Communities Act, SC 2012, c 1.

Savage, H.S., McKague, C., & Johnson, S. (1987). *Mental health law in Canada*: Butterworths.

Schneider, R. (1988). *Ontario mental health statutes*. Toronto: Carswell.

Schneider, R., Glancy, G., Bradford, J., & Seibenmorgen, E. (2000). Canadian landmark case, *Winko v. British Columbia*: Revisiting the conundrum of the mentally disordered accused. *Journal of the American Academy of Psychiatry and the Law, 28*(2), 206–12.

Warrants not cruel, district court rules. (1985, 12 June). *Globe and Mail*.

Winko v Forensic Psychiatric Institute, [1999] 2 SCR 625, 175 DLR (4th) 193.

Winko v Forensic Psychiatric Institute, 112 CCC (3d) 31, 84 BCAC 44 (CA) (additional reasons).

Winko v Forensic Psychiatric Institute, 1996 CarswellBC 1732, 79 BCAC 1 (CA).

5. Clarifying Wrongfulness

Baxter, D. (2017, 29 October). Lives in the balance: Robert Chaulk was found not guilty by reason of insanity for killing an elderly man in 1985; after receiving treatment, he killed two more people in 1999. *Winnipeg Free Press*. Retrieved from https://www.winnipegfreepress.com/local/lives-in-the-balance-453930593.html.

Beltrame, J. (1999, 6 January). Insane plea "too easy": Reform MP vows to press for tougher law. *Ottawa Citizen*.

Bill C-30, *An Act to amend the Criminal Code (mental disorder) and to amend the National Defence Act and the Young Offenders Act in consequence thereof*, 3rd

Sess, 34th Parl, 1991 (as passed by the House of Commons November 21, 1991).

Brodbeck, T. (2013, 15 May). Mentally ill killers can kill again, and here's an example. *Winnipeg Sun*.

Cabbie cleared. (1995, 20 January). *Medicine Hat News*. Retrieved from https://newspaperarchive.com/medicine-hat-news-jan-20-1995-p-4/.

Criminal Code, RSC 1970, c C-34, s 16(3).

Crown must prove sanity, top court told. (1990, 30 May). *Toronto Star*.

Deutscher, D.B. (1991). *R. v. Chaulk* and *R. v. Swain*: Insanity and the Constitution. *Forum Constitutionnel*, 2(99).

Duffy, A. (1987, 11 June). Accused teens tied to the occult. *Winnipeg Free Press*. Retrieved from https://newspaperarchive.com/winnipeg-free-press-jun-11-1987-p-5/.

Self-defense claimed. (1991, 26 February). *Lethbridge Herald*. Retrieved from https://newspaperarchive.com/lethbridge-herald-feb-26-1992-p-14/.

Law Reform Commission of Canada. (1987). *Report on Recodifying Criminal Law*. (30). Retrieved from https://archive.org/details/reportonrecodify00lawr.

McIntyer, M. (2009, 3 June). Four months, then liberty. *Winnipeg Free Press*.

McRuer, J., Desrochers, G., Kinnear, H., Jones, R., & Harris, J. (1956). *Report of the Royal Commission on the Law of Insanity as a Defense in Criminal Cases*. Hull, QC: Edmond Cloutier Queen's Printer and Controller of Stationery. Retrieved from http://publications.gc.ca/collections/collection_2014/bcp-pco/CP32-99-1956-eng.pdf.

Murray, M. (1987, 28 June). Inseparable duo baffled classmates *Winnipeg Free Press*. Retrieved from https://newspaperarchive.com/winnipeg-free-press-jun-28-1987-p-8/.

R v Oommen (1993), 135 AR 321, 21 CR (4th) 117 (CA).

R v Oommen, [1994] 2 SCR 507, 155 AR 190, online: Lexum < https://scc-csc.lexum.com/scc-csc/scc-csc/en/item/1153/index.do>.

R v Chaulk, 53 Ma. R (2d) 297, 4 WCB (2d) 218 (CA).

R v Chaulk, [1990] 3 SCR 1303, 62 CCC (3d) 193.

Rogers, R., Turner, R.E., Helfield, R., & Dickens, S. (1988). Fo ensic psychiatrists' and psychologists' understanding of insanity: Misguided expertise? *Canadian Journal of Psychiatry*, 33(8), 691–5.

Schneider, R.D., & Nussbaum, D. (2007). Can the bad be mad? *Criminal Law Quarterly*, 53, 206.

Workers' History Museum. (2014). The Battle of 66th Street – How the Gainers strike rallied a nation. Retrieved from http://workershistorymuseum.ca/the-battle-of-66th-street/.

6. Voluntariness

Adam, L. (2010, 25 March). The science of defending sleepwalkers that kill. *BBC News*. Retrieved from http://news.bbc.co.uk/2/hi/health/8583408.stm.

Aird, E. (1995, 12 October). Living in fear: Domestic violence never seems to take a holiday. *Vancouver Sun*, p. B1.

American Psychiatric Association. (2013). *Diagnostic and Statistical Manual of Mental Disorders* (5th ed.) Washington, DC: Author.

Arboleda-Flórez, J. (2002). On automatism. *Current Opinion in Psychiatry, 15*(6), 569–76.

Baker, D., & Knopff, R. (2014). Daviault dialogue: The strange journey of Canada's intoxication defence. *Review of Constitutional Studies, 19*, 35.

Bindman, S. (1998a, 22 June). "But she just wouldn't stop yelling at me": Bert Stone got four years for killing his wife. Now B.C. wants the Supreme Court to get tough on men with excuses for domestic murder. *Ottawa Citizen*, p. A1.

Bindman, S. (1998b, 27 June). Keep wife-killer behind bars, top court urged: B.C. attorney general appears in person to beg judges to make sentence consistent with society's "abhorrence" for crime. *Ottawa Citizen*, p. A4.

Birnie, P. (2009, 1 October). To sleep, perchance to sleepwalk; Pair returns to Vancouver with play meditating on dreams, night terrors. *Vancouver Sun*, p. D8.

Bratty v Attorney-General for Northern Ireland, [1963] AC 386 (HL (NI). Brieger, P. (2006, 28 October). Sleepwalking killing hangs over Durham trustee candidate: Acquitted 20 years ago. *National Post*.

Callwood, J. (1990). *The sleepwalker: The trial that made Canadian legal history.* Toronto: Lester & Orpen Dennys.

Bill C-72, *An Act to amend the Criminal Code (self-induced intoxication)*, 1st Sess, 35th Parl, 1996 (assented to 13 July 1995)

Chisholm, P. (1994, 14 November). Sobering questions: An Alberta case raises new debate over the so-called drunk defence. *Maclean's*, 100–2.

Cooper v R, [1983] 1 SCR 240, 133 APR 263, 2 CCC (3d) 64.

Criminal Code, RSC 1985, c C-46.

Davie v Magistrates of Edinburgh, [1953] SC 34 (Ct Sess).

Director of Public Prosecutions v Beard, [1920] AC 479 (HL (Eng)).

Director of Public Prosecutions v Majewski, [1977] AC 443 (HL (Eng)).

Ekirch, A.R., & Shneerson, J. (2011). Nineteenth-century sleep violence cases: A historical view. *Sleep Medicine Clinics, 6*(4), 483–91.

Fenwick, P. (1990). Automatism, medicine and law. *Psychological Medicine, 17* (Suppl.), 1–27.

Fiorentini, A., Volonteri, L.S., Dragogna, F., Rovera, C., Maffini, M., Mauri, M.C., & Altamura, C. (2011). Substance-induced psychoses: A critical review of the literature. *Current Drug Abuse Reviews, 4*(4), 228–40.

Glancy, G., Bradford, J., & Fedak, L. (2002). A comparison of *R. v. Stone* with *R. v. Parks*: Two cases of automatism. *Journal of the American Academy of Psychiatry and the Law Online, 30*(4), 541.

Gold, A. (1978). *Leary v. The Queen. Osgoode Hall Law Journal, 16*(3), 735–40.

Goldhill, O. (2015, 11 February). Murder, artistry and sex: The mysterious horrors of sleepwalking. *The Telegraph.*

Grant, I., Spitz, L., Ogilvie, M., Wells, P., Shi, C., Lambert, D., & Donald, G. (1993). Case comments: Accused killing while sleepwalking – Acquittal or not guilty by reason of insanity. *Canadian Bar Review, 72*(2).

Hall, N. (1995a, 27 September). Mother rushed into fateful trip, jury told. *Vancouver Sun,* p. B5.

Hall, N. (1995b, 6 October). No memory of stabbing a lie, court told: Prosecution attacks Winfield man's claim he can't emember. *Vancouver Sun,* p. B4.

Hall, N. (1995c, 7 October). Whole story denied jury, victim's sister claims. *Vancouver Sun,* p. A8.

Hutchinson, A. (1990, 1 December). When sleep becomes a nightmare: The sleepwalker. *Globe and Mail,* p. C18.

Idzikowski, C. (2014). An essay on sleep-related sexual behaviours and offences related to sexual behaviours. In *Sleep and its disorders affect society.* InTech Open, DOI: 10.5772/59140.

Idzikowski, C., & Rumbold, J. (2015). Sleep in a legal context: The role of the expert witness. *Medicine, Science and the Law, 55*(3), 176–82.

Killer gets parole after 20 months. (1997, 5 July). *Vancouver Sun,* p. A2.

Lobbyists want abuse law changed. (1995, 30 November). *Edmonton Journal,* p. H6.

Lawrence, M.S. (2017). Voluntary intoxication and the Charter: Revisiting the constitutionality of section 33.1 of the Criminal Code. *Manitoba Law Journal, 40,* 391.

LEAF. (2019). Women's Legal Education and Action Fund. Retrieved from https://www.leaf.ca/

Leary v The Queen, [1978] 1 S.C.R. 29.

MacLeod, L. (1987). *Battered but not beaten: Preventing wife battering in Canada.* Ottawa: Canadian Advisory Council on the Status of Women.

McQuigge, M. (2018, 29 August). Ontario court ruling clears the way for intoxication to be used as a defence in sexual assault cases. *Global News.* Retrieved from https://globalnews.ca/news/4417278/ontario-court-intoxication-sexual-assault/.

Middleton, G. (1994, 25 March). Husband hunted in killing. *The Province,* p. A6.

Moldofsky, H., Gilbert, R., Lue, F.A., & MacLean, A.W. (1995). Sleep-related violence. *Sleep, 18*(9), 731–9.

Ogilvie, C. (1995a, 8 October). Provoked into manslaughter. *The Province*, p. A30.

Ogilvie, C. (1995b, 26 September). Yes, I killed her: Accused. *The Province*, p. A6.

Okanagan man charged with murder in death of his wife. (1994, 26 March). *Vancouver Sun*, p. A4.

Pressman, M.R., Mahowald, M.W., Schenck, C.H., & Bornemann, M.C. (2007). Alcohol-induced sleepwalking or confusional arousal as a defense to criminal behavior: A review of scientific evidence, methods and fo ensic considerations. *Journal of Sleep Research, 16*(2), 198–212.

Calendar. (2016, 14 July). *The Province*, p. A37.

R c Bouchard-Lebrun, 2010 QCCA 402.

R c Daviault, 1991 CarswellQue 1049, [1991] R J.Q. 1794 (CQ crim & pén).

R c Daviault (1993), 80 CCC (3d) 175, 19 C.R (4th) 291 (Qc CA).

R v Bouchard-Lebrun, 2011 SCC 58.

R v Daviault, [1994] 3 SCR 63, 118 DLR (4th) 469.

R v Leary, [1978] 1 SCR 29, 74 DLR (3d) 103.

R v McCaw, 2018 ONSC 3464.

R v Parks (1990), 73 OR (2d) 129, 39 OAC 27 (CA).

R v Parks, [1992] 2 SCR 871, 95 DLR (4th) 27.

R v Quick, [1973] QB 910.

R v Rabey (1977), 17 OR (2d) 1, 79 DLR (3d) 414 (CA).

R v Rabey, [1980] 2 SCR 513, 114 DLR (3d) 193.

R v Stone (1997), 113 CCC (3d) 158, 86 BCAC 169 (BC CA).

R v Stone, [1999] 2 SCR 290, [173 DLR (4th) 66.

R v Szymusiak, [1972] 3 OR 602, 8 CCC (2d) 407 (CA).

Regehr, C., & Glancy, G. (1995). Battered woman syndrome defense in Canadian courts. *Canadian Journal of Psychiatry, 40*(3), 130–5.

Shum, D. (2018). Toronto man who used intoxication defence found guilty of sexual assault. *Global News* [Television news broadcast]. Retrieved from https://globalnews.ca/news/4785012/toronto-man-intoxication-defence-sexual-assault/.

Siclari, F., Khatami, R., Urbaniok, F., Nobili, L., Mahowald, M.W., Schenck, C.H., … Bassetti, C.L. (2010). Violence in sleep. *Brain, 133*(12), 3494–509.

Starzer, M.S.K., Nordentoft, M., & Hjorthøj, C. (2017). Rates and predictors of conversion to schizophrenia or bipolar disorder following substance-induced psychosis. *American Journal of Psychiatry, 175*(4), 343–50.

Thompson, J. (1995, 6 December). Loony law lets killers walk: Eager shrinks help sharp lawyers claim their clients were temporarily bonkers when they did their deadly deeds. *The Province*.

Tibbetts, J. (1998, 21 June). Supreme Court to look at sentences for crimes of passion [Donna Smith murdered by husband Bert Stone]. *Canadian Press Newswire*, n.p.

Tibbetts, J. (1999, 17 March). Passion may be erased as legal factor in slayings: Justice minister ponders pressures to revise Criminal Code. *National Post,* p. A5.

Tibbetts, J. (2001, 6 February). Ottawa drops plan to abolish "passion" defence for murder. *Observer,* p. B5.

Umanath, S., Sarezky, D., & Finger, S. (2011). Sleepwalking through history: Medicine, arts, and courts of law. *Journal of the History of the Neurosciences, 20*(4), 253–76.

Vienneau, D. (1994, 9 November). Judges under fi e for drunkenness defence: Top court ruling "wreaked havoc" on other judges. *Toronto Star,* p. A2.

Watts, J. (2013). Updating toxic psychosis into 21st-century Canadian: *Bouchard-Lebrun v. R. Journal of the American Academy of Psychiatry and the Law Online, 41*(3), 374–81.

7. Fitness to Stand Trial

American Academy of Psychiatry and the Law. (2005). Ethical guidelines for the practice of forensic psychiatry. Retrieved from http:// www.aapl.org /ethics.htm.

Blackstone, W. (1825/1979). *Commentaries on the laws of England* (Vol. 2). Chicago: University of Chicago Press.

Bloom, H. (2006). Fitness to Stand Trial. In H. Bloom & R. Schneider (Eds), *Mental disorder and the law: A primer for legal and mental health professionals* (pp. 211–47): Toronto: Irwin Law.

Buchanan, A. (2006). Competency to stand trial and the seriousness of the charge. *Journal of the American Academy of Psychiatry and the Law Online, 34*(4), 458–465.

Chaimowitz, G. ., Furimsky, I., Singh, N., & Kolawole, O. (2018). The utility of treatment orders in the restoration of fitness to stand trial: A Canadian study. *International Journal of Risk and Recovery, 1*(1), 12–20.

Criminal Code, RSC 1985, c C-46.

Davis, S. (1994). Fitness to stand trial in Canada in light of the recent Criminal Code amendments. *International Journal of Law and Psychiatry, 17*(3) 319–29.

Dusky v United States, 362 U.S. 402 (1960).

Felthous, A.R. (2011). Competence to stand trial should require rational understanding. *Journal of the American Academy of Psychiatry and the Law Online, 39*(1), 19–30.

For the record: Lawyer not guilty. (1988, 17 October). *Globe and Mail,* p. A17.

Haliechuk, R. (1988, 6 August). Right ruling is mind-boggling lawyers say. *Toronto Star,* p. D5.

In Brief: Lawyer Disbarred. (1983, 7 June). *Globe and Mail,* p. 4.

Law society looks at disbarring lawyer held in stabbing. (1987a, 30 January). *Toronto Star,* p. C15.

Lawyer is declared unfit to stand trial on assault cha ge. (1987, 7 March). *Globe and Mail*, p. A11.

Lawyer stabbed twice in the chest at Osgoode Hall office (1987b, 7 January). *Toronto Star*, p. A8.

Lawyer unfit to stand trial in wounding (1987c, 12 March). *Toronto Star*, p. D8.

Mossman, D., Noffsinger, S.G., Ash, P., Frierson, R.L., Gerbasi, J., Hackett, M., … Sieg, K.G. (2007). AAPL practice guideline for the forensic psychiatric evaluation of competence to stand trial. *Journal of the American Academy of Psychiatry and the Law Online, 35*(Suppl. 4), S3–S72.

Nussbaum, D., Hancock, M., Turner, I., Arrowood, J., & Melodick, S. (2008). Fitness/competency to stand trial: A conceptual overview, review of existing instruments, and cross-validation of the Nussbaum Fitness Questionnaire. *Brief Treatment and Crisis Intervention, 8*(1), 43.

R c Demers, 2002 CarswellQue 1045, [2002] JQ No. 590 (Qc CS).

R v Adam, 2013 ONSC 373.

R v B (D), 2003 SKPC 155.

R v Demers, 2004 SCC 46.

R v John Doe, 2011 ONSC 92.

R v Morrissey, 2003 CarswellOnt 3871, [2003] OJ No. 3961 (Sup Ct J).

R v Morrissey, 2007 ONCA 770.

R v Muschke (1997), 121 CCC (3d) 51, 1997 CarswellBC 2703.

R v Swain, [1991] 1 SCR 933, 63 CCC (3d) 481.

R v Taylor (1992), 11 OR (3d) 323, 77 CCC (3d) 551 (CA).

R v Whittle (1992), 59 OAC 218, 78 CCC (3d) 49 (CA).

R v Whittle, [1994] 2 SCR 914, 116 DLR (4th) 416.

Roesch, R., Zapf, P.A., & Eaves, D. (2006). *FIT-R: Fitness Interview Test-Revised. A structured interview for assessing competency to stand trial.* Sarasota, FL: Professional Resource Press/Professional Resource Exchange.

Rogers, R., Grandjean, N., Tillbrook, C. E., Vitacco, M.J., & Sewell, K.W. (2001). Recent interview-based measures of competency to stand trial: A critical review augmented with research data. *Behavioral Sciences & the Law, 19*(4), 503–18.

Rogers, R., & Johansson-Love, J. (2009). Evaluating competency to stand trial with evidence-based practice. *Journal of the American Academy of Psychiatry and the Law Online, 37*(4), 450–60.

Schneider, R.D. (1998). Fitness to be Sentenced. *Criminal Law Quarterly, 41*, 261.

Schneider, R.D., & Bloom, H. (1995). *R. v. Taylor*, a decision not in the best interests of some mentally ill accused. *Criminal Law Quarterly, 38*, 183.

Scott, C. (2018). Evaluation of criminal responsibility. In L. Gold & R.L. Frierson (Eds), *Textbook of Forensic Psychiatry* (pp. 281–96). Arlington, VA: APA Press.

Stabbing suspect to undergo psychiatric exam. (1987a, 7 January). Stabbing suspect to undergo psychiatric exam. *Vancouver Sun*, p. A14.

Stabbing suspect to undergo psychiatric exam. (1987b, 8 January). *Toronto Star*, p. A4.

Wilson v United States, 391 F 2d 460 (DC Cir, 1968).

8. Access to Treatment

A (LL) v B (A), [1995] 4 SCR 536, 103 CCC (3d) 92.

B.C. bishop disputes stories linking him to child sex abuse. (1991, 9 January). *Edmonton Journal*, p. A4.

Bill C-46, *An act to amend the criminal code (production of records in sexual offence proceedings)*, 2nd Sess, 35th Parl. 1996 (as passed by the House of Commons April 17, 1997).

Bill C-49, *An Act to amend the Criminal Code (sexual assault)*, 3rd Sess, 34th Parl, 1992, (as passed by the House of Commons June 15 1992).

Bindman, S. (1995, 3 January). Feds may join shredded document fray: Rock says access to counselling records could be restricted. *Windsor Star*, p. A1.

Bishop denounces "vicious" allegation of child molestation. (1991, 9 January). *Waterloo Record*, p. D12.

Bishop denies "vicious" reports of abuse probe. (1991, 9 January). *Ottawa Citizen*, p. A16.

Bishop faces six sex charges. (1991, 5 February). *Vancouver Sun*, p. A1.

Busby, K. (1999). Third party records cases since *R. v. O'Connor. Manitoba Law Journal*, 27, 355.

Canadian Charter of Rights and Freedoms, Part 1 of the Constitution Act, 1982, being Schedule B to the Canada Act 1982 (UK), 1982, c. 11.

Canadian Council of Bishops. (1991). Statement by the National Meeting on Indian Residential Schools [Press release]. Retrieved from http://www .cccb.ca/site/eng/media-room/files/2630-apology-on- esidential-schools -by-the-catholic-church.

Canadian Medical Association. (2004). *CMA code of ethics*. Retrieved from https://www.cma.ca/Assets/assets-library/document/en/advocacy /policy-research/CMA_Policy_Code_of_ethics_of_the_Canadian_Medical _Association_Update_2004_PD04-06-e.pdf.

Cockburn, L. (1993, 3 January). O'Connor case: Gender bias in action. *The Province*, p. A31.

Criminal Code, RSC 1985, c C-46.

Draft Committee, United Nations General Assembly. (1948). *Universal Declaration of Human Rights*. Retrieved from http://www.un.org/Overview/rights .html.

Edge, M. (1991, 8 December). Bishop walks free: Angry judge throws out sex charges, blames prosecutors. *The Province*, p. A5.

Feldthusen, B. (1996). Access to the private therapeutic records of sexual assault complainants. *Canadian Bar Review*, 75, 537.

G (JA) v R (R J), 1998 CarswellOnt 1487, [1998] OJ No 1415 (Ct J (Gen Div)).

Glancy, G., Regehr, C., & Bryant, A. (1998a). Confidentiality in crisis: Part I – The duty to inform. *Canadian Journal of Psychiatry, 43*(10), 1001–5.

Glancy, G., Regehr, C., & Bryant, A. (1998b). Confidentiality in crisis: Part II – Confidentiality of t eatment records. *Canadian Journal of Psychiatry, 43*(10), 1006–11.

Glancy, G., Regehr, C., Bryant, A., & Schneider, R. (1999). Another nail in the coffin of confidentiali . *Canadian Journal. of Psychiatry, 44*(5), 440.

Gotell, L. (2002). The ideal victim, the hysterical complainant, and the disclosure of confidential ecords: The implications of the charter for sexual assault law. *Osgoode Hall Law Journal, 40*, 251.

Gotell, L. (2008). Rethinking affirmative consent in Canadian sexua assault law: Neoliberal sexual subjects and risky women. *Akron Law Review, 41*, 865.

Hunter, J. (1992, 9 December). Special prosecutor appointed to consider appeal. *Vancouver Sun*, p. B4.

Indigenous and Northern Affairs Canada. (2018). Indian Residential Schools. Retrieved from https://www.aadnc-aandc.gc.ca/eng/1100100015576 /1100100015577.

Judge quashes RC bishop's sex charges. (1992, 8 December). *Hamilton Spectator*, p. A3.

Kenna, K. (1991, 19 February). Jury trial sought by B.C. bishop in sex-abuse case. *Toronto Star*, p. A11.

Koshan, J. (2002). Disclosure and production in sexual violence cases: Situating *Stinchcombe*. *Alberta Law Review, 40*, 655.

Legal Education and Action Fund. (1999). *R. v. Mills* [Factum].

Makin, K. (1995, 15 December). Court rules against rape victims: Advocates shocked as judges give accused right to demand private counselling records. *Globe and Mail*, p. A1.

Makin, K. (1999, 27 November). Ruling "a sign of things to come": Lamer's influence said to be waning *Globe and Mail*, p. A3.

Marshall, M. (2004). Canada – Production of private records of victims of sexual assault in *R. v. Shearing*. *International Journal of Constitutional Law, 2*, 139–48.

Mate, S. (1991, 24 July). RC order apologizes to natives. *Calgary Herald*, p. A1.

Neufeld, A. (1995). A.(L.L.) v. B.(A.): A case comment on the production of sexual assault counselling records. *Saskatchewn Law Review, 59*, 335.

Ontario College of Social Workers and Social Service Workers. (2005). *Privacy toolkit for social workers and social service workers*. Retrieved from http://www.ocswssw.org/wp-content/uploads/2015/01/PHIPA-Toolkit.pdf.

Personal Information Protection and Electronic Documents Act, SC 2000, c. 5.

Powell, K. (1997, 27 December). Privacy vs. fair trial; Debate is raging over a new law that restricts people charged with sex crimes from obtaining their accuser's counselling records. *Edmonton Journal*, p. F1.

Privacy Act, R SC 1985, c P-21.

R v Carosella (1995), 26 OR (3d) 209, 102 CCC (3d) 28 (CA).

R v Carosella, [1997] 1 SCR 80, 142 DLR (4th) 595.

R v Carosella, 1994 CarswellOnt 119, 35 CR (4th) 301 (Ct J (Gen Div)).

R v E (AW), [1993] 3 SCR 155 (SCC), cited in *R v Mills.*

R v Lee (1997), 35 OR (3d) 594, 1997 CarswellOnt 3636 (Ct J (Gen Div)).

R v Mills, [1999] 3 SCR 668, 180 DLR (4th) 1.

R v Mills, [1999] 3 SCR 668, 180 DLR (4th) 1.

R v O'Connor (1994), 89 CCC (3d) 109, 42 BCAC 105 (BC CA).

R v O'Connor (1994), 90 CCC (3d) 257, 43 BCAC 70 (BC CA) (additional reasons).

R v O'Connor, [1995] 4 SCR 411, 130 DLR (4th) 235.

R v O'Connor, 1992 CarswellBC 475, 18 CR (4th) 98(BC SC).

R v Osolin, [1993] 4 SCR 595, 109 DLR (4th) 478.

R v Stinchcombe, [1991] 3 SCR 326, 68 CCC (3d) 1.

R v Stinchcombe, [1991] 3 SCR 326, 68 CCC (3d) 1.

R v Mills (1997), 56 Alta. LR (3d) 277, 12 CR (5th) 138 (QB).

R v Mills (1997), 56 Alta. LR (3d) 301, 12 CR (5th) 163 (QB) (additional reasons).

Regehr, C., Glancy, G., & Bradford, J. (2000). Canadian landmark case: *L.C. and the Attorney General for Alberta v. Brian Joseph Mills. Journal of the American Academy of Psychiatry and the Law, 28*(4), 460–4.

Roberts, D. (1991, 5 February). B.C. bishop charged with sex offences: Incidents involving women allegedly occurred while accused was head of Indian school. *Globe and Mail,* p. A4.

Schneider, R. (1996). Confidentiality and privilege. In H. Bloom & M. Bay (Eds), *A practical guide to mental health capacity and consent law of Ontario* (pp. 379–406). Toronto: Carswell.

Solomon, R., & Visser, L. (2005). *A legal guide for social workers* Toronto: Ontario Association of Social Workers.

Temkin, J. (2002). Digging the dirt: Disclosure of records in sexual assault cases. *Cambridge Law Journal, 61*(1), 126–45.

9. Duty to Warn

Ahmed v Stefaniu (2006), 216 OAC 323, 275 DLR (4th) 101 (Ont CA).

Buchanan, A., Binder, R., Norko, M., & Swartz, M. (2012). Psychiatric violence risk assessment. *American Journal of Psychiatry, 169*(3), 340.

Buchanan, A., Binder, R., Norko, M., & Swartz, M. (2015). Resource document on psychiatric violence risk assessment. https://doi.org/10.1176/appi.focus.130402.

Buckner, F., & Firestone, M. (2000). Where public peril begins? 25 years after *Tarasoff. Journal of Legal Medicine, 21*(2), 187–222.

Cal. Civ. Code § 43.92 (1985).

Carlisle, J. (1996). Duty to warn: Report from council. *Canadian Medical Association Journal, 21* (July / August).

Casswell, D.G. (1989). Disclosure by a physician of AIDS-related patient information: An ethical and legal dilemma. *Canadian Bar. Review, 68,* 225.

Chaimowitz, G., & Glancy, G. (2002). *Position paper: The duty to protect.* Retrieved from http:/ / ww1.cpa-apc.org / Publications / Position_Papers / duty.asp.

Chaimowitz, G., Glancy, G., & Blackburn, J. (2000). The duty to warn and protect – impact on practice. *The Canadian Journal of Psychiatry, 45*(10), 899–904.

The disappeared. (2005, 5 August). The disappeared. *The Guardian.* Retrieved from https:/ / www.theguardian.com / world / 2005 / aug / 05 / features11.g2.

Ferris, L.E., Barkun, H., Carlisle, J., Hoffman, B., Katz, C., & Silverman, M. (1998). Defining the physician's duty to warn: Consensus statement of Ontario's Medical Expert Panel on Duty to Inform. *Canadian Medical Association Journal, 158*(11), 1473–9.

Flanagan, W.F. (1988). Equality rights for people with AIDS: Mandatory reporting of HIV infection and contact tracing. *McGill Law Journal, 34,* 530.

Fournier, S. (2011, 30 November). Vancouver police task force referred to missing and murdered women as "whores," inquiry hears. *National Post.* Retrieved from https:/ / nationalpost.com / news / canada / vancouver-police -task-force-referred-to-missing-and-murdered-women-as-whores-inquiry -hears.

Glancy, D., & Glancy, G. (2009). The case that has psychiatrists running scared: *Ahmed v. Stefaniu. Journal of the American Academy of Psychiatry and the Law Online, 37*(2), 250–6.

Glancy, D., Glancy, G., Felthous, A., & Chaimowitz, G. (2015). *From Hippocrates to Tarrasoff and beyond: An update on duty to warn and protect.* Paper presented at the International Association of Law and Mental Health, Vienna.

Harcourt, B.E. (2005). From the asylum to the prison: Rethinking the incarceration revolution. *Texas Law Review, 84,* 1751.

Hume, M. (1999, 17 May). Doctor's report may lead to prosecution: Confide - tial talks with psychiatrist ended up with police. *National Post,* p. A4.

Lamb, H., & Bachrach, L. (2001). Some perspectives on deinstitutionalization. *Psychiatric Services, 52*(8), 1039–45.

Lamb, H., & Weinberger, L. (2001). *Deinstitutionalization: Promise and problems*: San Francisco: Jossey-Bass.

Makin, K. (2006, 21 October). Psychiatrist held responsible for patient's action. *Globe and Mail.* Retrieved from https:/ / www.theglobeandmail.com / news / national / psychiatrist-held-responsible-for-patients-action / article954318 /.

Makin, K. (2007). Who killed Roslyn Knipe? *Toronto Life,* 81–6.

Mental Health Act, RSO 1990, c M.7.

Missing women timeline. (2012, 7 December). *Vancouver Sun*. Retrieved from http://www.vancouversun.com/news/Missing+women+timeline/7710337/story.html.

O'Shaughnessy, R.J., Glancy, G.D., & Bradford, J.M. (1999). Canadian landmark case, *Smith v. Jones*, Supreme Court of Canada: Confidentiality and privilege suffer another blow. *Journal of the American Academy of Psychiatry and the Law Online, 27*(4), 614–20.

Owens, A. (1999, 26 March). Sexual sadist's murder fantasies to be made public: Top court sets aside lawyer-client privilege in B.C. case. *National Post*, p. A9.

Picard, E., & Robertson, G. (2007). *Legal liability of physicians and hospitals in Canada* (4th ed.). Toronto: Thomson Carswell.

Pittman Estate v Bain (1994), 112 DLR (4th) 257, 19 CCLT (2d) (Ont Ct J (Gen Div)). Regehr, C., & Glancy, G. (2014). *Mental Health Social Work Practice in Canada* (2nd ed.). Toronto: Oxford University Press.

Regehr, C., & Kanani, K. (2010). *Essential law for social work practice in Canada*. Toronto: Oxford University Press.

Smith v Jones, 1997 CarswellBC 3048 (BC SC).

Smith v Jones (1998), 62 BCLR (3d) 198, 120 BCAC 145 (BC CA) (Reasons in Full).

Smith v Jones, [1999] 1 SCR 455, 169 DLR (4th) 385.

Spillane, S. (1989). AIDS: Establishing a physician's duty to warn. *Rutgers Law Journal, 21*, 645.

Tarasoff v Regents of the University of California, 188 Cal. Rptr. 129, 529 P2d 533 (1974).

Vitaly Tarasoff v University of California, 551 P.2d 334 (US Cal 1976).

Truscott, D., & Crook, K.H. (1993). *Tarasoff* in the Canadian context: Wenden and the duty to protect. *The Canadian Journal of Psychiatry, 38*(2), 84–9.

Vancouver Eastside missing women. (2016). Retrieved from http://www.missingpeople.net/robert_pickton.htm.

Wenden v Trikha (1993), 135 AR 382, 14 CCLT (2d) 225 (Alta CA).

Willems, M., & Robertson, D. (2007). Psychiatrist liable for actions of patient released from detention under the Mental Health Act. *Faskin Martineau Health Law Bulletin* (January), 1–4.

10. Consent to Treatment

Amdur, R. (2003, 14 June). Supreme Court decision permits people to stay sick. *Waterloo Record*, p. A19.

Appelbaum, P.S., & Grisso, T. (1995). The MacArthur treatment competence study. I. *Law and Human Behavior, 19*(2), 105–26.

Bailey, S. (2003, 6 June). A mother mourned Friday as her genius, psychotic son won his top-court fight against fo ced drugging. *Canadian Press*.

Brean, J. (2013). A beautiful mind of his own; Once the centre of a landmark case, Professor Starson is now free, but still fighting to escape medication *National Post*, p. A3.

Bricker, J. (2001, 5 June). Physicist wins right to refuse psychiatric drugs: Says medication for bipolar disorder slows his brain, impedes his research. *National Post*, p. A7.

Cairns, R., Maddock, C., Buchanan, A., David, A.S., Hayward, P., Richardson, G., .. Hotopf, M. (2005). Reliability of mental capacity assessments in psychiatric in-patients. *British Journal of Psychiatry, 187*(4), 372–8.

Canadian Medical Protective Association. (2018). Good practices guide: Informed consent. Retrieved from https://www.cmpa-acpm.ca/serve /docs/ela/goodpracticesguide/pages/communication/Informed _Consent/documenting-e.html.

Capponi, P. (1992). *Upstairs in the crazy house: The life of a psychiatric survivor*: Viking.

Ciarlariello v Schacter, [1993] 2 SCR 119, 100 DLR (4th) 609.

Consent to Treatment and Health Care Directives Act, RSPEI 1988, c C-17.2.

Dhir, A.A. (2008). Relationships of force: Reflections on la , psychiatry and human rights. *Windsor Review of Legal & Social Issues, 25*, 103.

Dickens, B. (2002). Informed consent. In J. Downie, T. Caulfield, & C. Flood (Eds), *Canadian health law and olicy* (2nd ed., pp. 129–55). Toronto: Butterworths.

Frelick, K. (2003). *Starson v. Swayze*: Patient wins right to refuse recommended psychiatric treatment. Toronto: Miller Thompson LLP Health Industry Practice Group. https://www.millerthomson.com/…/health-communique /october-24-2003-health-communique.

Gray, J.E., & O'Reilly, R.L. (2009). Supreme court of Canada's "beautiful mind" case. *International Journal of Law and Psychiatry, 32*(5), 315–22.

Grisso, T., & Appelbaum, P.S. (1995). The MacArthur treatment competence study. III. *Law and Human Behavior, 19*(2), 149–74.

Gutheil, T.G. (1980). In search of true freedom: Drug refusal, involuntary medication, and "rotting with your rights on." *American Journal of Psychiatry, 137*(3), 327–8.

Hardin, H. (1993, July). Far from respecting civil liberties, legal obstacles to treating the mentally ill limit or destroy the liberty of the person. *Vancouver Sun*. Retrieved from http://www.herschelhardin.ca/commentaries/misc /Uncivil_liberties.htm.

Hawkes, E. (2012, 18 June). Erin L. Hawkes: Forced medication saved my life. *National Post*. Retrieved from https://nationalpost.com/opinion /erin-l-hawkes-forced-medication-saved-my-life.

Health Care (Consent) and Care Facility (Admission) Act, RSBC 1996, c 181.

Health Care Consent Act, 1996, SO 1996, c 2, Schedule A.

Hiltz, A., & Szigeti, A. (2005). *A guide to consent and capacity law in Ontario*. Toronto: LexisNexis.

Hunter, I. (2003, 8 August). The rights-mad Supremes. *National Post*, p. A15.

Kim, S.Y., & Caine, E.D. (2002). Utility and limits of the mini mental state examination in evaluating consent capacity in Alzheimer's disease. *Psychiatric Services, 53*(10), 1322–4.

Kress, K. (2006). Rotting with their rights on: Why the criteria for ending commitment or restraint of liberty need not be the same as the criteria for initiating commitment or restraint of liberty, and how the restraint may sometimes justifiably continue after its p erequisites are no longer satisfied. *Behavioral Sciences & the Law, 24*(4), 573–98.

Makin, K. (2003, 5 May). Brilliant man in an asylum fights doctors in top court. *Globe and Mail*, p. A3.

McLachlin, B. (2005) Medicine and the Law: the Challenges of Mental Illness, Remarks of the Right Honourable Beverley McLachlin, P.C. Chief Justice of Canada. Retrieved from https://www.scc-csc.ca/judges-juges/spe-dis/bm-2005-02-17-eng.aspx.

Morris, J., Ferguson, M., & Dykeman, M. (1999). *Canadian nurses and the law* (2nd ed.). Toronto: NexisLexis.

Neilson, G., & Chaimowitz, G. (2015). Informed consent to treatment in psychiatry. *Canadian Journal of Psychiatry /Revue canadienne de psychiatrie, 60*(4), 1.

Noyes, H.P., & Starson, S. (1991). *Discrete antigravity*. Retrieved from https://www.slac.stanford.edu/pubs/slacpubs/5250/slac-pub-5429.pdf.

O'Neill, J., & Fischer, D. (2005, 11 June). Fighting for the right to refuse treatment. *Ottawa Citizen*, p. E1.

O'Reilly, R. (2004, 31 August). The catch-22 of Ontario's Health Care Consent Act. *National Post*, p. A13.

Physicist wins right to refuse medication. (2003, 7 June). *Times Colonist*, p. A3.

Regehr, C., & Antle, B. (1997). Coercive influences: Informed consent in court mandated social work practice. *Social Work, 42*(3), 300–6.

Regehr, C., Kanani, K., McFadden, J., & Saini, M. (2015). *Essential law for social work practice in Canada* (3rd ed.). Toronto: Oxford University Press.

Reibl v Hughes, [1980] 2 SCR 880, 114 DLR (3d) 1.

Reville, D., & Church, K. (2012). Mad activism enters its fifth decade: Psychia - ric survivor organizing in Toronto. In A. Chaudrey, J. Hanley, & E. Schragge, (Eds), *Organize!*, 189–201. https://books.google.ca/books?hl=en&lr=&id=xm_7BgAAQBAJ&oi=fnd&pg=PA189&dq=Reville,+D.,+%26+Church,+K.+(2012).+Mad+activism+enters+its+fifth+decade:+Psychiatri+survivor+organizing+in+Toronto.+Organize,+189%E2%80%93201.&ots=r5Xl_oZMpi&sig=o6wrRBBLBOIqVMDvh-0JT5SwtBY#v=onepage&q&f=false.

Rozovsky, L. (2003). *The Canadian law of consent to treatment*. Toronto: Butterworths.

Sklar, R. (2007). *Starson v. Swayze*: The Supreme Court speaks out (not all that clearly) on the question of "capacity." *Canadian Journal of Psychiatry, 52*(6), 390–6.

Sorrentino, R. (2014). Performing capacity evaluations: What's expected from your consult: Core components of a capacity evaluation are understanding, free choice, and reliability. *Current Psychiatry, 13*(1), 41.

Starson v Swayze, 2003 SCC 32.

Szigeti, A. (2019, 1 January). [Legal Point on Consent and Capacity]. [Personal communication].

Tibbetts, J. (2003, 7 June). Psychotic genius can refuse treatment. *Ottawa Citizen*, p. A1.

Tremblay, M., Gobessi, L., Spinks, T., Srivstava, S., Bush, C., Graham, L., & Richardson, I. (2007). Determining capacity to consent: Guiding physicians through capacity and consent to treatment. Retrieved from https://www.cpso.on.ca/uploadedFiles/policies/policies/policyitems/capacity_consent_july07dialogue.pdf.

Tyler, T. (2001a, 16 December). Mentally ill genius fights for the right to efuse treatment. *Toronto Star*, p. 08.

Tyler, T. (2001b, 15 June). Prodigy wins right to refuse drugs; Medication could slow mentally ill man's thinking, court says. *Toronto Star*, p. A2.

11. Assessing Damages

American Academy of Psychiatry and the Law. (1999). AAPL Task Force: Videotaping of forensic psychiatric evaluations. *Journal of the American Academy of Psychiatry and the Law, 27*, 345–8.

American Academy of Psychiatry and the Law. (2005). *Ethical guidelines for the practice of forensic psychiatry*. Retrieved from http://www.aapl.org/ethics.htm.

American Psychiatric Association. (2013). *Diagnostic and statistical manual of mental disorders* (5th ed.). Washington, DC: Author.

Athey v Leonati, [1996] 3 SCR 458, 140 DLR (4th) 235.

Athey v Leonati, 1993 CarswellBC 2838, [1993] BCJ No. 2777, (BC SC).

Athey v Leonati, 1995 CarswellBC 3007, [1995] BCJ No. 666 (BC CA).

B (KL) v British Columbia, 2003 SCC 51.

Bonnington Castings Ltd v Wardlaw, [1956] AC 613 [1956] (HL (Eng)).

Buchanan, A., & Norko, M. (2011). *The psychiatric report: Principles and practice of forensic writing*. Cambridge, UK: Cambridge University Press.

Calandrillo, S.P., & Buehler, D.E. (2013). Eggshell economics: A revolutionary approach to the eggshell plaintiff rule. *Ohio State Law Journal, 74*, 375.

Canadian Academy of Psychiatry and the Law. (2018). Ethical guidelines. Retrieved from http://www.capl-acpd.org/ethical-guidelines/.

Corfield v Shaw, 2011 BCSC 1529.

Drukteinis, A. (2018). Psychiatric disability. In L. Gold & R. Frierson (Eds), *Textbook of Forensic Psychiatry* (pp. 247–259). Arlington, VA: APA Press.

Dulieu v White and Sons, [1901] 2 KB 669 (KB (Eng)).

Eden, S.M. (2001). I am having a flashback . all the way to the bank: The application of the thin skull rule to mental injuries – *Poole v. Copland, Inc. North Carolina Central Law Review, 24*, 180.

Gerbasi, J. (2004). Forensic assessment in personal injury litigation. In R.I. Simon & L.H. Gold (Eds), *The American Psychiatric Publishing textbook of forensic psychiatry* (pp. 231–61).

Washington, DC: American Psychiatric Publishing Co.

Glancy, G., Ash, P., Bath, E., Buchanan, A., Fedoroff, P., Frierson, R. L., ... Knoll, J. (2015). AAPL practice guideline for the forensic assessment. *The Journal of the American Academy of Psychiatry and the Law, 43* (2 Suppl.), S3.

Gold, L., Anfang, S., & Drukteinis, A. (2008). AAPL Practice guideline for the forensic evaluation of psychiatric disability. *Journal of the American Academy of Psychiatry and the Law, 36* (Suppl. 4), S3-S50.

Gordon v Ahn, 2017 BCCA 334.

Graham v Rourke (1990), 74 DLR (4th) 1, 75 OR (2d) 622 (Ont CA).

Hoffman, B., & O'Shaughnessy, R. (2013). Malingered mental illness in compensation cases. In R.D. Schneider & H. Bloom (Eds), *Law and mental disorder: A comprehensive and practical approach*. Toronto, ON: Irwin Law.

Klar, L. (1991). Recent developments in Canadian tort law: Tort Law. *Ottawa Law Review, 23*, 177–268.

Klar, L. (2013). Torts in Canada. Retrieved from https://www .thecanadianencyclopedia.ca/en/article/torts/.

Klimchuk, D., & Black, V. (1997). A comment on *Athey v. Leonati*: Causation, damages and thin skulls. *University of British Columbia Law. Review, 31*, 163.

McGhee v National Coal Board (1972) 3 All ER 1008 (HL (Eng)).

McInnes, M. (1996). Causation in tort law: Back to basics at the Supreme Court of Canada. *Alberta Law Review, 35*, 1013.

Mustapha v Culligan of Canada Ltd, 2008 SCC 27.

Piel, J. (2012). Causation and legal cases. Paper presented at the Annual Meeting of the American Academy of Psychiatry and the Law, 26 October, Montreal.

Poole v Copland, Inc, 125 NC App. 235 (NC Ct App, 1997).

Poole v Copland, Inc, 348 NC 260 (NC Sup Ct, 1998).

Regehr, C., Kanani, K., McFadden, J., & Saini, M. (2015). *Essential law for social work practice in Canada* (3rd ed.). Toronto: Oxford University Press.

Reid, L., Wilberforce, L., of Glaisdale, S., Kilbrandon, L., & Salmon, L. (1973). *McGhee v. National Coal Board. Managerial Law, 13*(6), 471–85.

Rose, R.V., Wallace, A.N., & Piccard, A.M. (2010). Another crack in the thin skull plaintiff rule: Why women with post traumatic stress disorder who suffer physical harm from abusive environments at work or school should

recover from employers and educators. *Texax Journal of Women & Law,*
20, 165.

Shaw v Clark (1986), 11 BCLR (2d) 46, 1986 CarswellBC 28 (BC SC).

Snell v Farrell, [1990] 2 SCR 311, [72 DLR (4th) 289.

Waddams, S.M. (1998). The valuation of chances. *Canadian Business Law*
Journal, 30, 86.

Weiss, K., & Watson, C. (2018). Personal injury. In L. Gold & R. Frierson (Eds),
Textbook of Forensic Psychiatry (pp. 201–12). Arlington, VA: APA Press.

Case Index

General Index

Figures and tables indicated by page numbers in italics.

(somnambulism), 109–11, 127–9, *128*; landmark cases: *R v Bouchard-Lebrun* (2011), 123–5, 129–30, *134*; *R v Daviault* (1994), 9, 119–22, *133*; *R v Parks* (1992), 9, 108–12, 118, 121, 127, *133*, 134–5; *R v Quick* (1973), 126; *R v Rabey* (1980), 112–14, 132, *133*, 134; *R v Stone* (1999), 9, 114–19, 124–5, 126–7, 130, *133*, 135

Waddams, S.M., 218, 220
warn and protect. *See* duty to warn and protect
Watts, J., 125
Wensleydale, Lord, 22
wild beast test, 53
Women's Legal Education and Action Fund (LEAF), 112–13, 168

World Health Organization: Disability Assessment Schedule (WHO-DAS), 228
Wren, Justice, 139
wrongfulness, 93–107; introduction and summary, 8–9, 106–7, *107*; definition issues, 96–8; implications for forensic mental health practice, 105–6, *107*; presumption of sanity and, 95–6; specific delusions as alternative defence and, 98–9, 103–5; landmark cases: *R v Chaulk* (1990), 8, 93–100, 104–5, 106, *107*; *R v Oommen* (1994), 9, 68, 100–5, 106–7, *107*

Yukon, *203*

www.ingramcontent.com/pod-product-compliance
Lightning Source LLC
Chambersburg PA
CBHW030239030426
42336CB00009B/169